If Adam Had Not Sinned

If Adam Had Not Sinned

THE REASON FOR THE INCARNATION
FROM ANSELM TO SCOTUS

Justus H. Hunter

THE CATHOLIC UNIVERSITY OF AMERICA PRESS
WASHINGTON, D.C.

The paper used in this publication meets the minimum
requirements of American National Standards for
Information Science—Permanence of Paper for Printed
Library Materials, ANSI Z39.48-1984.
∞

Cataloging-in-Publication Data available from
the Library of Congress
ISBN 978-0-8132-3285-0

for Ellen

Contents

Acknowledgments

This book is only possible thanks to the many teachers, colleagues, friends, and family members who supported it. At several key moments, Bruce Marshall listened carefully and offered guidance with his unique combination of patience, freedom, and uncompromising demand for rigor. William Abraham was always available to discuss my arguments, adding his own more perceptive arguments and counterarguments, and refining my thought. Natalia Marandiuc helped me to clarify what was really central to my text. Trent Pomplun gave me invaluable advice early in the preparation of the manuscript and again once it was drafted.

My colleagues and friends at Southern Methodist University spent countless hours reading chapters, hashing out arguments, and offering companionship. Daniel Houck, Jared Maddox, David Mahfood, Nathan McLellan, and Adam Van Wart all read chapters along the way. Colleagues at United Theological Seminary have been a source of continuous support and encouragement. In particular, Tom Dozeman and Anthony Le Donne guided me through the preparation and revision of the manuscript for publication. The Board of Trustees of United Theological Seminary granted a sabbatical leave for the fall of 2018 to finalize the manuscript. Finally, I am grateful to the Catholic University of America Press for its care with my manuscript, and for the insightful reviewers whose close reading and perceptive comments made for a much improved text and argument.

My parents, Wayne and Melinda Hunter, always prioritized my education, often at great personal cost. This work became possible with their sacrifices. Our sons, Justus II and Miles, gave me the laughs and breaks I needed along the way. Baby Lucy joined the fun at the end. But no one sacrificed so long and so consistently for this book as my wife, Ellen Ann Hunter. I could never repay your love, support, and faith in me; I simply accept it with gratitude.

Abbreviations

CDH	*Cur Deus homo* (Anselm of Canterbury)
DCL	*De cessatione legalium* (Robert Grosseteste)
Defensiones	*Defensiones theologiae Divi Thomae Aquinatis* (John Capreolus)
De veritate	*Quaestiones disputatae de veritate* (Thomas Aquinas)
Glossa	*Glossa in quatuor libros Sententiarum Petri Lombardi* (Alexander of Hales)
In Sententiarum	*Commentarii in III Sententiarum* (Albert the Great)
Ord.	*Ordinatio* (John Duns Scotus)
PL	Patrologia Latina (ed. Migne)
Quaestio	*Quaestio de conceptione Christi* (Albert the Great)
Quodl.	*Quaestiones de Quolibet* (Guerric of Saint-Quentin)
Reportatio	*Reportatio Parisiensis* (John Duns Scotus)
SCG	*Summa contra Gentiles* (Thomas Aquinas)
Scriptum	*Scriptum super libros Sententiarum* (Thomas Aquinas)
Sent.	*Commentaria in quatuor libros Sententiarum Magistri Petri Lombardi* (Bonaventure)
Sentences	*Sententiae in IV libris distinctae* (Peter Lombard)
SH	*Summa theologica seu sic ab origine dicta "Summa fratris Alexandri"* (*Summa Halensis*) (Alexander of Hales [?])
ST	*Summa theologiae* (Thomas Aquinas)

Introduction

Since the twelfth century, theologians have found a counterfactual question irresistible: "If Adam had not sinned, would the Son have become incarnate?" In the latter half of the twentieth century, Hans Urs von Balthasar, Hans Küng, Gerhard Ludwig Müller, Karl Rahner, Karl Barth, Wolfhart Pannenburg, Jürgen Moltmann, and Robert Jenson all considered this question on the reason, or motive, for the incarnation. Nearly every case refers to the classic disagreement between those who follow Thomas Aquinas and those who follow John Duns Scotus. Recently, several book- or chapter-length proposals on the reason for the incarnation have emerged. Marilyn McCord Adams follows the solution of Robert Grosseteste and John Duns Scotus in order to address problems in contemporary theodicy.[1] Edwin Chr. Van Driel develops a response in conversation with Friedrich Schleiermacher, Isaak August Dorner, and Karl Barth, whose putatively Scotist positions he variously labels "supralapsarian."[2] In conversation with John Calvin and Francis Turretin, Oliver Crisp develops a position that presses in a "Scotist" direction.[3] Frederick Christian Bauerschmidt develops an

---

1. Marilyn McCord Adams, "Cosmic Coherence and the Primacy of Christ: Christ the One in Whom All Things Hold Together," in *Christ and the Horrors: The Coherence of Christology* (Cambridge: Cambridge University Press, 2006), 170–204.

2. Edwin Chr. van Driel, *Incarnation Anyway: Arguments for Supralapsarian Christology* (Oxford: Oxford University Press, 2008).

3. Oliver Crisp, "John Calvin (1509–1564) on the Motivation for the Incarnation,"

innovative argument in conversation with John Paul II that aims to mediate the Thomist and Scotist positions.[4]

Though it is common to claim Thomas or Scotus as one's authority, the theological debates among which Thomas and Scotus developed their own positions remain largely neglected. This study fills that gap. *If Adam Had Not Sinned* is a study of the medieval debates over the motive for the incarnation from Anselm of Canterbury to John Duns Scotus. While the study is chiefly focused on thirteenth-century debates at the University of Paris, it also supplies necessary historical background to those debates. As a result, the larger context within which Thomas Aquinas and John Duns Scotus developed their influential responses is detailed. This larger context permits an analysis that leads to the surprising claim, against widespread assumptions, that the responses given by Thomas and Scotus are substantially reconcilable.

The heart of this study is an analysis of the debates over the motive for the incarnation in three moments. In the first moment—represented by Robert Grosseteste, Alexander of Hales, and the *Summa Halensis* (*SH*)—theologians supplied deductive arguments for the conclusion that the Son would become incarnate in any possible world. Theologians of the second moment—represented by Guerric of Saint-Quentin, Odo Rigaldi, and Albert the Great—rejected the deductive arguments of the first moment in order to secure God's freedom over creation. Theologians of the third moment—such as Thomas Aquinas and Bonaventure of Bagnoregio—likewise preserve divine freedom, but also appropriate the arguments of the first moment as arguments from congruity or fittingness (*convenientia*). These third-moment theologians effectively resolve the set of questions raised in the first two moments. John

in *Revisioning Christology: Theology in the Reformed Tradition* (Burlington, Vt.: Ashgate, 2011), 23–42.

4. Frederick Christian Bauerschmidt, "Incarnation, Redemption, and the Character of God," *Nova et Vetera* 3, no. 3 (2005): 459–72; *Thomas Aquinas: Faith, Reason, and Following Christ* (Oxford: Oxford University Press, 2013), 180–88.

Duns Scotus's reflections on the motive for the incarnation, which shift from these modal debates to an analysis of the order of divine intentions, marks a new moment in the history of considering the motive for the incarnation. However, the new moment inaugurated by Scotus is conceptually consistent with third-moment strategies. Hence, in the larger context of thirteenth-century debates on the reason for the incarnation, Scotus and Thomas are substantially reconcilable. It was not inevitable that the "Scotist position" and the "Thomist position" on the reason for the incarnation developed in contradistinction to one another.

Overview of the Argument

The following reading of the thirteenth-century debates highlights the important way in which the counterfactual question is nested within a larger set of considerations regarding both the reasons for divine operations *ad extra* and the rules that govern the articulation of those reasons. This systematic concern is shared by all the thirteenth-century theologians considered in this study. In the commentaries on Peter Lombard's *Sentences*, it was standard to introduce reflections on the reason for the incarnation with an extended reflection on the modal status of the incarnation.[5] We will see that the interrelation between broader theological issues and the reason for the incarnation was a major concern that permitted thirteenth-century theologians to develop both highly refined accounts of divine action, in general, and theologies of the incarnation, in particular. In order to clarify the key systematic junctures raised by the counterfactual question, the first chapter clarifies the term *ratio* (reason) and refines the set of questions thirteenth-century theologians considered in relation to the reason for the incarnation.

---

5. See, for instance, Thomas Aquinas, *Summa Theologiae*, vols. 4–12, *Opera omnia iussu Leonis XIII P.M. edita* (Rome: Typographia Polyglotta, 1886–1906), III, q. 1–3, (hereafter, *ST*).

Following this introductory chapter, I turn to Anselm of Canterbury's *Cur Deus homo* (*CDH*). Anselm's text greatly influenced early thirteenth-century Christology at both Oxford and Paris. Although Anselm does not address the counterfactual question, his argument on the necessity of the incarnation was massively influential for thirteenth-century treatments of the reason for the incarnation. The influence is largely attributable to Anselm's method for reasoning about divine operations *ad extra* in *CDH*. Close analysis of Anselm's arguments on the incarnation yields several theses on divine reasons for divine operations, which Anselm's thirteenth-century followers variously developed.

The third chapter turns to the first development of Anselm's method into a thorough position on the reason for the incarnation: Robert Grosseteste's *De cessatione legalium* (*DCL*). Grosseteste produces well over a dozen arguments for the affirmative response to the counterfactual question. The third chapter shows how Grosseteste's arguments develop Anselm's approach into deductive arguments that there will be incarnation in all worlds compossible with Grosseteste's God. Moreover, Grosseteste's arguments are reducible to two strategies, one proceeding from some divine attribute, the other deriving from some created effect.

We transition from Oxford to Paris in the fourth chapter, the first of two on the reason for the incarnation at the University of Paris. Chapter four considers, first, the revisions Peter Lombard's *Sentences* made to discussions of the reason for the incarnation at Paris. The chapter then moves through the positions of Guerric of Saint-Quentin, Albert the Great, and Thomas Aquinas, three occupants of the Dominican Chair for Externs in the early- to mid-thirteenth century. The subsequent, fifth chapter treats several occupants of the Franciscan Chair over the same period: Alexander of Hales, the various authors of the *SH*, Odo Rigaldi, and Bonaventure of Bagnoregio.

The sixth and final chapter draws together all the arguments and positions encountered in the fourth and fifth chapters. I show

how the debates over the motive for the incarnation at Paris developed in three moments. Moreover, I argue that Bonaventure and Thomas, who offer substantially the same solution, mark a summative resolution to the two preceding moments of the debate. Thus, they provide an alternative reception of Anselm's theses to the one developed by Robert Grosseteste and favored by Alexander in the first moment of the debates at Paris. Finally, the sixth chapter briefly considers the reception of Bonaventure's argument by three subsequent Franciscan Masters: Matthew of Aquasparta, Richard Middleton, and John Duns Scotus. While Matthew and Richard follow Bonaventure closely, Scotus augments Bonaventure's influential treatment with a new set of considerations on the reason for the incarnation. Thus, Scotus marks the beginning of a new moment in the debates over the reason for the incarnation, one that both assumes and moves beyond the summative achievement of Bonaventure and Thomas.

If Adam Had Not Sinned

ONE

The Reason for the Incarnation

The question "Why the incarnation?" has exercised theologians for centuries, and rightly so. The reasons we give for the incarnation carry significant implications for the doctrines of sin and redemption. Both medieval and modern theologians argue that one's answer—the reason for the incarnation—is determinative for ascribing the proper primacy to Jesus Christ in Christian theology. The reason for the incarnation, or *ratio incarnationis*, is located at an important juncture of several dogmatic loci: divine will and operation, Christology, soteriology, and faith. Few other questions afford such opportunities to think across so many Christian doctrines. Hence, the question is a rigorous test for the coherence of Christian theology. As a result, it has proven a fruitful site for theological disputation, speculation, and discovery.

Most important, the question stands at the heart of the Christian faith. The incarnation is God's central operation in creation. Thus, a theologian's position on the *ratio incarnationis* will be determinative for her speech both about that central mystery of the faith and its varied and extensive implications for Christian spirituality and practice. It is therefore unsurprising that the *ratio incarnationis* has endured as a central topic on the agenda of theologians for centuries.

The thirteenth century was a high point for systematic reflection on the *ratio incarnationis*. Contemporary discussions of the *ratio incarnationis*, even when theologians manifest engagement with thirteenth-century investigations of the question, often wander from important and highly persuasive thirteenth-century approaches to the question. This is regrettable, as thirteenth-century theologians showed remarkable insight into the challenges the question presents, the possible responses, and where to locate the question in Christian theology.

Ratio

What is a *ratio*, and what do we mean to answer a question with a *ratio*? A *ratio* is a kind of explanation. It supplies a specific kind of answer to the question "Why?" In the event that my notebook falls from my desk to the floor, it is natural to inquire, "Why did my notebook fall?" In response, I could give a number of explanations. I might respond that it was because my elbow nudged it over the edge as I swiveled in my chair, or that I picked up another book whose weight was preventing the force of gravity from pulling the notebook off the desk and onto the floor, or that an earthquake shook it off the desk, or simply that gravitational force is such that notebooks fall from desks when a certain percentage of their weight is distributed in a certain way. Any of these explanations could be true so long as we ask the question generically. Moreover, it is possible for more than one of these explanations to be true regarding the same event. But to give a *ratio* is to give a particular kind of explanation, an explanation for an action that involves intention. As Elizabeth Anscombe puts it, what distinguishes intentional actions from unintentional actions "is that they are the actions to which a certain sense of the question 'Why?' is given application; the sense is of course that in which the answer, if positive, gives a reason for acting."[1] Or, in Donald Davidson's terms, an intentional action is

---

1. G. E. M. Anscombe, *Intention*, 2nd ed. (Cambridge, Mass.: Harvard University Press, 1963), 9.

an event that, under some description, has a reason (pro-attitude + belief) for its explanation.[2]

Of course, not all acts performed by a human agent are intentional actions. Reflexes, for instance, are not intentional. Aristotle distinguishes intentional actions from actions of the reflexive sort in terms of their sources.[3] That is, he distinguishes between "things that come to be ... as a result of thought or nature."[4] Later thinkers develop these comments into a distinction between (1) willed and (2) natural acts. Both come to the same: willed, or intentional, actions are distinguished by their source in the free deliberations of an agent, while natural actions come to be necessarily, so long as certain conditions are satisfied. For example, if my dog is functioning properly, and the bone is visible and not out of reach (nor are any other mitigating factors present), he will chew the bone. This bone-chewing is a natural action.

Willed actions are distinguished from natural actions in that they are free. Multiple analyses of freedom can be given. For instance, Duns Scotus thinks of freedom in terms of the will's ability to will opposite acts (volition or nolition) with regard to the same object. The will can determine whether to elicit an act of volition or nolition when presented with its proper object. The intellect, on the other hand, is a natural faculty. That is, the intellect is not free to choose between opposite acts when presented with its proper object. Rather, the intellect necessarily elicits an act of intellection when presented with an intelligible object, as my dog necessarily elicits the act of chewing when presented with the bone. Alternatively, Aquinas conceives of the will as a rational appetite. That is,

2. Donald Davidson, "Actions, Reasons, and Causes," *Journal of Philosophy* 60, no. 23 (1963): 685–700.

3. From this point forward, my analysis will be deliberately medieval in articulation. If there are counterparts in the contemporary philosophy of action, all the better, but I will not develop my analysis here in conversation with contemporary philosophy of action.

4. Aristotle, *Physics*, in *The Complete Works of Aristotle*, ed. Jonathan Barnes, 2 vols. (Princeton: Princeton University Press, 1984), II.5, 196b22–3.

the will pursues an end insofar as it is perceived, by the intellect, to be good. Moreover, the intellect directs the will by its deliberation upon the means whereby that end might be attained.[5] Whatever analysis of the will one prefers, the distinction between natural and willed acts in terms of freedom remains. And so, prima facie, it does not make a determinative difference which philosophy of action one prefers when it comes to the *ratio incarnationis*.

We have, then, a basic distinction between two kinds of action, natural and willed, that have different kinds of explanations.[6] The latter are free, and therefore they have *rationes* (reasons) for their explanation. Thus, if we are to pursue the *ratio* for some divine operation, our description of divine *rationes* will have to develop on analogy with the willed action of humans, and so in the argument that follows I will utilize the language of human agency: will and intellect.[7]

While that "God has a will and intellect" is accepted by all theologians considered in this study, this is not to say (1) why it is necessary do so, or (2) what it is to say such a thing. Various arguments have been given in response to (1). For instance, Scripture speaks regularly of God's knowledge (Romans 11:33) and will (Romans 12:2). St. Anselm of Canterbury argues that God must have an intellect and will because they are pure perfections (i.e., it is always better to have them than to lack them). Scotus finds Anselm's argument unpersuasive. Instead, he argues that if there is at least one contingent event in creation, then the first efficient cause must be a willing agent since this is the only kind of cause, to our knowledge,

---

5. See Alan Donagan, "Thomas Aquinas on Human Action," in *The Cambridge History of Later Medieval Philosophy: From the Rediscovery of Aristotle to the Disintegration of Scholasticism 1100–1600*, ed. Norman Kretzmann, Anthony Kenny, and Jan Pinborg (Cambridge: Cambridge University Press, 1982), 642–54; Robert Pasnau, *Thomas Aquinas on Human Nature: A Philosophical Study of Summa Theologiae Ia 75–89* (New York: Cambridge University Press, 2002), esp. ch. 8.

6. Specifically, while both might admit of several similar or identical explanations, only the latter will include the agent's reasons as one of those explanations.

7. To speak of the "willed actions of humans" is not to preclude the application of willed actions to other agents, such as angels.

that can produce contingent results. Our experience shows us that there is at least one contingent event in creation—one event that could have come about otherwise. Thus, it must be that the first efficient cause is a willing agent.[8] Any of these responses suggest (1) why it is necessary to speak of divine knowledge and will. However, they do not yet clarify (2) what it is to say such a thing.

Thomas Aquinas reflects, in *Summa Theologiae* (*ST*) I, q. 14, a. 1, on whether there is knowledge (*scientia*) in God. He first raises the objection that "knowledge is a habit, which is not appropriate for God, because (a habit) is a mean between potency and act."[9] Since God is pure actuality, a point already established by Thomas in *ST* I, q. 3, a. 1, God cannot have the habit of knowledge. How, then, can God be said to have knowledge? Aquinas responds as follows:

Because perfections proceeding from God to creatures are in God in a greater way, as is said above, whenever some name taken from some created perfection is attributed to God, all of that which pertains to the imperfect way which befits a creature should be excluded from its signification. Thus knowledge is not a quality or habit in God, but substance and pure actuality.[10]

Aquinas's procedure for attributing terms and concepts of created perfections to God is to exclude anything inappropriate from the signification of the term in order to eminently attribute the perfection to God. I will refer to this procedure as analogical, and speech of this sort as analogical speech, or speech by way of anal-

---

8. For an overview of Scotus's argument, see Ludger Honnefelder, "John Duns Scotus on God's Intellect and Will," in *John Duns Scotus 1308–2008: The Opera Theologica of Scotus. Proceedings of "The Quadruple Congress" on John Duns Scotus, Part 2*, ed. Richard Cross, *Archa Verbi Subsidia* 4 (St. Bonaventure, N.Y.: Franciscan Institute Publications, 2012), 73–88.

9. "Scientia enim habitus est, qui Deo non competit, cum sit medius inter potentiam et actum." All translations, unless otherwise indicated, are my own.

10. *ST* I, q. 14, a. 1, ad 1: "Quia perfectiones procedentes a Deo in creaturas, altiori modo sunt in Deo, ut supra dictum est, oportet quod, quandocumque aliquod nomen sumptum a quacumque perfectione creaturae Deo atribuitur, secludatur ab eius signifcatione omne illud quod pertinet ad imperfectum modum qui competit creaturae. Unde scientia non est qualitas in Deo vel habitus, sed substantia et actus purus."

ogy.[11] Analogical speech moves from a familiar predication, taken from the created realm, and stipulates those senses in which that predication fails due to their imperfection.

With this methodological principle in mind, I can now respond to (2) above: What does it mean to say "God has a will and intellect"? We say it analogically. In certain senses I mean the same thing as when I say "My brother, John, has a will and intellect." In certain senses I mean something different. The task, then, is to specify which senses are which.

Determining with some degree of precision what these similarities and differences are will be a major factor in determining the reason for the incarnation. If my predications of volitions and *rationes* to God are analogical, the way in which I reason about them will have to be consistent with how I conceive the analogy. To give an absurd example, if I take creaturely and divine volitions to be similar insofar as they are mutable, the following premises are both possibly true:

1.1 God wills to beatify some humans at time t_1.

1.2 God wills not to beatify any humans at time t_2.

The possible truth of (1.1) and (1.2) would render Anselm's argument in *Cur Deus homo* unsound, as Anselm's argument hinges on God's immutable desire to beatify some humans at any time *t*. Alternatively, if I take creaturely and divine volitions to be distinct with respect to their mutability, then I can only take one of the two premises to be true, and, presuming I take (1.1) to be true, I might argue to Anselm's conclusion in *CDH*.[12]

The theologians surveyed in subsequent chapters work simulta-

---

11. This is not to say that "being" is also analogous. My analogical procedure is equally descriptive of language used by Scotus, for whom the univocity of being, when predicated of God and creatures, is a condition of the possibility of the analogical predications discussed here. All that is meant by analogical here is deflationary: similar in some sense and different in another.

12. For a more detailed analysis of Anselm's argument and the important function of immutability therein, see chapter 2.

neously at two exercises: (1) supplying reasons for the incarnation, and (2) rendering those reasons consistent with their theologies of divine action. These two exercises provoked theologians to refine their understanding of the relation between divine and human volitional acts.

A typical thirteenth-century strategy for performing these two exercises coherently was *nesting* specific questions within more general topics and questions. So, for instance, when Thomas Aquinas asks the famous counterfactual in the *Summa Theologiae*—"if humanity had not sinned, would God have become incarnate?"—the question follows a series of inquiries into whether the incarnation was fitting or necessary for the reparation of human nature.[13] These modal questions on the necessity and fittingness of the incarnation frame the counterfactual question, thereby bringing to bear considerations of divine action and human access to divine reasons.

Even when scholastic reflections on the reason for the incarnation do not follow Thomas's order of questions in the *Summa Theologiae*, they evince attention to this nesting relationship between the reason for the incarnation and broader questions about divine action and human access to divine reasons. For instance, when Bonaventure considers "the primary reason (*ratio praecipua*) for the incarnation," his rephrasing of the question is motivated by his commitment to a broader consideration of whether and how we can determine divine reasons for divine operations *ad extra*. This broader consideration provokes him to rephrase the specific question about the reason for the incarnation in terms of primacy amongst reasons, rather than in the counterfactual as Thomas does. This revision was broadly accepted, at least among subsequent Franciscan theologians.[14]

Observing this nesting relationship between scholastic questions allows us to isolate the critical systematic junctures that pro-

13. *ST* III, q. 1, aa. 1–3. Hereafter, Aquinas's counterfactual will be called "the hypothetical question."
14. See chapter 5.

voke and animate the debates over the reason for the incarnation. Whatever reasons are supplied for the incarnation, they must be consistent with a theological account of what divine *rationes* are and how they are known. Across various configurations, the critical juncture in the thirteenth-century debates can be isolated by specifying a generic question: How can we determine reasons for divine operations *ad extra*?[15] Observing the relationship between a theologian's response to this generic question and the nested specific question on the reason for the incarnation (a particular divine operation *ad extra*) will allow us to observe the significant moments in the series of debates over the reason for the incarnation in the thirteenth century. Moreover, it will allow us to connect those thirteenth-century debates to their historical precedents, in particular to Anselm of Canterbury's *Cur Deus homo*.

Finally, it must be noted that *ratio* is a notoriously ranging term in scholastic theology. In nearest semantic proximity to its use here, it is translated "reason," "intention," or "motive." As I specified above, we are concerned with the *ratio* for some willed action. Some have insisted upon "reason" as opposed to "motive," insofar as "motive" implies an external causality unfitting for God, whereas *ratio* is restricted to internal causality.[16] However, this argument seems to misunderstand the analogical nature of such predications. It is perfectly acceptable to use the language of "motive" while retaining the freedom of divine action from external causality, simply by stipulating this external causality as one dissimilarity. The semantic preference for *ratio* or "reason" is no better for guarding against this worry, as human reasons often include external referents. Neither is it clear what sense of "external causality" is at stake here. If this "external causality" is simply that "for the sake of which" the act is, then there is nothing objectionable so long as the act is free. Anything more seems difficult to defend as consti-

---

15. Hereafter, this question will be referred to as "the generic question."

16. See, for instance, Jean Francois Bonnefoy, *Christ and the Cosmos*, trans. Michael D. Meilach (Paterson, N.J.: St. Anthony Guild Press, 1965), 6.

tutive of the meaning of "motive." Moreover, human reason differs
from divine reason insofar as it proceeds by composition and division, and divine reason is simple.[17] So we do not avoid challenges
with a move from "motive" to "reason." I will therefore make use of
both "motive" and "reason" in translating *ratio*.[18] The *ratio* for some
divine operation is God's reason for performing that operation,
which I take to be synonymous with God's motive for performing
that operation. Both will require similar analogical revisions.

Rationes, Priority, and Primacy

In subsequent chapters, I will use language of primacy and priority to clarify the various positions on the *ratio incarnationis* developed in the thirteenth century. It will be worthwhile, briefly, to
clarify and warrant my use of this language.

Every theologian in the thirteenth century recognized that
there are many reasons for the incarnation. Broadly, we can distinguish two sources for determining divine reasons for the incarnation: (1) recorded revelation and (2) observation. The first is
conveyed to us by divine revelation recorded in Scripture. For instance, Ephesians 1 states, "(God) chose us in Christ before the
foundation of the world to be holy and blameless before him in
love." 1 Timothy 1:15, on the other hand, states that "Christ Jesus
came into the world to save sinners." The second source for determining divine reasons for the incarnation is the set of created
goods that follows from the incarnation. These created goods allow for human observation and reflection. Whether or not we can
comprehend or specify all of those goods, we can identify many of
them. For instance, the set of goods achieved by the incarnation
includes the creation of an individual creature, the deliverance of
revelation, and the outpouring of the Holy Spirit. All these goods,

---

17. *ST* I, q. 14, a. 7.
18. No inferences should be made from which term is used in which cases; the
terms vary for stylistic reasons, and so should be read synonymously.

and many others, are specified by scholastic theologians. Each of these is an observable good, achieved by the incarnation, for which we can infer God has an intention, or reason. That is, these goods achieved by the incarnation are among the many reasons for the incarnation, distinguished from the aforementioned reasons in terms of the source of our knowledge of them; the latter reasons derive from our observation of the historic event of the incarnation, rather than recorded revelation. Of course, in a broader sense, both sets of reasons are revealed.[19]

In short, myriad reasons can be given in response to the question "Why the incarnation?" When Thomas Aquinas considers whether or not the incarnation was necessary in the *Summa Theologiae*, he recites ten reasons, an uncharacteristically lengthy list for this concise *Summa*. Among six other reasons, he notes that the incarnation greatly raises hope, excites charity, takes away presumption, and liberates from servitude.[20] Thomas then concludes the *corpus*: "There are many other usefulnesses (*utilitates*) which are accomplished (by the incarnation), beyond the comprehension of human sense."[21] Neither the set of revealed goods nor the set of observable goods exhaust the set of divine reasons for the incarnation.

Late in the thirteenth century, and especially over the course of the fourteenth, theologians became concerned with a challenge arising from the diversity of divine reasons for divine operations

19. It is granted by everyone in these debates that the mystery of the incarnation itself can only be known by revelation.

20. *ST* III, q. 1, a. 2, *corpus*.

21. *ST* III, q. 1, a. 2, *corpus*: "Sunt autem et aliae plurimae utilitates quae consecutae sunt, supra comprehensionem sensus humani." Thomas, here, prefers the term *utilitates*, as the *corpus* opens with a distinction between two ways of saying something is necessary: (1) *sine quo aliquid esse non potest*—that without which something is not able to be—and (2) *per quod melius et convenienitus pervenitur ad finem*—that through which an end is better and more fittingly obtained. Appeal to "usefulnesses" implies this latter sense of "necessary" while supplying a litany of reasons for the incarnation; that is, "usefulnesses" are goods achieved by the incarnation, which must be among the set of reasons for which God became incarnate. I will give a fuller account of these passages in the context of Thomas's fuller view on the *ratio incarnationis* in its historical moment in chapter 4.

ad extra. Divine simplicity seems to require that we recognize the unity of the divine will and action. There must be some story to tell about how, in spite of these diverse reasons, the divine intention is one. Some might object, then, that we should not speak of multiple reasons, but rather of one divine reason, volition, and operation.[22] This is one of the problems Bonaventure's consideration of order among reasons seeks to resolve through the language of "primacy." The unity of divine volitions and operations can be conceived as a unity of order, with one reason having relative primacy or priority vis-à-vis the others in a single order.[23]

The situation is not entirely disanalogous with human reasons for human operations. Consider the following example: this morning I instructed my son to eat both the white and the yolk of his egg. What was my reason? Immediately, it was to see that he consume the entirety of the egg. That reason was further motivated by my desire to see that he develops a healthy and strong body. And that desire was motivated by my desire for him to have a happy life. Motives, then, can form a sequence wherein certain motives are prior and others posterior in the order of motives. But, as the egg example indicates, the order of motives need not follow the order of execution. Furthermore, there are other motives for my whole-egg-eating directive: to ensure he does not become overly hungry before lunchtime, to reduce malodorous trash, and so on. These motives, at some point, connect with the earlier order of motives, such that while they might be distinct at a posterior level, they come into union with the order of motives as we proceed to more primary motives (see figure 1).

22. In the sixteenth century, Luis Molina advances this objection forcefully, and well beyond the topic of the reason for the incarnation. As this study will demonstrate, the concerns this objection raises are both anticipated in Bonaventure and advanced by John Duns Scotus when they come to the reason for the incarnation. See Juniper Carol's treatment in *Why Jesus Christ? Thomistic, Scotistic, and Conciliatory Perspectives* (Manassas, Va.: Trinity Communications, 1986), 483–85.

23. For Alston's attempt to reckon with this problem, see William P. Alston, "Divine and Human Action," in *Divine Nature and Human Language: Essays in Philosophical Theology* (Ithaca, N.Y.: Cornell University Press, 1988), 81–102.

FIGURE 1

		Instructing him to eat the egg
	Physical health	
		Walking him to school
Happiness		
		Instructing him to eat the egg
	Avoiding hunger	
		Packing him a full lunch box

There are, then, two senses of priority. First, to speak of priority is to speak of the relationship between two individuals. The seventh batter in a batting lineup is prior to the eighth and ninth batters. I will refer to this sense of priority simply as priority. Second, to speak of priority can also be to speak of the original, the first, the primary thing to which all other individuals in that order are secondary, tertiary, and so on. In this latter sense, when I speak of a primary or prior motive I intend the most generic level of motivation, the level that ranges over the broadest set of actions and motivations for actions. I will refer to this sense of priority as primacy.

So, my son's happiness is both primary and a prior motive to his health among my motivations for action in the chart above, whereas my son's health is not primary but is a prior motive to his eating the entire egg. Alternatively, his eating the entire egg is a posterior motive to his having health, which is a posterior motive to his happiness, which is posterior to nothing in this order.

I have now given both a specific account of my order of motives and a general account of the human order of motives. As I distinguished divine and human reasons earlier, so I must also account for the difference between divine and human orders of reasons or motives. For instance, one will note that the sequence of motives adumbrated above for my instruction to my son is a well-ordered sequence. However, we humans are also capable of producing disordered sequences of motivations. For instance, if I instructed my son to consume his entire fork in order to conserve my time by washing fewer dishes, some lesser good (conserving time) is given priority to some greater good (the health of my son). Such disordered motivations would be entirely unworthy of God.

Divine simplicity demands clarification of another sense in which divine motives differ from creaturely motives. Priority and posteriority among divine motives do not include any temporality, as God is eternal. Thus, primacy and priority do not entail succession, but only order. Primacy among divine reasons in no way implies a temporal before and after, but merely logical order. In this way, they are more akin to the order between the first principles of logic and principles derived from the first principles, all of which hold simultaneously in time. All the reasons are one in God, even as God is one. Nevertheless, we must make do with language and concepts familiar to us, which will demand talk of priority, posteriority, first, next, and primary.[24]

Even when theologians of the thirteenth century do not use language of priority and primacy as explicitly as does Bonaventure, they evince concern about the interrelation between diverse reasons for the incarnation. I have already noted that Thomas supplies diverse reasons for the incarnation. From the earliest reflections on the reason for the incarnation at both Paris and Oxford we can see a prominent concern over the relation between one particular motive—the redemption from sin—and myriad others. After all, in the first phases of the debates, the conversation centered on a subjunctive conditional that specifies a reason in the protasis, "If Adam had not sinned...." It seems, therefore, worthwhile to follow closely the developing understanding of priority and primacy among the myriad reasons in the texts we will encounter ahead. As I specified a generic question to track the nesting relations between answers to the hypothetical question and broader concerns about divine

24. Jean Francois Bonnefoy comments at some length on this point in Bonnefoy, *Christ and the Cosmos*, 11–14.

operation *ad extra*, I will also specify a primacy question: What is the primary reason for the incarnation?[25] Like the generic question, the primacy question allows us to clarify the contours of a theologian's position on the reason for the incarnation, thereby tracking development across the thirteenth century and connecting the thirteenth-century debates to their historical precedents in Anselm.

Possibility, Possible Worlds, and Compossibility

We have now specified three questions:

- If humanity had not sinned, would God have become incarnate? (hypothetical question)
- What is the primary reason for the incarnation? (primacy question)
- How can we determine reasons for divine operations *ad extra*? (general question)

Both the hypothetical question and the primacy question are "nested" within the general question. That is, how one responds to "Whether and how can we determine reasons for divine operations *ad extra*?" will be determinative for whether and how one responds to both the hypothetical and the primacy question. In fact, to answer either the hypothetical question or the primacy question is to issue a partial response to the general question. Taking up the hypothetical question or the primacy question entails certain assertions with respect to the general question.

For example, the hypothetical question is a subjunctive conditional, or counterfactual. Subjunctive conditionals specify a state of affairs contrary-to-fact designated by the protasis (e.g., "if Adam had not fallen"). To pose a counterfactual is to provoke speculation on possible worlds other than our actual world.[26] Thus, simply

---

25. Hereafter, this will be called "the primacy question."

26. This implication of counterfactuals has been developed by R. Trent Pomplun, "The Immaculate World: Predestination and Passibility in Contemporary Scotism,"

to pose the hypothetical question is to provoke speculation on a range of possible worlds open to the divine will, which entails some account of divine freedom analyzable according to possible worlds semantics.

Theologians, scholastic and otherwise, are sometimes more (Bonaventure) and sometimes less (Grosseteste) reflective about the implications of counterfactuals for broader accounts of divine action. In the thirteenth century, it was somewhat pro forma to acknowledge discomfort with the hypothetical question, and then to proceed in issuing responses. The theologians we will be surveying in subsequent chapters raise various concerns with counterfactual arguments, even while they continue to produce them.

Even when theologians are less reflective about the implications of a question like the hypothetical question for accounts of divine action, they often express anxiety about these implications. Robert Grosseteste, for instance, following a litany of deductive arguments on why the Son would become incarnate even if there were no fall, notes: "These and similar reasons seem to be able to show that God would become man, even if man had never sinned. Nevertheless, I know myself to be ignorant as to whether this is true, and for this ignorance I am not lightly sorrowed."[27]

The nesting relationships between these questions, the implica-

---

Modern Theology 30, no. 4 (2014): 544–48. See also William Marshner, "A Critique of Marian Counterfactual Formulae: A Report of Results," *Marian Studies* 30 (1979): 108–39. Pomplun, following the lead of Marshner, gives a rigorous analysis of Baroque debates over the possibility of Christ by utilizing counterfactual analysis of protasis-worlds (or *p*-worlds). Protasis-worlds are the range of possible worlds for which the conditional of the protasis is true. My analysis is similar insofar as it will (1) consider sets of protasis-worlds, and (2) seek to be as deflationary as possible. However, I will use set-theoretic distinctions among various classes of possible worlds that together comprise the entire union of sets compossible with the existence of some God (I will leave open which God is under consideration), including possible worlds outside the set of protasis-worlds, such as our actual world. A serviceable orientation to set theory can be found in Part I of David Papineau, *Philosophical Devices: Proofs, Probabilities, Possibilities, and Sets* (Oxford: Oxford University Press, 2012).

27. *DCL* III.2.1. "Hiis et huiusmodi raciocinacionibus videtur posse astrui Deum esse hominem licet numquam peccasset homo. Quod tamen an verum sit me ignorare scio, et meam in hac parte ignorantiam non mediocriter doleo."

tions of responses to one question for another, and varying degrees of reflection on the implications across the thirteenth century present challenges to the intellectual historian. But they also present certain opportunities. In order to manage the challenges and pursue opportunities, it is necessary to have some means of clarifying and refining the implications of arguments across questions and topics.

In order to clarify and refine the scholastic arguments, I will make use of set theoretic distinctions across possible worlds. I will be distinguishing between several sets of possible worlds on the basis of the presence or absence of (a) a fall and (b) an incarnation, the two variables specified in the hypothetical question. Let W-worlds be the set of possible worlds in which there is a fall and an incarnation (including our own), X-worlds be the set of possible worlds in which there is neither a fall nor an incarnation, F-worlds be the set of possible worlds in which there is a fall but no incarnation, and I-worlds be the set of possible worlds in which there is an incarnation but no fall. To ask the hypothetical question, then, is to ask whether or not there are I-worlds.

But I have not yet refined the concepts enough. First of all, we must be clear as to what sort of possibility I have in mind. Logical possibility? Surely this must be true. Physical possibility? This seems to be the consideration at the forefront of protracted medieval debates over the metaphysics of the incarnation. But neither class of possibility isolates the relevant sense of "possible" we are interested in here. For our purposes, we will need to stipulate a narrower sense of "possible," which I will pursue by deploying the concept of "compossibility."

Two things are compossible when they are possibly true for the same possible world. For instance, it is compossible both that I am 5 feet, 9 inches tall and that I am about 140 pounds at some time t. It is not compossible that I am both 5 feet, 9 inches tall and that I am 6 feet, 9 inches tall at some time t. There is no possible world in which I am at the same time and in the same sense 5 feet, 9 inches tall and 6 feet, 9 inches tall. Certain states of affairs foreclose other logically or physically possible states of affairs from obtaining in the same possible world.

Perhaps we are no better off with compossibility than we were with possibility. After all, we are no more interested in physical compossibilities than we are with physical possibilities. I will specify a narrower sense of compossibility with the phrase "compossible with x-God," which I will call theological compossibility.[28] Theological compossibility has the decided advantage of restricting the domain of possible worlds to the relevant ones, those that are compossible with x-God. Moreover, the flexibility of the variable x permits us to clarify multiple descriptions of God (Grosseteste's God, Thomas's God, Anselm's God, and so on) by observing the domain of theologically compossible worlds over which the relevant x-God ranges.

The latter insight is particularly important, as it clarifies an implication deriving from my earlier observation that the hypothetical question and the primacy question are "nested" within the general question. As we will see, the response of some theologian x to the hypothetical question, in restricting or expanding the domain of possible worlds "compossible with x-God," implies or entails various assertions on the general question. For instance, imagine theologian x gives a negative response to the hypothetical question. In this case, I-worlds will be incompossible with x-God. Moreover, the reasons supplied for that negative response may imply or entail an understanding of the properties of x-God that permit or foreclose certain forms of inference to divine reasons for divine operations *ad extra*.

Consider the following example: In *DCL* III, Robert Grosseteste gives an affirmative response to the hypothetical question and supplies the reason that God is supremely generous and will therefore bestow the greatest gift, namely union with divinity, upon His creatures. But this argument entails that divine reasons for (at least)

---

28. The value of x will be some possessive proper noun, such as "Grosseteste's," and so the phrase "compossible with Grosseteste's God."

this operation *ad extra* can be given by deduction from divine attri-butes such as generosity. Therefore, Grosseteste's argument entails, minimally, a partial response to the general question. Moreover, Grosseteste's response to the hypothetical question entails that some reason exists for the incarnation prior to redemption from sin: the expression of supreme generosity in creation. Hence, Gros-seteste's response to the hypothetical question both entails a partial response to the general question and a response to the primacy question. These are the benefits of distinguishing the questions as I have done, considering them together, and clarifying them in terms of compossibility.

A final clarification should be made concerning similarity across possible worlds. David Lewis, in his classic essay "Causation," refers to comparative overall similarity and develops the notion as follows:

> I take as primitive a relation of *comparative over-all* similarity among pos-sible worlds. We may say that one world it *closer to actuality* than another if the first resembles our actual world more than the second does, taking account of all the respects of similarity and difference and balancing them off one against another. . . . I have not said just how to balance the respects of comparison against each other, so I have not said just what our relation of comparative similarity is to be. Not for nothing did I call it primitive.[29]

A more thorough analysis of similarity is given in Lewis's early and influential 1979 essay "Counterfactual Dependence and Time's Ar-row."[30] On both occasions, Lewis insists, the concept of similarity across possible worlds is vague. Much will depend upon how partic-ular kinds of similarity are prioritized against others.[31]

---

29. David Lewis, "Causation," *The Journal of Philosophy* 70, no. 17 (1973): 559.

30. Lewis stipulates a set of priorities for similarity relations across possible worlds. They run as follows: "(1) It is of the first importance to avoid big, widespread, diverse violations of law. (2) It is of the second importance to maximize the spatio-temporal region throughout which perfect match of particular fact prevails. (3) It is of the third importance to avoid even small localized, simple violations of law. (4) It is of little or no importance to secure approximate similarity of particular fact, even in matters that concern us greatly." David Lewis, "Counterfactual Dependence and Time's Arrow," *Nous* 13, no. 4 (1979): 472.

31. In Lewis's own examples natural laws and matters of fact are considered. Thus,

This vagueness of similarity across possible worlds calls for stipulating the specific similarity-relations I will be prioritizing in the analysis that follows. For example, I will prioritize the similarity of reasons for divine operations *ad extra* over the fact of those operations. Thus, among the set of *I*-worlds (with an incarnation and without a fall), of which there are many (logically speaking), those most similar to our *W*-world (with a fall and an incarnation), in the relevant sense of "similar," will be those in which God possesses the same reasons for divine operations *ad extra*. If we grant that the primary reason for the incarnation in our actual *W*-world is redemption from sin, then *I*-worlds (which must possess some prior reason for an incarnation other than redemption from sin) will be less similar to our *W*-world than any *X*-world (without a fall or an incarnation) in which God possesses the same reasons for divine operations *ad extra*, even though these worlds are dissimilar with regard to the fact of an incarnation.

Before we move on, let us consider a possible objection to my application of possible worlds semantics to the arguments of the thirteenth century. After all, it is the schoolmen of the fourteenth century with whom we associate possible worlds as an extension of the famed absolute-ordained power distinction.[32] The latter distinction, between God's absolute power (within which multiple possi-

---

even if we accept Lewis's prioritization schema in this domain, some theological re-tuning will be necessary in order to arrive at the relevant sense of similarity for this investigation.

32. The secondary literature is extensive. Of special note are Hester Goodenough Gelber, *It Could Have Been Otherwise: Contingency and Necessity in Dominican Theology at Oxford, 1300–1350* (Leiden: Brill, 2004); Simo Knuuttila, *Modalities in Medieval Philosophy* (London: Routledge, 1993); Eugenio Randi, *Il sovrano e l'orologiaio: Due immagini di Dio nel dibattito sulla "potentia absoluta" fra XIII e XIV secolo* (Florence: La Nuova Italia Editrice, 1987). A helpful study of thirteenth-century formulations of the absolute-ordained distinction can be found in Lawrence Moonan, *Divine Power: The Medieval Power Distinction up to Its Adoption by Albert, Bonaventure, and Aquinas* (Oxford: Clarendon Press, 1994). William Courtenay offers the finest diachronic analysis of the debates over the absolute-ordained power distinction from the eleventh to the fourteenth century in *Capacity and Volition: A History of the Distinction of Absolute and Ordained Power* (Bergamo: Pierluigi Lubrina Editore, 1990).

ble worlds reside) and God's ordained power (actualized in our own possible world), was long associated with nominalism and late medieval theology. Indeed, wherever issues of contingency, necessity, and modality arose, the absolute-ordained power distinction and the investigation of *possibilia* were at hand.[33] It would seem, then, that I am reading the fourteenth into the thirteenth century.

And yet, the scholastic theologians of the thirteenth century did not refrain from posing the hypothetical question, the critical opening for possible worlds analysis. Ironically, Thomas's use of the hypothetical question is a more expansive opening for possible worlds analysis than Scotus's more refined formulation of the question at the end of the thirteenth century, which set the tone for the fourteenth-century debates.

Neither did thirteenth-century theologians refrain from, at times, introducing the absolute-ordained power distinction when the hypothetical question is raised. For instance, Thomas Aquinas states that, although he prefers the negative response to the hypothetical question, "nevertheless the power of God (*potentia Dei*) is not limited to this, for it is possible, even if sin did not exist, that God would become incarnate."[34] Moreover, as William Courtenay has shown, the absolute-ordained power distinction "was not a late medieval innovation nor a distinction whose use characterized the theology of (the fourteenth century) far more than that of the thirteenth century."[35] Rather, as Courtenay shows, the distinction "was a product of early scholasticism and reached its technical formulation in the opening years of the thirteenth century within the theological faculty at Paris."[36]

But perhaps a more subtle objection is still afoot. As many Thomists have noted, thirteenth-century theology, while occasion-

---

33. See the summary evaluation of the distinction in late medieval theology in Courtenay, *Capacity and Volition*, 189–91.

34. *ST* III, q. 1, a. 3, *corpus*: "Quamvis potentia Dei ad hoc non limitetur: potuisset enim, etiam peccato non existente, Deus incarnari."

35. Courtenay, *Capacity and Volition*, 189.

36. Courtenay, *Capacity and Volition*, 190.

ally engaging in speculative exercises about other possibilities available to the divine will, is finally oriented to the wisdom (*sapientia*) of the world actually ordained by the Triune God. Does a rigorous possible worlds analysis of the thirteenth-century debates endanger this "sapiential" character of thirteenth-century theology? Does an orientation to possibility distract from the thirteenth-century orientation to wisdom embedded in the good order willed by God in fact?

Thomas Aquinas exemplifies such a "sapiential" approach. Jean-Pierre Torrell has described Thomas's practice of *sacra doctrina* as consisting of three main lines (*lignes de force*): (1) speculative, (2) historical-positive, and (3) mystical.[37] *Sacra doctrina*, as practiced by Thomas, consisted in a careful integration of all three lines, joined together in "undivided unity." However, shortly after his death, and particularly in the fourteenth century, theology underwent "a fragmenting of theological knowledge into various fields of specialization and perhaps even to its utter breakdown."[38] Torrell describes one impact of this fragmentation as follows:

> Thomas's speculative line has been sidetracked into a "science of conclusions" in which the theologian's art lies in discovering, by means of syllogisms, *new* conclusions, candidates for adoption by the magisterium by virtue of their theological certitude. That way of doing theology is so out-of-fashion today that, in disappearing, it has taken with it the speculative theology itself as an attempt to understand faith.[39]

Torrell's historical claims, extending well beyond the fourteenth century, are beyond the scope of this argument. The theological problem Torrell isolates, on the other hand, is the very one we are considering.

---

37. Jean-Pierre Torrell, *Saint Thomas d'Aquin, Maitre Spirituel* (Fribourg: Editiones Universitaires de Fribourg, 1996); *Saint Thomas Aquinas*, vol. 2, *Spiritual Master*, trans. Robert Royal (Washington, D.C.: The Catholic University of America Press, 2003), 2–3.

38. Torrell, *Saint Thomas*, 2:3.

39. Torrell, *Saint Thomas*, 2:3.

The sapiential orientation of thirteenth-century theology, according to Torrell, is sustained by an integration of the multiple dimensions of *sacra doctrina*. The process of disintegration or "fragmentation" led to the loss of a theology integrated around the faith the theologian seeks to understand. As a result, Torrell suggests, the spiritual wisdom embedded in Thomas's theology is lost in the fragmented disciplines of speculative, historical, and mystical theology.

There might be reason to suspect the fourteenth-century interest in the absolute-ordained power distinction and orientation to *possibilia* is instrumental in this disintegration. After all, Thomas's Christology is anxious about some of the tendencies within the speculative Christologies of the thirteenth century. Such speculative Christologies, it would seem, distract Christology from its true object—our own Jesus Christ—in reflecting on alternative possibilities. As Joseph Wawrykow has shown, while Thomas includes speculative Christology in his analysis of the incarnation, these speculations are (1) far outstripped by Thomas's historical interests, and (2) strategically deployed so as not to detract from his overarching focus upon the good order willed by God.[40] While Thomas does consider some counterfactual possibilities (e.g., the assumption of a human nature by the Father or the Spirit), such hypotheticals are "warranted, ultimately, by the light (they) can shed on the actual Christian dispensation."[41] Is Thomas's reticence toward hypotheticals a reflection of the sapiential orientation of *sacra doctrina*? Is the fourteenth-century move toward possibility a move away from the actual Christian dispensation? If so, are the fourteenth-century *possibilia* perversions of the thirteenth-century pursuit of *sacra doctrina*? Will my possible worlds analysis eventuate in similar perversions?

Perhaps there is nothing to worry about here. After all, Thom-

40. Joseph Wawrykow, "Hypostatic Union," in *The Theology of Thomas Aquinas*, ed. Rik Van Nieuwenhove and Joseph Wawrykow (Notre Dame, Ind.: University of Notre Dame Press, 2005), 222–51; "Wisdom in the Christology of Thomas Aquinas," in *Christ among the Medieval Dominicans*, ed. Kent Emery Jr. and Joseph Wawrykow (Notre Dame, Ind.: University of Notre Dame Press, 1998), 175–96.

41. Wawrykow, "Wisdom in the Christology of Thomas Aquinas," 181.

as not only considers counterfactuals (the hypothetical question, for instance), but he also took the time to carefully refine a modal category—*convenientia*—to suit his sapiential purposes. As Corey Barnes has shown, this exercise was both carefully developed and systematically deployed in Thomas's Christology.[42] Nor was Thomas alone in seeking such modal categories. The *Summa Halensis* distinguishes necessity from *convenientia* in its opening questions as well, taking a cue from Anselm's repeated use of the term in *CDH*.[43] In fact, possible worlds analysis helps to clarify thirteenth-century uses of necessity, possibility, and other modal categories such as *convenientia* (as in the *Summa Halensis* or Thomas's *Summa Theologiae*) or *congruitas* (as in Bonaventure's *Sentences* commentary). Such analysis will offer greater clarity about what was truly achieved when thirteenth-century theologians turned to various modal categories in considering the reason for the incarnation. This study will demonstrate that greater precision of concepts and development is to be gained by careful application of possible worlds analysis to the thirteenth century.

Ratio Incarnationis: A History in Brief

Recently, one book-length study and one extended investigation by a Regius Professor of Divinity have advanced innovative responses to the question of the *ratio incarnationis*: Edwin Chr. van Driel's *Incarnation Anyway* and Marilyn McCord Adams's *Christ and Horrors*. Van Driel interprets the debates over the reason for the incarnation as a conflict over whether the Son would have become incarnate in spite of the fall, and conflates the supralapsarian thesis in election debates of Reformed dogmatics with what he calls the "incarnation anyway" conclusion. Robert Jenson makes a similar

---

42. Corey Barnes, "Necessary, Fitting, or Possible: The Shape of Scholastic Christology," *Nova et Vetera* 10, no. 3 (2012): 669–78.

43. See *Doctoris irrefragabilis Alexandri de Hales Ordinis minorum Summa theologica,* ed. PP. Collegii S. Bonaventurae (Quaracchi: Collegium S. Bonaventurae, 1928), *SH* IV, P3, In1, Tr1, Q2. On Anselm, see chapter 2.

conflation between supralapsarianism and the incarnation anyway conclusion when he rephrases the hypothetical question as follows:

> Did God decree that the Incarnation should take place in view of foreseen and permitted sin, or did He allow sin in view of the unconditionally decreed Incarnation? Did God decide that Jesus Christ should come in view of some third factor? Is an "in view of" involved here at all?[44]

While thirteenth-century theologians were certainly interested in the relation between prevision, election, and incarnation, those issues do not occupy the central place they take in Reformed dogmatics. Both van Driel and Jenson are guided by Barth's long excursus on supralapsarian-infralapsarian debates in the famous *CD* II, 2, §33.1 on the election of Jesus Christ.[45] Following Barth, they conflate two issues: (1) the status of the incarnation in the hypothetical state of affairs wherein the fall does not obtain, and (2) debates internal to Reformed dogmatics over whether the object of predestination is *homo creatus et lapsus* (humanity created and fallen) or *homo creabile et labile* (humanity creatable and fallible). Thus, they pass over the important and preliminary issue of the relation between predestination and Christ, where thirteenth-century theologians finally located the question of the *ratio incarnationis*. As a result, Edwin Chr. van Driel is persuaded by the very sorts of arguments that thirteenth-century theologians, with the possible exception of Robert Grosseteste, found entirely unpersuasive, even while he claims Scotus as part of his "supralapsarian family tree." Van Driel's arguments for the "incarnation anyway" position, for him equivalent to supralapsarianism, are by appeal to (1) eschatological superabundance, (2) the vision of God, and (3) divine friendship. Thirteenth-century theologians considered variants of these arguments, at least formally, and developed important objections to them.[46]

44. Robert W. Jenson, *Alpha and Omega: A Study in the Theology of Karl Barth* (New York: Nelson, 1963), 55.

45. Karl Barth, *Church Dogmatics*, ed. G. W. Bromiley and T. F. Torrance, trans. G. W. Bromiley (New York: T&T Clark, 2004), 127–45.

46. Whether van Driel can resolve them by appeal to "eschatology," a common strategy in *Incarnation Anyway*, is unclear to me.

Marilyn McCord Adams's treatment is characteristically prob-
ing with respect to the thirteenth-century debates. Chapter seven
of *Christ and Horrors,* entitled "Cosmic Coherence and the Primacy
of Christ," reflects a close reading of Grosseteste's *De cessatione legalium,* Aquinas's *Summa Theologiae,* and the relevant distinctions
of Scotus's *Opus Oxoniense.* Nevertheless, certain aspects of her argument suggest that she, too, has passed over important features
of the thirteenth-century debates too hastily. Adams construes the
issue as a debate over the primacy of two distinct cosmic goods
achieved by the incarnation: (1) some cosmic good of creation or
(2) redemption from sin. As a result, she gives the following characterization of the thirteenth-century debates:

> The disputed question—whether God would have become Incarnate
> anyway, even if human beings never sinned—forced Latin medieval the-
> ology to examine whether God's decision to become Incarnate issues
> out of Divine purposes for *creation,* or whether it arises out of the hu-
> man need for *redemption,* or both. Middle-third-of-the-thirteenth-century
> "Incarnation-anyway" authors answer "both-and": God's creative aim at
> universal excellence would have been enough, and the human need for
> redemption would have been enough. Bonaventure and the later Aquinas
> reply that only the soteriological demand was decisive. Scotus replies, "First
> and foremost, God's goals in creation." On Scotus' scheme, human need
> for redemption does not function as a reason for Incarnation. Rather, only
> because the Incarnation is already in place (at the earlier instant of nature)
> does it seem wise and efficient (at the later instant of nature) for the Incar-
> nate One to supply the remedy for sin.[47]

Adams's description of the situation is relatively apt. If the matter
is presented as a creation-versus-redemption debate, the positions
seem to shake out as she describes. But the debate is not (primarily)
a matter of creation-versus-redemption, and to present it as such is
to skew the debates themselves. For Scotus, for instance, "first and
foremost, God's goals in creation" is at best a partial summary. In *Ordinatio* III, d. 7, q. 3, he identifies a particular created good, the human nature of Christ, as the object worthy of priority among those

47. Adams, *Christ and Horrors,* 187–88.

things actually effected by God in the incarnation. Among those things, for Scotus, is of course redemption from sin. This is decidedly not the sort of cosmic unity argument Adams has in mind. That argument is given by Robert Grosseteste early in the thirteenth century. As we will see, Scotus knew this argument and found it as problematic as any other thirteenth-century theologian at Paris.

Many scholars attribute similar positions to Grosseteste and Scotus. The Grossetestean reading of Scotus is commonly given by those who read him as the great champion of the affirmative response to the hypothetical question.[48] But this was a position for which Scotus expressed reluctance. Collations of figures, according to their responses to the hypothetical question, skew the focus away from the central concerns of the thirteenth century and toward other issues. In the thirteenth century, even the formulation of the hypothetical question was a site of contention. Moreover, on nearly all the substantial issues that divide thirteenth-century theologians, Grosseteste and Scotus disagree. Instead, these skewed recent accounts supplant the central concerns of the thirteenth-century debates with modern Christological considerations: contrasting redemptive and cosmic goods achieved (Adams) and unifying Christ's person and work or economic and immanent existence (Jenson and van Driel).

These contemporary approaches to the reason for the incarnation, which have their precedents in modern theology, skew the thirteenth-century debates to their own detriment. Careful analysis of the thirteenth-century debates yields a different set of animating concerns, a series of substantial arguments and objections, and potential strategies for rearticulating the contemporary theologians' arguments. Moreover, careful reflection on the thirteenth-century

---

48. To cite a few examples, Daniel P. Horan, "How Original Was Scotus on the Incarnation? Reconsidering the History of the Absolute Predestination of Christ in Light of Robert Grosseteste," *Heythrop Journal* 52, no. 3 (2011): 374–91; Juniper B. Carol, *Why Jesus Christ?*; Francis Xavier Pancheri, *The Universal Primacy of Christ*, trans. Juniper B. Carol (Front Royal, Va.: Christendom, 1984).

debates shows that the question of the *ratio incarnationis* is properly Christian; it is a question that the logic of Christian theology naturally raises and to which a response is required.

At the close of the eleventh century, St. Anselm of Canterbury inquired after the reason for the incarnation most succinctly: *Cur Deus homo?* "Why the God-man?" While Anselm's actual question is more specific than his title suggests, from the thirteenth century on his contribution to the *ratio incarnationis* in *CDH* was recognized as a cornerstone of Christian reflection on the incarnation in the West. As his thirteenth-century reception demonstrates, Anselm has much to teach beyond his account of satisfaction.[49]

The first instance we have of the hypothetical question, which became standard in thirteenth-century *quaestiones* and commentaries on the *Sentences*, is found early in the twelfth century, in Rupert of Deutz's commentary on Matthew's Gospel, *De gloria et honore Filii hominis*.[50] At Oxford, around 1230–35, Robert Grosseteste gives the first extended discussion of the hypothetical question in his *DCL*. Grosseteste is clearly inspired by Anselm's *CDH* and regularly deploys Anselm's arguments with counterfactual revisions. Roughly concurrently, and likely independently, students of Alexander of Hales at Paris placed Anselm's *CDH* as the central authority in their discussions of the modality of the incarnation and passion, consider-

---

49. Michael Robson has produced two very insightful essays on the rise of Anselm's influence in the thirteenth century: "The Impact of the Cur Deus Homo on the Early Franciscan School," in *Anselm: Aosta, Bec and Canterbury: Papers in Commemoration of the Nine-Hundredth Anniversary of Anselm's Enthronement as Archbishop, 25 September 1093*, ed. David E. Luscombe and Gillian R. Evans (Sheffield: Sheffield Academic Press, 1996), 334–47; "Saint Anselm, Robert Grosseteste, and the Franciscan Tradition," in *Robert Grosseteste: New Perspectives on His Thought and Scholarship*, ed. James McEvoy, Instrumenta Patristica 27 (Turnhout: Brepols, 1995), 257–76. See also Andrew Rosato, "The Interpretation of Anselm's Teaching on Christ's Satisfaction for Sin in the Franciscan Tradition from Alexander of Hales to Duns Scotus," *Franciscan Studies* 71 (2013): 411–44.

50. Rupert of Deutz, *De gloria et honore Filii hominis super Mattheum*, ed. H. Haacke, Corpus Christianorum continuatio mediaevalis 29 (Turnhout: Brepols, 1979), 13.696: "Hic primum illud quaerere libet utrum iste Filius Dei, de quo hic sermo est, etiam si peccatum, propter quod omnes morimur, non intercessisset, homo fieret, an non."

ations they located in the first and twentieth distinction of the *Summa Halensis* III.[51] Later in the thirteenth century, St. Thomas Aquinas includes the counterfactual form of the question in *ST* III, q. 1, a. 3: Whether, if there had not been sin, God would have become incarnate?[52] By that time, Thomas observes, his contemporaries are engaged in a substantial debate over the *ratio incarnationis*: "Concerning this, some have thought differently. For some say that, even if man had not sinned, the Son of God would have become incarnate. But others assert the contrary."[53] The same disputed state of the question was earlier attested by both Guerric of Saint-Quentin and Albert the Great. While all three find the question rather problematic, Thomas prefers the negative response against his teacher Albert.

Bonaventure's treatment of the question is notable for his revision of its formulation away from the hypothetical. When he treats the reason for the incarnation in III *Sent.* d. 1, a. 2, q. 2, he asks: "What is the principal reason for the incarnation?"[54] In this restatement, Bonaventure formulates the question in the manner both Albert and Aquinas preferred: focused upon the de facto incarnation of the Son in Jesus Christ.

---

51. Michael Robson gives a thorough overview of the rise of Anselm's influence among the Franciscans at both Oxford and Paris in the thirteenth century, and the *CDH*'s important infusion into the *Sentences* commentaries. "The inquisitive spirit of the Sentences offered a more fertile ground for the *rationes Anselmi* and a vast amount of his teaching was incorporated into the commentaries by Alexander, the two anonymous commentaries, Odo Rigaldi, Bonaventure and Richard Rufus of Cornwall, who also abbreviated Bonaventure's commentary, and the *Quaestiones disputatae* by Jean de la Rochelle and William of Melitona. The *Cur Deus Homo* supplied these theologians with a framework for the discussion of the mode of the incarnation and redemption." As we will see, the influence was not limited to the Franciscan school. Robson, "The Impact of the Cur Deus Homo," 338–39.

52. *ST* III, q. 1, a. 3: "Utrum, si non fuisset peccatum, Deus incarnatus fuisset?"

53. *ST* III, q. 1, a. 3, *corpus*: "Aliqui circa hoc diversimode opinantur. Quidam enim dicunt quod, etiam si homo non peccasset, Dei filius fuisset incarnatus. Alii vero contrarium asserunt."

54. Bonaventure, *Commentaria in quatuor libros Sententiarum Magistri Petri Lombardi*, vols. 1–4, *Opera theologica selecta*, ed. PP. Collegii S. Bonaventurae (Quaracchi, Italy: Collegii S. Bonaventurae, 1934–49), III, d. 1, a. 2, q. 2 (III, 21): "Quae fuerit incarnationis ratio praecipua?"

When John Duns Scotus treats the question at the end of the thirteenth century, he follows Bonaventure in directing the focus of his question to the de facto order of God's work in this world by including his argument under the heading of the predestination of Christ.[55] This reformulation features a dimension of the question that will take on increased importance in the ensuing debates: election. As a result, Scotus is more explicit and systematic in his deployment of the absolute-ordained power distinction than earlier theologians.

Juniper Carol, OFM, has produced an extensive, thorough, and invaluable compendium and analysis of the subsequent history of the debates over the *ratio incarnationis*.[56] Carol divides the various theological positions after Scotus into three groups: the "Thomistic school," the "Scotistic school," and the conciliatory, intermediate, or *tertia via* perspective. As he shows, while a few significant contributions to both the "Thomistic" and "Scotistic" positions are notable in the fourteenth and fifteenth centuries, beginning in the sixteenth century and especially throughout the seventeenth a massive flowering of innovation and debate arises over the *ratio incarnationis*. The debates are largely characterized by the Dominican-Franciscan-Jesuit polemics of the period. Along the way, the central concerns of the thirteenth-century debates were replaced with increasingly complex and ramified accounts of the *instantia rationis* and the genera of priority and primacy.[57]

In this period, both Luis de Molina and Francisco Suárez at-

---

55. John Duns Scotus, *Ordinatio*, vols. 9–10, *Opera omnia*, ed. B. Hechich et al. (Civitas Vaticana: Typis Vaticanis, 2006-07), III, d. 7, q. 3; *Reportatio Parisiensis*, vol. 3, *Ioannis Duns Scoti, doctoris Mariani, theologiae marianae elementa*, ed. Carl Balić (Sibenici: Kačić, 1933), III, d. 7, q. 4.

56. Carol, *Why Jesus Christ?*

57. The *signa* or *instantia rationis* are the logical distinctions between successive divine determinations of the in-fact-simple divine decree. They serve as a means for distinguishing the relations among divine volitions. By various genera of priority and primacy, I have in mind the distinction between primacy in the order of efficient and final causality, and the like. Both dimensions of the *ratio incarnationis* enjoyed increased attention over the course of the sixteenth and seventeenth centuries.

tempted to mediate between the affirmative and negative responses to the hypothetical question. Molina holds that God selects our
world from many possible worlds, all of which God sees through
His *scientia media,* prior to freely willing any possible world. Suárez
posits coordinated, as opposed to subordinated, reasons for the incarnation; that is, both the glory of Christ's humanity and the redemption from sin are complete, sufficient, and adequate reasons
for the incarnation such that, absent either motive (but not both),
a sufficient condition for the incarnation still obtains such that it
would be actualized. Neither position was accepted by the Dominican or Franciscan mainstream, although both enjoyed some support among Jesuit theologians.

In Protestant theology, the *ratio incarnationis* has also enjoyed a
lengthy and labyrinthine history. In the mid-sixteenth century, John
Calvin, at *Institutes* 2.12.4, asserts "since all Scripture proclaims that
to become our Redeemer (Christ) was clothed with flesh, it is too
presumptuous to imagine another reason or another end."[58] He
proceeds to argue this position against Alexander Osiander's assertion that the Son would have become incarnate even if Adam had
not sinned. However, in the same chapter of the *Institutes,* Calvin
also asserts "even if man had remained free from all stain, his condition would have been too lowly for him to reach God without
a Mediator."[59] Calvin's apparent equivocation sparked continuous
debate over the question in subsequent Protestant theology. Oliver
Crisp has recently attempted to clarify Calvin's position.[60]

Calvin's polemical framing of the issue (contra Osiander) is
reflected in the debates over the *ratio incarnationis* throughout Reformed Scholasticism. By the time of Turretin the question is subordinated to the larger concerns of the Socinian controversy:

As the Son of God became incarnate only on account of sin, so it would not
have been necessary for him to become incarnate if man had not sinned.

58. John Calvin, *The Institutes of the Christian Religion,* 2.12.4.
59. Calvin, *Instit.,* 2.12.4.
60. Crisp, "John Calvin (1509–1564) on the Motivation for the Incarnation."

It is opposed to the old Scholastics, who rashly and without Scripture authority asserted it (as Alexander of Hales, Occam, Bonaventure and others). Osiander, a Lutheran, in a former century interpolated their error. In recent times, the Socinians renew the same for no other object than to seek from it some support for their most pestilent heresy concerning the metaphorical redemption of Christ and the improper satisfaction.[61]

Turretin's polemical interpretation of the thirteenth-century theologies of the *ratio incarnationis* is evident. His final assertion, composed late in the seventeenth century, shows the increasing pressure of the Socinian controversy on the doctrine of the incarnation. That pressure would only grow as theologians increasingly reckoned with Enlightened rationalism throughout Europe and North America over the eighteenth century.

Edwin Chr. van Driel contends that "an almost unanimous rejection among the Reformed of the supralapsarian position on the incarnation" endured into the nineteenth century.[62] By "the supralapsarian position" he has in mind any position that holds that Christ would have become incarnate apart from the fall. However, van Driel contends, Protestant theology in the nineteenth century, under the influence of Hegel and Schleiermacher, developed a renewed interest in the *ratio incarnationis*, even while drastically revising the nature of the question and the relevant issues raised by it.[63] As van Driel shows, Isaak August Dorner's *History of the Development of the Doctrine of the Person of Christ* encapsulates the nineteenth-century iteration of the debate.

Two key features of twentieth-century Protestant theology bear upon the recent history of the debate over the *ratio incarnationis*.

---

61. François Turrettini, *Institutes of Elenctic Theology*, ed. James T. Dennison, trans. George Musgrave Giger, vol. 1 (Phillipsburg, N.J.: Protestant and Reformed, 1994), II.13.3.

62. Van Driel, *Incarnation Anyway*, 173.

63. Van Driel, *Incarnation Anyway*, 174. While van Driel's analysis of the medieval and Catholic debates is severely lacking, he gives a superb overview and careful analysis of the modern debates over the *ratio incarnationis*, the issues that animate them, and the key arguments, which trace their roots to Friedrich Schleiermacher.

First, Karl Barth's radical Christocentrism suggested to many theologians new possibilities for resolution of the old question of the *ratio incarnationis*, both in Protestant and Catholic theology. Second, the rise of ecumenical interests brought together several sets of debates over the *ratio incarnationis*: the detailed debates among Dominican, Franciscan, and Jesuit theologians; the debates of Reformed orthodoxy; and various direct and indirect modern Protestant engagements with the *ratio incarnationis*. As van Driel points out, Karl Barth still occupies the center of gravity in Protestant circles for contemporary reflection on the *ratio incarnationis*, but now there is, as in van Driel, a renewed interest in connecting Barth's Christocentrism to the scholastic debates.

TWO

After Anselm

After Alexander of Hales introduced Peter Lombard's *Sentences* as the basis for theological lectures at Paris, it became standard to include a series of questions on the necessity, possibility, and fittingness of the incarnation in the first distinction of book three of the commentaries on Lombard's text.[1] This is fitting, as Peter explicitly considers the necessity, possibility, and fittingness of the incarnation when he asks (1) why the Son was incarnate, and not the Father or the Spirit, and (2) whether the Father or the Spirit could have, or could become incarnate (*potuerit incarnari vel possit*).[2] Lombard's set of topics and arguments on the necessity and possibility of the incarnation underwent significant expansion over the course of the thirteenth century.[3] This expansion reflects an

1. See, for instance, Bonaventure, III *Sent.* d. 1; Aquinas, *Scriptum super libros Sententiarum*, ed. P. Mandonnet and M. F. Moos (Paris: Lethielleux, 1929–47), III, d. 1.

2. Peter Lombard, *Sententiae in IV libris distinctae*, ed. PP. Collegii S. Bonaventurae, Spicilegium Bonaventurianum 4–5 (Grottaferrata, Italy: Collegii S. Bonaventurae, 1971–81), III, d. 1, c. 1–2.

3. The debates over the metaphysics of the incarnation, extending well beyond the "three opinions" posited by Lombard in *Sentences* III, d. 6, are themselves investigations into the metaphysical possibility of the incarnation. On these debates as expressed by Peter, see Marcia Colish, *Peter Lombard*, 2 vols. (Leiden: Brill, 1994), I: 399–437. Lauge Olaf Nielsen gives unparalleled analysis of the historical precedents of the "three opinions" in *Theology and Philosophy in the Twelfth Century: A Study of Gilbert of Porreta's Thinking and Theological Expositions of the Doctrine of the Incarnation*

increasing concern about how to reason consistently about divine operations *ad extra*, especially the incarnation and the passion.

From the earliest commentaries on the *Sentences*, scholastic theologians placed great value on Anselm of Canterbury's reflections on the incarnation in *CDH*. As Michael Robson has shown, there was a marked increase in references to Anselm's *CDH* in book three of the *Sentences* commentaries of the thirteenth century.[4] When thirteenth-century theologians considered questions about the necessity, possibility, and fittingness of the incarnation and the passion, they turned to Anselm of Canterbury.[5]

Anselm's influence in thirteenth-century Christology was not limited to Paris. At Oxford, around the time when Alexander was redacting the third book of the *Glossa in quatuor libros Sententiarum Petri Lombardi* (*Glossa*), Robert Grosseteste wrote:

That one ought to be, in person, both God and human, who is liberator of fallen humanity from guilt (*culpa*) and punishment (*poena*) and leader of humanity to the glory which [was] lost by sin through the passion of the cross, is shown more clearly than light by blessed Augustine, Gregory, and Anselm, maximally in his book which is entitled *Cur Deus homo*; and here and there all the expositors of sacred scripture declare reasonably that the fall of humanity ought to be restored through the passion of the God-man.[6]

---

during the Period 1130–1180 (Leiden: Brill, 1982). For later reception of Lombard's "three opinions," see the somewhat dated yet still helpful volumes by Walter Principe, *The Theology of the Hypostatic Union in the Early Thirteenth Century*, 4 vols. (Toronto: Pontifical Institute of Mediaeval Studies, 1963–75). More recently, Richard Cross has analyzed the later debates of the thirteenth century, in a manner attuned to the increasing philosophical rigor of those later debates, in his *Metaphysics of the Incarnation* (Oxford: Oxford University Press, 2002). A helpful bibliography and brief summation of the debates over Lombard's preferences among the "three opinions" can be found in Corey L. Barnes, *Christ's Two Wills in Scholastic Thought: The Christology of Aquinas and Its Historical Contexts* (Toronto: Pontifical Institute of Mediaeval Studies, 2012), 39–41.

4. Michael Robson, "The Impact of the *Cur Deus Homo* on the Early Franciscan School," in *Anselm Aosta, Bec, and Canterbury: Papers in Commemoration of the Nine-Hundredth Anniversary of Anselm's Enthronement as Archbishop, 25 September 1093*, ed. D. E. Luscombe and G. R. Evans (Sheffield: Sheffield Academic Press, 1996), 334–47.

5. Robson, "The Impact of the *Cur Deus Homo*," 345.

6. *DCL* III.1.1: "Quod autem oporteat unum in persona esse Deum et hominem, liberatorem hominis lapsi a culpa et pena et reductorem illius ad gloriam quam

Grosseteste observes that Anselm does not consider the hypothetical question commonly associated with thirteenth-century debates over the *ratio incarnationis*. Grosseteste writes, "Whether God would have become human even if humanity had not fallen is not determined by any of the sacred expositors in their books which I have inspected, unless my memory fails me."[7] Rather, Anselm seeks to show "by what logic or necessity did God become man."[8]

Focused on the de facto state of affairs, Anselm engages in no hypothetical speculation on the incarnation in possible worlds without the fall. What contribution, then, does Anselm make to the early thirteenth-century Parisian debates over the reason for the incarnation, where the hypothetical question abounds? We can gain some clarity on Anselm's contribution by thinking through the relationship between Anselm's question in *CDH* and our three questions.

---

peccando amiserat, et hoc per crucis passionem, luce clarius ostendunt beatus Augustinus, Gregorius, et Anselmus, maxime in libro suo qui intitulatur *Cur Deus homo*; et sparsim omnes expositores sacre pagine rationabiliter declarant quod hominis lapsi restauracionem oportuit fieri per Dei hominis passionem." Latin text supplied from Robert Grosseteste, *De cessatione legalium*, ed. Richard C. Dales and Edward B. King, Auctores Britannici Medii Aevi 7 (London: British Academy, 1986). Though translations are my own, I much benefitted from the work of Stephen Hildebrand in Robert Grosseteste, *On the Cessation of the Laws*, trans. Stephen M. Hildebrand, The Fathers of the Church Mediaeval Continuation 13 (Washington, D.C.: The Catholic University of America Press, 2012).

7. *DCL* III.1.2: "Verumtamen, an Deus esset homo etiam si non esset lapsus homo non determinant aliqui de sacris expositoribus in libris suis quos ego adhuc inspexerim, nisi fallat me memoria mea. Sed magis videntur insinuare quod si non esset lapsus homo, non esset Deus homo; et ideo solum Deus factus sit homo ut hominem perditum repararet. Videntur tamen esse raciones efficacies ad ostendendum simpliciter quod Deus esset homo etiam si numquam lapsus fuisset homo. Quapropter, omittentes ad presens illas rationes per quas probant sacri expositores quod oportuit Deum esse hominem ut restauraret perditum hominem, querimus an Deus esset homo etiam si non fuisset lapsus homo."

8. *CDH* I.1 (S II, 48, 2–3): "Qua scilicet ratione vel necessitate deus homo factus sit." Anselm of Canterbury, *Cur Deus homo* in *S. Anselmi opera omnia*, ed. F. S. Schmitt, 2 vols. (Edinburgh: Thomas Nelson and Sons, 1946). Unless otherwise noted, English translations are taken from Anselm of Canterbury, "Why God Became Man," trans. Janet Fairweather, in *The Major Works*, ed. G. R. Evans and Brian Davies (Oxford: Oxford University Press, 1998), 260–356. References to Anselm's works in Schmitt's critical edition note the abbreviated title of the work, the book and chapter numbers, in addition to the volume, page, and line numbers in Schmitt's edition.

Since he is focused on the state of affairs in our world, Anselm assumes that the reason for which the Son became incarnate and died was the redemption of humanity from sin. His chief interest is the method whereby that redemption was effected. We might, therefore, restate the question of *CDH* as follows: "Ought the redemption of humanity have been effected by the passion of the God-man?" (Anselm's question)

Granting to Grosseteste that, at most, Anselm implies a response to the hypothetical question, we should focus our attention on the general question in order to clarify Anselm's contribution to the thirteenth-century debates. Thus, we are interested in what Anselm's response to his own question entails for the general question: "How can we determine reasons for divine operations *ad extra*?"

While I will not seek a fully developed response to either the hypothetical question or the primacy question from *CDH*—such a response will be impossible—I will seek to clarify the way in which Anselm's argument entails or implies a partial response to the general question. Thus, we will be able to observe ways in which Anselm shaped thirteenth-century debates about the general question and how these debates influenced thirteenth-century responses to the hypothetical question and the primacy question.

Thirteenth-century theologians worked systematically across the general question and the primacy question to produce a coherent vision of divine action. Their concern for systematic coherence is further reflected in their return to similar questions regarding necessity, possibility, and fittingness with respect to other divine operations *ad extra*, like Christ's passion. Unsurprisingly, then, Anselm emerges again in later questions on Christ's passion in the commentaries on Lombard's *Sentences*. In clarifying Anselm's position on the general question, we will be in position to observe the impact he had on the subsequent responses to the hypothetical question and the primacy question.

Since Anselm's argument in *CDH* implies a partial response to the general question, I will say that Anselm presents a series of theses on the general question, rather than a full response. Anselm admits as much, noting that in his argument "power (*potestatis*) and necessity (*necessitas*) and will (*voluntatis*)" are only treated briefly and in a manner "sufficient for the present work."[9] Since Anselm does not produce a full response to the general question, but rather several theses, it is difficult to arrive at a purely Anselmian conclusion to the hypothetical question, a point that Grosseteste notes in his introduction to *DCL* III, cited above. Thus, I will limit my focus here to Anselm's response to the general question.

In the pages to come, I will derive Anselm's theses on the general question from his extended reflection on the incarnation in *CDH*.[10] Careful analysis of *CDH* and other select texts by Anselm will clarify his key commitments on divine operations *ad extra*. These commitments will be specified as theses. Once I have derived and analyzed Anselm's theses on the general question, I will briefly note the central contributions and difficulties Anselm's theses bequeathed to the thirteenth-century theologians who were eager to incorporate the *CDH* into their reflections on the incarnation and passion.[11]

9. *CDH* I.1 (S II, 49, 14–16): "Sic breviter de his suis locis dicere poteris, ut et quod sufficiat ad praesens opus habeamus, et quod plus dicendum est in aliud tempus differamus."

10. While my analysis of Anselm's theses on the general question focuses on *CDH*, I clarify relevant passages in *CDH* by drawing upon Anselm's discussion of "capacity and incapacity, possibility and impossibility, necessity and freedom" in his philosophical fragments, available in Anselm of Canterbury, *Memorials of St. Anselm*, ed. R. W. Southern and F. S. Schmitt, Auctores Britannici Medii Aevi 1 (London: British Academy, 1969), 341.2–3. Eileen F. Serene helpfully clarifies Anselm's conceptions of necessity, capacity, and so on in "Anselm's Philosophical Fragments: A Critical Examination" (PhD diss., Cornell University, 1974); "Anselm's Modal Conceptions," in *Reforging the Great Chain of Being: Studies of the History of Modal Theories*, ed. Simo Knuuttila, 177–62, Synthese Historical Library 20 (Dordrecht: D. Reidel, 2010). See also Desmond Paul Henry, *The Logic of Saint Anselm* (Oxford: Clarendon Press, 1967).

11. This is not to say that Anselm did not enjoy influence prior to the thirteenth-century commentaries, as we have a clear manuscript tradition throughout the twelfth century; see Robson, "The Impact of the *Cur Deus Homo*." Nevertheless, Anselm is notably brought into systematic reflection on the incarnation and the passion at both Oxford and Paris in the thirteenth century, beginning with Grosseteste and the *SH*.

Cur Deus homo: An Outline

Before I turn to the Anselmian theses on the general question, a brief recitation of Anselm's central argument in *CDH* is in order. Numerous summaries of Anselm's arguments have been produced. What follows is my own, although it closely follows that of John Duns Scotus, itself in no way unique.[12] I lay the argument out propositionally below, so that we can isolate the particular conjunctions where Anselm's theses contribute to his overarching argument.

2.1   If God wills to redeem humans, humans are redeemed.

2.2   God wills to redeem humans.

2.3   Humans are redeemed.

2.4   If humans are redeemed, it must be by satisfaction for sin.

2.5   If there is satisfaction for sin, then it must be by the God-man.

2.6   If humans are redeemed, then the God-man satisfies.

2.7   The God-man satisfies.

2.8   Satisfaction is the offering of something proportionate to the offense which restores the offenders.

2.9   The passion of the God-man is proportionate to the offense of sin and restores the offenders (sinners).

2.10 There is no more fitting means of satisfaction.

2.11 The passion of the God-man satisfies for sin.

This argument is Anselm's basic solution to the titular question *Cur Deus homo*—why the God-man? God wills the God-man because the passion of the God-man is the most fitting means for redemption from sin.

Once again, our concern here is not with the plausibility of the

---

12. John Duns Scotus, *Lectura* III, vols. 20–21, *Opera omnia*, ed. Barnaba Hechich et al., (Vatican City: Typis Vaticanis, 2003–04), d. 20. The critical edition notes the similarity of Scotus's recitation to that of Matthew of Aquasparta. The shape of the argument is also similar to Aquinas's recitation in *Scriptum* III, d. 1, q. 1, a. 2, *resp.*, albeit Aquinas makes use of his preferred category of *convenientia* in making his own argument.

central argument of *CDH* per se, interesting as that subject may be. Rather, we are concerned with Anselm's argument as a provocation for subsequent debate; we are interested in Anselm as received (and transformed) by those who read *CDH* in the thirteenth century. Thus, I will focus on Anselm's theses on the general question, which are reinterpreted, challenged, and accepted in the ensuing scholastic disputations. Along the way, I will note how the Anselmian theses on the general question function within the overarching argument of *CDH.*

Anselmian Theses on the General Question

Thesis 1: Divine operations *ad extra* cannot be necessary

Anselm is clear; God does not operate necessarily with respect to creation. He writes:

> We have already said that it is incorrect to say of God that he "cannot do something" or that he "does it of necessity." For all necessity, and all impossibility, is subject to his will. Moreover his will is not subject to any necessity or impossibility. For nothing is necessary or impossible for any reason other than that he himself so wills it. . . . Hence, from the fact that he does all things which are his will and does nothing other than the things which are his will, two consequences follow: no necessity or impossibility precedes his volition or non-volition and, similarly, neither precedes his action or inaction, no matter how many things he may unchangeably wish or do.[13]

But what does Anselm mean by "necessity"? By clarifying the sense of "necessity" for Anselm, we can see both (1) what it is to deny necessity of divine operations *ad extra,* and (2) why Anselm does so. In defining "necessity," we can also clarify Anselm's other modal cat-

---

13. *CDH* II, 17 (S II, 122, 25–123, 3): "Iam diximus quia deus improprie dicitur aliquid non posse aut necessitate facere. Omnis quippe necessitas et impossibilitas eius subiacet voluntati; illius autem voluntas nulli subditur necessitati aut impossibilitati. Nihil enim est necessarium aut impossibile, nisi quia ipse ita vult. . . . Quare quoniam omnia quae vult, et non nisi quae vult facit: sicut nulla necessitas sive impossibilitas praecedit eius velle aut nolle, ita nec eius facere aut non facere, quamvis multa velit immutabiliter et faciat."

egories (i.e., possibility and contingency), as well as the metaphysical categories he coordinates with his account of necessity (i.e., nature, will, and capacity). This will allow us to derive further theses on the general question. Toward this end, I will sketch the modal and metaphysical categories as they are developed in *CDH* and clarified in Anselm's broader *corpus*.[14]

In *CDH* Anselm uses three terms and their negations to clarify necessity (*necessitas*): freedom (*libertas*), capacity (*potentas*), and possibility (*possibilitas*). For Anselm, the most fundamental distinction is between necessity and freedom. We can note, then, that Anselm is chiefly concerned not with logical necessity (in which case the distinction would be between necessity and possibility), but rather with the necessity (or freedom) that attends the action of an agent.[15] Necessity and freedom are mutually exclusive properties of actions issuing from an agent. Acts are necessary or free; agents act necessarily or freely. Any individual agent will be capable of (have a capacity for) either necessary acts, or free acts, or both. Humans, for instance, are capable of both necessary and free acts. Alternatively, some agents perform only necessary, that is, natural, acts. Anselm distinguishes between the agent action of a human and the natural action of a horse in *De libertate arbitrii* 5:

In the horse there is not the will to subject himself, but naturally, always and of necessity he is the slave of sense appetite, whereas in man, as long as his will is right, he does not serve nor is he subject to what he ought not to do, nor can he be diverted from that rectitude by any other force, unless he willingly consents to what he ought not to do, which consent does not come about naturally or of necessity as in the horse, but is clearly seen to be from itself.[16]

---

14. Specifically, I will draw upon *De libertate arbitrii* and *Proslogion* to clarify the account given in *CDH*. Both *De libertate arbitrii* and *Proslogion* are found in *S. Anselmi opera omnia*, ed. F. S. Schmitt, vol. 1 (Edinburgh: Thomas Nelson and Sons, 1946).

15. Here, I am utilizing a deflated account of "agent," equivalent to *agentis, operantis,* actor, or doer. Thus, agents include both those who act freely (in virtue of will) or necessarily (naturally).

16. *De libertate arbitrii* 5 (S I, 216, 6–11): "In equo namque non ipsa voluntas se

According to Anselm, necessary and free acts have distinct metaphysical sources: nature (*natura*) and will (*voluntas*), respectively. The distinction between natural and volitional acts adds to necessary and free acts the notion of their metaphysical source. Thus, for any action *x*, if the action issues from an agent capable of willed acts, *x* will be either necessary or free. If the action issues from an agent incapable of willed acts, *x* will be necessary. Again, on these points Anselm is unoriginal.

Following St. Augustine, Anselm introduces the concept of rectitude (*rectitudine*) into his account of the will in *De libertate arbitrii* 5. Rectitude is a necessary condition of the freedom of the human will. Sans rectitude, the will lacks freedom because volitional creatures are thereby "subject to what they ought not do." Subjection, for Anselm as for Augustine, properly includes subjection to the "ought not," to actions that are not right (*non recte*). Moreover, even when the human agent has a subjected will (coincident with a lack of rectitude), and therefore acts necessarily on account of its subjection, the will's freedom remains a necessary condition for the lack of rectitude. This is because the human can only lose rectitude by some prior willing consent to that which ought not be, namely, that which is not right, or disordered. Insofar as consent issues from the will, rather than from nature, even that subjection of the will, which determines the human agent to act against the rectitude that is a condition of its freedom, has for itself as a necessary condition some free act of the will.

This Augustinian account of freedom has the advantage of encompassing both God and creatures. Since God is right (*recte*) and the source of all rectitude, and is likewise free and the source of all freedom, rectitude and freedom must finally be coincident. Simi-

---

subicit, sed naturaliter subiecta semper necessitate appetitui carnis servit; in homine vero quamdiu ipsa voluntas recta est, nec servit nec subiecta est cui non debet, nec ab ipsa rectitudine ulla vi aliena avertitur, nisi ipsa cui non debet volens consentiat; quem consensum non naturaliter nec ex necessitate sicut equus, sed ex se aperte videtur habere."

larly, the beatified share in the perfection of rectitude, which permits no disorder. They, like God, enjoy total freedom and their impeccability is unrestricted freedom.[17] This, in brief, is the account of necessity and freedom in relation to nature and will that Anselm gives in *De libertate arbitrii*. As we will see, *CDH* accepts and extends this line of thought.

We now have a brief account of *human* will and freedom. Our question, however, concerns divine operation *ad extra*. In denying necessity in Thesis 1, Anselm has asserted that any divine operation *ad extra* is characterized by freedom. Accordingly, the act will issue from the divine will. But there seem to be several problems with constructing a parallel notion of divine freedom and denying divine necessity. Anselm gives his first extended treatment of this issue in *CDH* II, 5. His interlocutor, Boso, asks how it could be that God's act of bringing about salvation is free, given that Anselm seems to argue for its necessity in order to avoid unfittingness (*inconvenientia*). Boso ascribes the following argument to Anselm:

2.12 It is unfitting that God not complete what he has begun (premise; II, 4).

2.13 God created (began) humanity to attain blessed happiness (premise; II, 1).

2.14 It is unfitting that humanity not attain blessed happiness (2.12, 2.13).

2.15 If God does not redeem humanity from sin, humanity will not attain blessed happiness (premise; I, 20).

2.16 It is unfitting that God does not redeem humanity from sin (2.14, 2.15).

2.17 If it is unfitting that God do *x*, then necessarily not *x* (premise; I, 10).

---

17. For a thoughtful account of these topics, as developed in the high middle ages, see Simon Gaine, *Will There Be Free Will in Heaven?: Freedom, Impeccability, and Beatitude* (New York: Continuum, 2003).

2.18 It is necessarily not the case that God does not redeem
humanity from sin (2.16, 2.17).

2.19 It is necessarily the case that God redeems humanity
from sin.

Boso objects that Anselm's argument seems to undermine the grace
of salvation because divine freedom is a necessary condition of
grace. "How is it that we are to attribute our salvation to his grace,
if it is of necessity that he saves us?"[18] Underlying this worry over the
gratuity of salvation is the violation of our Thesis 1. Since God's salvation of humanity from sin is a divine operation *ad extra*, the assertion of 2.19 entails that "some divine operation *ad extra* is necessary"
and, therefore, Thesis 1 is false. And if some divine operation *ad
extra* is necessary, then it is not gratuitous.

Anselm responds that, even if the argument stands, the act is
nevertheless free and therefore gratuitous, because it is not compelled. Compulsion, in this case, distinguishes necessary from free
acts. Moreover, we must distinguish compulsion from obligation.
Obligation is a necessary but not sufficient condition of necessity
proprie (i.e., proper necessity). God is both free *and* obligated to
save humanity according to the argument above. "For it was no se-
cret to God what man was going to do, when he created him, and
yet, by his own goodness in creating him, he put himself under an
obligation to bring his good beginning to fulfillment."[19] Compulsion adds to the concept of obligation a source of obligation external to the obliged agent. Compulsion does not obtain in God's case
insofar as the obligation derives from "the unchangeability of God's
honor, which he possesses of himself, and from no one apart from
himself."[20] That is to say, God's obligation to save is an internal ob-

18. *CDH* II, 5 (S II, 99, 21–22): "Quomodo etiam imputabimus nostram salutem
eius gratiae, si nos salvat necessitate?"

19. *CDH* II, 5 (S II, 100, 18–20): "Non enim illum latuit quid homo facturus
erat, cum illum fecit, et tamen bonitate sua illum creando sponte se ut perficeret
inceptum bonum quasi obligavit."

20. *CDH* II, 5 (S II, 100, 24–25): "Quae scilicet necessitas non est aliud quam
immutabilitas honestatis eius, quam a se ipso et non ab alio habet."

ligation derived from the immutable character of the divine will.

Anselm permits the application of "necessary" to acts just in case they include the character of obligation, whether internal or external. But he distinguishes between two classes of necessity according to the source of the obligation. Necessity *proprie* adds to obligation a source external to the agent, whereas necessity *improprie* adds an internal source. Since necessity *improprie* includes the concept of obligation but lacks the external source of that obligation, it is *properly* freedom. Necessity *proprie* is obligation from an external source, or compulsion. God's act of salvation is properly free because the source of the obligation is God's own immutable and spontaneous will. It is improperly necessary because salvation is obligated by the determinations of God's own willing. So even the apparent necessity of obligation is only apparent, as it derives from the more basic free determination of God's spontaneous will to create humanity with freedom and for beatitude.

These are the basic contours of Anselm's distinction between necessity *proprie* and *improprie,* but several questions remain. For instance, granting that God's determination to save humanity is free insofar as it is not under external obligation (but, rather, internal obligation), what sense can be made of another class of assertions that seem to imply necessity to God by the predication of some "impossibility." For instance, is the assertion "God is incapable of lying" not tantamount to asserting that "For God, to lie is impossible"? And given that impossibility is equivalent to "necessarily not," we seem to have admitted the necessity problem in through the back door. Boso presents this objection at *CDH* II, 16, together with another that I will treat momentarily. These objections incite Anselm's most extended reflection on necessity in *CDH.*

From Anselm's response to Boso's objections in *CDH* II, 17 we can construct a fuller account of Anselm's modal categories of necessity and possibility and the correlated metaphysical concepts of capacity and incapacity. Anselm immediately denies the propriety of Boso's objection:

We have already said that it is incorrect (*improprie*) to say of God that he "cannot do something" or that he "does it of necessity." For all necessity, and all impossibility, is subject to his will. Moreover his will is not subject to any necessity or impossibility. For nothing is necessary or impossible for any reason other than that he himself so wills it.[21]

Anselm proceeds to give the following description of the order of divine action: "No necessity or impossibility precedes his volition or non-volition and, similarly, neither precedes his action or inaction, no matter how many things he may unchangeably (*immutabiliter*) wish or do."[22] Thus:

neither necessity nor impossibility → volition/nolition → action/inaction

Likewise, it seems:

freedom and possibility → volition/nolition → action/inaction

Every divine action (or inaction) issues from the divine will, which is in no way externally obligated by necessity or impossibility. Apparently, Anselm conceives "impossibility" as a negative instance of necessity *proprie*; it is an external obligation to *in*action. The distinction between necessity *proprie* and impossibility *proprie* is therefore coextensive with the distinction between compulsion and prohibition. With regard to some action or inaction *x*, it is not the case that God is externally compelled to perform or prohibited from performing *x*. Moreover, actions issue from the will of an intelligent agent unless the agent is prevented from acting on a volition by something extrinsic. Since God is an intelligent agent for whom nothing extrinsic can prevent any willed action, it must be that no external obligation whatsoever compels or prohibits a divine voli-

---

21. *CDH* II, 17 (S II, 122, 25–28): "Iam diximus quia deus improprie dicitur aliquid non posse aut necessitate facere. Omnis quippe necessitas et impossibilitas eius subiacet voluntati; illius autem voluntas nulli subditur necessitati aut impossibilitati. Nihil enim est necessarium aut impossibile, nisi quia ipse ita vult."

22. *CDH* II, 17 (S II, 123, 1–3): "Sicut nulla necessitas sive impossibilitas praecedit eius velle aut nolle, ita nec eius facere aut non facere, quamvis multa velit immutabiliter et faciat."

tion or nolition to action or inaction.[23] Finally, we should note an important implication of the *proprie-improprie* distinction: any assertion of necessity *improprie* to any divine operation ("It is necessarily the case that God *x*") includes (explicitly or implicitly) a causal clause ("because God wills *x*") that supplies a necessary condition of the truth of the assertion.[24]

I have clarified Anselm's ascription of impossibility to God and have made some headway into Anselm's philosophy of will and action. But we have not yet discovered what sense can be given to the assertion "God cannot tell a lie," or "For God, lying is impossible," such that Thesis 1 is upheld by withholding the ascription of necessity *proprie* for the divine act of truth-telling. Anselm's rebuttal runs as follows:

2.20 Nothing can compel God to act against God's will (premise).

2.21 God always wills to tell the truth (premise).

2.22 God always tells the truth (2.20, 2.21).

2.23 To tell the truth is not to lie (definition).

2.24 God always does not lie (2.22, 2.23).

2.25 For God, lying is impossible (2.24).[25]

---

23. To be explicit, both compulsion and prohibition must be denied of both (1) divine volitions and nolitions as well as (2) divine actions and inactions, or doings and not-doings. That is, the will is neither compelled to will nor prohibited from willing; neither is it compelled to not-will (nill) or prohibited from nilling.

24. Anselm makes a similar point in considering the capacity of Christ to lie in *CDH* II, 10.

25. The derivation of 2.21 from 2.20 holds so long as one accepts what Simo Knuuttila terms the "temporal frequency" conception of necessity and possibility. This conception operates according to the following rule: "To be possible is to be actual at some time and, consequently, what always is, is by necessity, and what never is, is impossible." See Simo Knuuttila, "Anselm on Modality," in *The Cambridge Companion to Anselm*, ed. Brian Davies and Brian Leftow, 111–131 (Cambridge: Cambridge University Press, 2006), 112. This account of necessity and possibility, and its correlative account of diachronic contingency, was highly influential on medieval modal theories prior to Duns Scotus and following Boethius's interpretation of Aristotle in his *Commentarium in librum Aristotlelis Perihermeneias I-II*. See Knuuttila, *Modalities in Medieval Philosophy* (London: Routledge, 1993). As Knuuttila notes, Anselm is not entirely consistent in his acceptance of this account, at least insofar as he accepts the

Anselm accepts this form of the argument as valid and sound. One can immediately note, however, why it is that "impossible" in 2.25 cannot be taken as a negative instance of necessity *proprie*. Were it so, we must then say that something external to God compels God to act against God's will to always tell the truth. Then, per impossibile, it would be true both that nothing can compel God to act against God's will (2.20) and that God's will goes unfulfilled.

When Anselm gives a sense to "for God, lying is impossible," he draws upon the earlier *proprie-improprie* distinction and his appeal to divine immutability:

> When we say that it is a necessary fact that God always speaks the truth, and that it is a necessary fact that he never lies, all that is being said is that there is such a high degree of constancy with regard to upholding the truth that nothing can make him not speak the truth, or tell lies.[26]

Whence this constancy? It seems, for Anselm, that the divine will here simply reflects the divine nature. "Neither the necessity for action or the impossibility of inaction is operative in this case, only the will of God who, being himself the Truth, always wishes the truth to be unchangeable, as he is."[27] Thus, premise 2.21 ("God always wills to tell the truth") is justified by appeal to the divine nature, which is the cause of the divine will's volition for truth always. Anselm is therefore confident in the truth of 2.21, but without positing anything external to God that obligates God's willing the truth always. Thus, God necessarily tells the truth in the sense that God always tells the truth, but not in the sense that God is externally ob-

Augustinian view of atemporal divine alternatives, which will lead Scotus to develop his own account of synchronic contingency and therefore undermine such accounts of temporal necessity. However, in this case, it is apparent that the "temporal frequency" conception is operative in Anselm's argument.

26. *CDH* II, 17 (S II, 123, 31–124, 2): "Nam cum dicimus quia necesse est deum semper verum dicere, et necesse est eum numquam mentiri, non dicitur aliud nisi quia tanta est in illo constantia servandi veritatem, ut necesse sit nullam rem facere posse, ut verum non dicat aut ut mentiatur."

27. *CDH* II, 17 (S II, 123, 6–8): "Nihil enim ibi operatur necessitas non faciendi aut impossibilitas faciendi, sed dei sola volunas, qui veritatem semper, quoniam ipse veritas est, immutabilem, sicuti est, vult esse."

ligated to do so; the necessity is necessity *improprie*. Likewise, the impossibility of God's lying is impossible *improprie*, in that the source of God's obligation for not lying is internal.

Interestingly, Anselm seems to think any true ascription of necessity or impossibility, whether *proprie* or *improprie*, must be *properly* applicable to some subject. For necessity or impossibility *proprie*, the application is straightforward: the subject of the sentence is externally obliged to some willing or nilling of action or inaction. For instance, when I say "It is necessary that I breathe to live," the order of nature that is caused by God places an external obligation upon me (the subject) such that I cannot act otherwise. In the case of necessity or impossibility *improprie*, however, the external obligation is applied elsewhere: "Nor is it because there is any necessity inherent in him that we say that God does something 'of necessity,' but rather because the necessity exists in something else."[28] Proper necessity (external obligation) is properly ascribed to the subject in necessity *proprie*, and improperly ascribed to something else in the case of necessity *improprie*. Or better yet, necessity is falsely ascribed to the subject but truly ascribed to that upon which the subject acts, thereby producing the external obligation, which is the proper sense of necessity.

We can now refine Anselm's Thesis 1, "Divine operations *ad extra* cannot be necessary." What is denied is necessity or impossibility *proprie*, an obligation from any external source. Divine operations *ad extra* can, however, be necessary or impossible *improprie*, insofar as they are obligated by the divine will to do that which is willed. The latter case entails no restriction of divine freedom whatsoever. Rather, the necessity simply reflects the immutability and spontaneity of the divine will. This internal obligation is essential for Anselm to supply human reasons for divine operations *ad extra*. This important function of necessity *improprie* can be seen in a second thesis.

---

28. *CDH* II, 17 (S II, 123, 19–22): "Nec dicimus deum necessitate facere aliquid, eo quod in illo sit ulla necessitas, sed quoniam est in alio."

Thesis 2: Attributes of the divine nature restrict the domain of possible divine operations *ad extra*

Thesis 2 is evident in Anselm's response to the lie-telling dilemma. The divine will itself is the source of any divine operation *ad extra*, and that will, qua divine, possesses the character of divinity. Since God is true and truthful, lie-telling is impossible for God, not in virtue of any external obligation, but because the divine will wills in accordance with the properties of the divine nature.

This account requires some revision to the category of capacity or power (*potentia*). *CDH* makes this revision in response to Boso's objection to Anselm's solution to the lie-telling dilemma, which runs as follows:

2.26 It is impossible for God to lie (2.25).

2.27 If impossible to *x*, then no capacity for *x* (premise).

2.28 God has no capacity for lying.

2.29 God lacks some capacity.

If 2.29 is true, then it seems to follow that God is not omnipotent since God, in lacking the capacity for lying, will not possess all capacities. Anselm's solution will be unsurprising by now. The problem arises with the sense of "capacity." What appears to be a capacity is in fact incapacity; being able to lie is actually an inability to maintain proper rectitude. Just as rectitude is a necessary condition of freedom, it is also a necessary condition of capacity. This account is once again substantiated by an Augustinian appeal to the divine nature as that which is supremely determinative of all perfections.[29]

Anselm reasons that since God is the freest possible being, our concept of freedom must begin with God's own freedom rather than the creature's lesser freedom. Likewise, since God is the most powerful possible being (omnipotent), our concept of power (or capacity) must begin with God's own power rather than with the

---

29. Perfections are anything it is better for a being to have than to lack.

creature's lesser power. Capacity *proprie*, to use the earlier distinction, can only be a capacity for right action. If the act is disordered, then it is properly incapacity, or capacity *improprie*. Capacity is said properly, then, of the source of rightly ordered action, and improperly of the source of wrongly ordered action.

This account of capacity renders intelligible Anselm's assertion that "on all occasions when it is stated that God is 'incapable' of something, this is not a negation of any capacity in him: rather, it is his insuperable power and might which is being signified."[30] Incapacity, when predicated of God, is not incapacity *proprie* (the lack of some capacity), but these instances of incapacity *improprie* actually signify maximal capacity. Just as necessity *improprie* signifies freedom (and in the divine case, maximal freedom), incapacity *improprie* signifies capacity (and in the divine case, maximal capacity). Nevertheless, that we can ascribe incapacity to God improperly does make possible certain modes of reasoning about God. For instance, we can deny any argument that entails "God lied" given the truth of our premise "God is incapable of lying" or "For God, lying is impossible," in spite of the fact that impossibility and incapacity are used in both cases *improprie*. The important point is that even improper uses of modal terms (necessity and impossibility) can serve a restrictive function in seeking out a reason for divine operations *ad extra*.

The best-known instance of Anselm's application of Thesis 2 is his reconciliation of divine mercy with divine justice in *CDH*. Throughout *CDH*, Boso defends the possibility of God extending the mercy of salvation to fallen humanity without satisfaction for sin, by fiat.[31] Anselm's objection to this possibility is an application of Thesis 2. Anselm argues that there are only two proportionate responses to the debt incurred by the fall: (1) punishment by damnation, or (2) repayment. Since "God saves by fiat" is an instance of

---

30. *CDH* II, 17 (S II, 123, 11–12): "Quotiens namque dicitur deus non posse, nulla negatur in illo potestas, sed insuperabilis significatur potentia et fortitudo."

31. See esp. *CDH* I, 12, 24–25.

neither, it would entail that "God saves disproportionately," which can be restated as "God performs some disproportionate act *x*." Furthermore, Anselm takes it that "God is just" entails "God always performs proportionate acts."[32] Thus, "God saves by fiat" is false as it is inconsistent with "God is just." This instance of impossibility is not tantamount to a denial of some capacity (capacity for salvation by fiat), but an expression of God's maximal capacity for right action, which is always in accordance with divine justice. Later theologians will object to various aspects of this argument, but Anselm's assent demonstrates his commitment to and application of our Thesis 2.

Finally, I should note the important function of Anselm's doctrine of the divine attributes for Thesis 2. For Anselm, the chief divine attribute is perfection (greatness), from which all the others can be derived. Anselm claims in the *Proslogion* that all the perfections of God can be determined from his principle *aliquid quo nihil maius cogitari possit*, something than which nothing greater can be thought.[33] Since the *aliquid* establishes the principle that God is "whatever it is better to be than not to be," all other perfections (such as, just, true, and happy) can be derived from it.[34] Leaving aside the plausibility of the *aliquid* as an argument for the existence of God, note the important function it serves in restricting the domain of possible reasons for divine operations *ad extra*. This central attribute, perfection, restricts any proposition or argument that entails something "lesser" in God. Anselm makes frequent use of this principle, as when he argues that Christ would be "more purely and honourably procreated from a man in isolation or from a woman in isolation, than from an intermingling of the two like that whereby all other human children are procreated."[35] But these attributes

---

32. *CDH* II, 12.

33. *Proslogion* 2. Hereafter, I will use *aliquid* as shorthand.

34. *Proslogion* 5.

35. *CDH* II, 8 (S II, 103, 28–30): "Mundius et honestius procreabitur homo ille de solo viro vel femina, quam de commixtione utriusque, sicut omnes alii filii hominum."

of the divine nature are not the only restrictions Anselm applies to human reasons for divine operations, which brings us to our third thesis.

Thesis 3: Prior divine operations *ad extra* and their reasons restrict the domain of possible subsequent divine operations *ad extra*

Since divine immutability guarantees the truth of Thesis 3, Thesis 3 is an extension of Thesis 2.[36] Since the divine will is simultaneously immutable and spontaneous, further reflection upon reasons for divine operations *ad extra* is possible without violating Anselm's view of divine freedom as expressed in Thesis 1. Thesis 2 renders possible a series of propositions that restrict the domain of possible divine operations without making any particular divine operation necessary. One of the most important of these restricting propositions for Anselm is "God is immutable," and, by extension, "divine willings are immutable" and "divine actions are elicited by immutable divine willings."

These assertions do not entail that any particular effect of some divine operation restricts the domain of subsequent divine operations. After all, efficient effects of divine operations *ad extra* are contingent and therefore rely upon divine providence for their preservation. However, Anselm argues, divine immutability and omnipotence require that any divine reason (*ratio* in the sense of final cause, or end) for a divine operation *ad extra* must be realized. Divine intentions cannot be thwarted. Thus, a *ratio*, the end God gives to any efficient effect of a divine operation *ad extra*, can restrict the domain of possible subsequent divine operations *ad extra*.

The primary instance of Thesis 3 in *CDH* is the creation of humans for the sake of beatitude. Since God wills these creatures to this end, the divine will is immutable, and divine power is omnip-

---

36. I say an extension because the specific divine attribute of "immutability" must also be supplied, hence it is not identical to Thesis 2.

otent, any other divine operation *ad extra* cannot entail either the change of that end of beatitude or that beatitude is not realized in some case.[37] Anselm makes this argument in an extended reflection on the purpose of the human creature. He argues that humans were created for the sake of beatitude, which they attain so long as they satisfy the condition of purity (i.e., lack of stain):

> Do you not understand ... that it is a necessity that some human beings should attain to happiness? For let us assume that God created mankind without stain with this state of bliss in view and thus that it is unfitting for him to bring to this state a human being who is in any way stained—otherwise he might seem to be having regrets about his good undertaking and to be incapable of bringing his plan to fulfillment.[38]

On this basis, Anselm proceeds to argue against the possibility of God either (1) allowing no human beings to attain that state for which humans are created, or (2) allowing for the attainment of that state without satisfying its condition. Thus, one divine operation *ad extra* (i.e., the creation of humans intended for beatitude if they remain pure) restricts the domain of possible subsequent divine operations *ad extra*.[39] Once again, the function of Thesis 3 is strictly negative: it rejects any beliefs inconsistent with prior divine reasons for divine operations. It does not adjudicate between those beliefs consistent with the divine reasons, many of which are incomposcible.

Earlier I summarized Anselm's central argument in *CDH* as follows:

---

37. Anselm argues that beatitude must be realized in all the elect who, together with the angels, comprise the perfect number in the heavenly host. Moreover, he argues that in every moment of human history some human has existed who was to realize beatitude.

38. *CDH* I, 25 (S II, 95, 24–28): "An non intelligis ex iis quae supra diximus, quia necesse est aliquos homines ad beatitudinem pervenire? Nam si deo inconveniens est hominem cum aliqua macula perducere ad hoc, ad quod illum sine omni macula fecit, ne aut boni incepti paenitere aut propositum implere non posse videatur."

39. "Subsequent" is taken, here, temporally.

2.1 If God wills to redeem humans, humans are redeemed.

2.2 God wills to redeem humans.

2.3 Humans are redeemed.

2.4 If humans are redeemed, it must be by satisfaction for sin.

2.5 If there is satisfaction for sin, then it must be by the God-man.

2.6 If humans are redeemed, then the God-man satisfies.

2.7 The God-man satisfies.

2.8 Satisfaction is the offering of something proportionate to the offense, which restores the offenders.

2.9 The passion of the God-man is proportionate to the offense of sin and restores the offenders (sinners).

2.10 There is no more fitting means of satisfaction for sin.

2.11 The passion of the God-man satisfies.

We can now observe the important function of Theses 1–3 in Anselm's central argument. Thesis 1 states that divine operations *ad extra* cannot be necessary. This rule is upheld in Anselm's decision to ground his argument in the divine will, which acts in perfect freedom. However, Anselm's distinction between proper and improper necessity makes possible internal obligations, which admits the negative epistemic rule of Thesis 2, that attributes of the divine nature restrict the domain of possible divine operations *ad extra*. To restate the point, any assertion inconsistent with some divine attribute (e.g., "God is just") will be false. This rule renders 2.4 as a conclusion of the following argument:

2.30 If humans are redeemed, then sins are satisfied or not satisfied.

2.31 If anything under God's governance is unregulated, then God is unjust (premise, *CDH* I, 12).

2.32 God is just (premise).

2.33 Nothing under God's governance is unregulated (2.31, 2.32).

2.34 Sin is under God's governance (premise, *CDH* I, 23).

2.35 No sin is unregulated (2.33, 2.34).

2.36 If sin is unsatisfied, then sin is unregulated (premise, *CDH* I, 12).

2.37 Sin is satisfied (2.35, 2.36).

2.38 If humans are redeemed, it must be by satisfaction for sin (2.30, 2.37).

Since "some sin is unregulated" is inconsistent with "God is just," it is therefore false. Anselm's application of Thesis 2 makes possible the conclusion that satisfaction is a necessary condition of redemption. A similar strategy is applied to conclude in 2.5: "If there is satisfaction for sin, then it must be by the God-man."

Finally, Thesis 3 is reflected in 2.2. Thesis 1 demands that it is not necessary that God create humans for beatitude.[40] Nevertheless, since God has immutably willed to create humans for beatitude, any assertion inconsistent with "God wills to create humans for beatitude" must be rejected.[41] One such assertion would be "God does not redeem humans" as redemption from sin is a necessary condition of beatitude in a fallen world. Otherwise, God would have begun something without finishing it, which can only be explained by a change in the divine will (denied by immutability) or divine impotence to realize something God wills to be (denied by omnipotence). Since either God does or does not will to redeem humans, and it cannot be the latter, 2.2 follows. An argument from Thesis 3 will be valid, then, on three conditions: (1) divine immutability, (2) divine omnipotence, and (3) revelation of the divine reason for some prior divine operation.

To this point, all of our theses have been negative. God does not act necessarily *ad extra, and* the reason for a divine operation *ad*

40. *CDH* II, 1–4. I take Anselm's Thesis 1 to require that it is neither necessary for God to create humans nor is it necessary for God to create humans for beatitude.

41. *CDH* II, 4 (S II, 99, 3–5): "Ex his est facile cognoscere quoniam aut hoc de humana perficiet deus natura quod incepit, aut in vanum fecit tam sublimem naturam ad tantum bonum (With regard to the nature of mankind, there are two alternatives: either God will complete what he has begun, or it was to no avail that he created this life-form—so sublime a life-form, and with such great good as its purpose).

extra cannot be inconsistent with either the divine attributes *or* with the divine reasons for divine operations *ad extra*. Our fourth and final thesis functions both positively and negatively, and substantiates the transition from 2.10 to 2.11 in the central argument of *CDH*. The application of this particular thesis became a significant site for the development of Anselm's Christology over the course of the thirteenth century.

Thesis 4: Reasons for divine operations *ad extra* possess fittingness (*convenientia*)

Anselm frequently refuses to accept positions that are "unfitting" (*inconvenientia*). He rejects, for instance, the assertion that "God allows anything in his kingdom to slip by unregulated" because it is unfitting.[42] In these instances, his use of *inconvenientia* seems indistinguishable from those arguments supported by our Thesis 2 above; unregulated sin requires a denial of divine immutability, omnipotence, or justice. However, on other occasions Anselm's arguments from fittingness seem to demand less rational confidence. Put simply, Anselm's use of fittingness in *CDH* is varied.

Convenientia and various derivatives of *convenio* occur fifty-five times in *CDH*. Many of those occurrences gather around central moments in the text's argument. In order to clarify our Thesis 4, while holding out the possibility for an underlying unity in Anselm's arguments from fittingness, I will first distinguish between three classes of arguments from fittingness among these fifty-five occurrences in *CDH*: (1) negative limitation arguments, (2) gradation arguments, and (3) embellishment arguments.[43] I will then consider their intersection and internal logic.

---

42. *CDH* I, 12 (S II, 69, 15): "Deum vero non decet aliquid inordinatum in suo regno dimittere."

43. This is excluding uses that carry the sense of "coming together" as in "combining," as when Anselm describes the hypostatic union of Christ's two natures with the verb *convenire*.

Negative Limitation Arguments

The first class of arguments from fittingness is difficult to distinguish from the arguments we encountered in Theses 2 and 3. Unfittingness obtains when some assertion is inconsistent with properties of the divine nature or the reasons for prior divine operations. In this case, the rule "if unfitting, then false" is applied. Or, as Anselm puts it, "no unfittingness where God is concerned—not even the smallest—shall be accepted by us."[44]

If "unfittingness where God is concerned" is impossible in negative limitation arguments, then "fittingness" must be that which is possible. Possibility here is conceived in a specifically theistic way, as reflected in the stipulation "where God is concerned." For Anselm in *CDH*, the relevant set of possible assertions is the set including all assertions composable with Anselm's account of the divine attributes and (by extension) all the divine reasons for prior divine operations *ad extra*. "Fitting" assertions, then, will be the set of assertions composable with fundamental commitments of Christian theism.[45] Or, fitting assertions are composable with Anselm's God.

---

44. *CDH* I, 10 (S II, 67, 1–4): "Quoniam accipis in hac quaestione personam eorum, qui credere nihil volunt nisi praemonstrata ratione, volo tecum pacisci, ut nullum vel minimum inconveniens in deo a nobis accipiatur, et nulla vel minima ratio, si maior non repugnat, reiciatur."

45. It is, admittedly, somewhat problematic to say "composable with certain fundamental assertions of Christian theism" when considering Anselm for two reasons. First, note the important apologetic feature of the beliefs in question: they are shared by Judaism and Christianity. Perhaps, then, we should say Judeo-Christian theism. This is the set of beliefs I intend by the term "Christian" theism. However, given that my interests here are for the sake of Christian theology, and I do not wish to raise any inquiries as to the degree to which Anselm's conception of common beliefs obtains, I will restrict myself to Christian theism. Second, possible worlds semantics ordinarily conceive of possibility as "exists in at least one possible world" and necessity as "exists in all possible worlds." That I am stipulating a certain class of possible worlds, namely those that are composable with the God of Christian theism, implies that there are possible worlds without the God of Christian theism for which the propositions of Christian theism perform no composable limitations. One could argue that Anselm takes this view of things as well insofar as he stipulates, at *CDH* I, 10, the set of beliefs he is allowing in order to continue with his investigation. Much will hinge on the status of the *aliquid* argument in the *Proslogion*. In any event,

Anselm makes this point explicit at the conclusion of *CDH* I, 10, when he describes his shared presuppositions with his apparently Jewish interlocutors in the renown *remoto Christo* passage:

> Let us posit, therefore, (1) that the incarnation of God and the things which we say about him as man had never happened, and (2) let it be agreed between us that man was created for a state of blessedness which cannot be had in this life, and (3) that no one can arrive at that state if his sins have not been got rid of, and (4) that no man can pass through this life without sin; (5) let us also accept the other matters in which we need to have faith in order to attain eternal salvation.[46]

We can see the importance of logical consistency and compossibility in the stipulation of both a general account of the divine nature, which must minimally be included in (5), as well as the reason for a prior divine operation *ad extra* (2), and an insight derived from experience and expressed in revelation (4).

Can we distinguish *inconvenientia* from "incompossible with Anselm's God," and *convenientia* from "compossible with Anselm's God?" At those times when Anselm deploys negative limitation arguments from fittingness, and there are many, there seems to be no distinction. Consider a few examples: Boso objects in I, 8 that it is unfitting to say that God could not save except by the condemnation of one who is just. Given divine omnipotence, it must be that God is capable of saving otherwise. Thus, if God chooses to save by the condemnation of the just one, then God is unwise and unjust, which is unfitting insofar as it is incompossible with the belief "God is just." In II, 1 Anselm insists that it would not be fitting for God to give rational creatures the ability to distinguish good from bad

---

such an argument is not necessary for the account I am giving here. I will therefore proceed with the language of compossibility insofar as it is (1) a viable interpretive option and (2) seems consistent with the reception of Anselm's *aliquid* argument in the thirteenth century.

46. *CDH* I, 10 (S II, 67, 12–16): "Ponamus ergo dei incarnationem et quae de illo dicimus homine numquam fuisse; et constet inter nos hominem esse factum ad beatitudinem, quae in hac vita haberi non potest, nec ad illam posse pervenire quemquam nisi dimissis peccatis, nec ullum hominem hanc vitam transire sine peccato, et alia quorum fides ad salutem aeternam necessaria est."

so that they might hate and avoid the bad and love and choose the good, all to no avail. Unfittingness, again, is synonymous with incompossibility. This argument is nearly indistinguishable from the argument in *CDH* I, 25 cited above as an expression of Thesis 3. Because *inconvenientia* is incompossible, it restricts the domain of compossibilities, but it does not determine which of the range of compossibilities obtains. Thus, it seems, in negative limitation arguments *inconvenientia* is equivalent to incompossibility, and *convenientia* to compossibility.

Embellishment Arguments

With our second class of arguments from fittingness, which I will call embellishment arguments, the rule "*inconvenientia* is incompossible" is strictly upheld.[47] While *inconvenientia* is incompossible and therefore necessarily not the case, *convenientia* is compossible and therefore possibly, but not necessarily the case. As Michael Root puts it:

To say that an act is fitting is to say only that God can appropriately perform such an act. No certain or necessary conclusions about what God will do follow from an assertion to fittingness. To say that an act is unfitting is to say that God necessarily will not perform such an act. A certain and necessary conclusion does follow, though only a negative one. When applied to God, the concepts "fitting" and "unfitting" come to operate like the concepts "possible" and "impossible," which display a similar asymmetry.[48]

Embellishment arguments, however, go beyond negative limitation arguments in that they select one possibility from the set of propositions compossible with Anselm's God and then demonstrate the "order" and "beauty" of that particular possibility. In this way, while not arriving at a demonstration, reason extends into the

47. Embellishment here should not be taken in the sense of embellishing a tale with falsity, but rather as illuminated medieval manuscripts were embellished with artistry, ornamentation, and color.

48. Michael Root, "Necessity and Unfittingness in Anselm's *Cur Deus Homo,*" *Scottish Journal of Theology* 40, no. 2 (1987): 220.

domain of divine operations *ad extra*. Thus, those operations remain both entirely free and entirely rational.

In Anselm's words, these arguments require some foundation, something "solid," in order to render them compelling to the unbeliever. A rational demonstration cannot be given for the conclusion that Christ, who "was to redeem the human race and bring it back from the way of death and destruction to the way of life and eternal happiness, should live in the company of human beings and, while he was teaching them verbally how they ought to live, should, through his very behavior, present himself as an example."[49] Nevertheless, given the "solid" foundation of Anselm's central argument (2.1–10), and our record of Christ's life and works in Scripture, Anselm must conclude that Christ's exemplary role is extremely fitting (*valde conveniat*).

Anselm holds consistently that embellishment arguments from fittingness do not arrive at necessary demonstrations from reason alone. Independently, such arguments do not persuade the unbeliever. At I, 4, following a series of embellishment arguments, Boso presents to Anselm the unbeliever's central objection to embellishment arguments:

All these are beautiful notions, and are to be viewed like pictures. But if there is nothing solid underlying them, they do not seem to unbelievers to provide sufficient grounds why we should believe that God wished to suffer the things of which we are speaking. . . . When we offer to unbelievers these notions which you say are appropriate (*conveniens*), like pictorial representations of an actual past event, they think we are, as it were, painting on a cloud.[50]

---

49. *CDH* II, 11 (S II, 111, 29–112, 1): "Quis enim explicet quam necessarie, quam sapienter factum est, ut ille qui homines erat redempturus et de via mortis et perditionis ad viam vitae et beatitudinis aeternae docendo reducturus, cum hominibus conversaretur et in ipsa conversatione, cum eos doceret verbo qualiter vivere deberent, se ipsum exemplum praeberet?"

50. *CDH* I, 4 (S II, 51, 16–18, 21–52, 3): "Omnia haec pulchra et quasi quaedam picturae suscipienda sunt. Sed si non est aliquid solidum super quod sedeant, non videntur infidelibus sufficere, cur deum ea quae dicimus pati voluisse credere debeamus. . . . Quapropter cum has convenientias quas dicis infidelibus quasi quasdam

Anselm accepts this criticism and proceeds to develop the central argument of *CDH* (2.1–11) as the solid base upon which the embellishment arguments can be added. Nevertheless, embellishment arguments are not trivial. Neither, for Anselm, is their rational status any lower than the necessary arguments underlying them. Negative limitation and embellishment arguments from fittingness are both true and therefore express the same metaphysical reality: the order, beauty, and justice of God imprinted upon creation.

Embellishment arguments also have an important function when it comes to expressing the *kind* of mystery we are attempting to reason about in our reflection on the incarnation; it is inexhaustible.[51] Anselm is unable to resist the temptation to wander off into the expansive fittingness of the incarnation of the Son of God. He gives embellishment arguments from fittingness in the sequence of parallelisms at I, 3, in his appeal to the perfect number of the heavenly host in I, 18, and in his reflections on the fittingness of the Son, rather than the Father or the Spirit, becoming incarnate in II, 9. These embellishments reach apogee when, in response to Anselm's argument that it is most fitting that the reward for Christ's death be applied to those for whom he became incarnate, Boso declares, "There can be nothing more logical, nothing sweeter, nothing more desirable that the world can hear. I indeed derive such confidence from this that I cannot now express in words with what joy my heart is rejoicing."[52] Fittingly, Anselm responds:

---

picturas rei gestae obtendimus, quoniam non rem gestam, sed figmentum arbitrantur esse quod credimus, quasi super nubem pingere nos existimant."

51. Marilyn McCord Adams gives a lovely expression of the rhetorical function of what I have called embellishment arguments and the important intellectual and conative engagement which they effect in the reader, as a distinct form of Anselmian dialogue, in "Elegant Necessity, Prayerful Disputation: Method in *Cur Deus Homo*," in *Cur Deus Homo: Atti del congresso Anselmiano internazionale: Roma, 21–23 Maggio 1998*, ed. Paul Gilbert, Helmut Kohlenberger, and Elmar Salmann, 367–96 (Rome: Pontificio Ateneo S. Anselmo, 1999).

52. *CDH* II, 19 (S II, 131, 3–5): "Nihil rationabilius, nihil dulcius, nihil desider-

I think I have now gone some little way towards a satisfactory reply to your question, although someone better than I could do it more fully, and there are more, and greater, reasons (*rationes*) for this thing than my intellect, or any mortal intellect, can comprehend.[53]

We have now determined two classes of arguments from fitting-ness and clarified their modal status. Negative limitation arguments are demonstrations of some unfittingness inconsistent with the set of propositions outlined by Anselm in *CDH* I, 10. That is, unfittin-gess obtains when a state of affairs is incompossible with Anselm's God. Thus, unfitting propositions are necessarily false. Alterna-tively, embellishment arguments consider one of multiple states of affairs all of which are compossible with Anselm's God. In these instances, revelation shows which compossibility obtains (e.g., that the Son, not the Father or the Spirit, is incarnated). Hence the theologian's task is the explication of fittingness in terms of beauty, justice, and order for that particular compossibility. These theolog-ical insights are turned up, as it were, by Anselm's ceaseless pursuit of necessary arguments (*rationes neccessarie*).

Gradation Arguments

Anselm gives arguments from fittingness in one further way. The modality of these particular arguments is murkier. Gradation argu-ments from fittingness are ordinarily marked by the comparative of *convenientia* (*convenientius*). A paradigmatic instance of this class of arguments, complete with methodological excursus, is found at *CDH* II, 16. In that chapter, Anselm presents a parable of a king whose entire city, with the exception of one man, sinned against him. The one innocent man enjoys such favor with the king that

---

abilius mundus audire potest. Ego quidem tantam fiduciam ex hoc concipio, ut iam dicere non possim quanto gaudio exultet cor meum."

53. *CDH* II, 19 (S II, 131, 13–15): "Puto me iam aliquantulum tuae satisfecisse quaestioni, quamvis hoc melior me facere plenius possit, et maiores atque plures quam meum aut mortale ingenium comprehendere valeat huius rei sint rationes."

he can, and does, render such a service to reconcile all the guilty to the king, both those present and those absent in space and time. Anselm argues that, like the parable, the reconciliation achieved by Christ can and does extend both to those present and to those absent, spatially and temporally. He then adds a further claim:

Nor is it to be believed that, since mankind's first creation, there has been any time in which this world, filled as it is with creatures which were created for the use of mankind, has been so barren that there was no one in it from the human race bearing any relation to the purpose for which mankind was created.[54]

The contrary, that there is some time in which no human exists who would join the heavenly city, is unfitting, and therefore false: "For they would seem to have their being in vain for as long as they did not seem to exist with a view to the purpose for which they were principally created."[55]

Boso, somewhat surprisingly, accepts this argument.[56] *Quod non solum conveniens sed etiam necessarium esse possumus concludere*: "We can conclude that this is not only fitting but even necessary." Why?

For, assume that this state of affairs is more fitting and logical than that there should have been at some time no one with regard to whom the intention of God in creating mankind was to be fulfilled; assume too that there is no obstacle to this logical state of affairs: in that case it is a necessary fact that there has always been someone connected with the reconciliation we have in mind. Hence it is not to be doubted that Adam and Eve

54. *CDH* II, 16 (S II, 119, 3–6): "Nec credendum est, ex quo factus est homo, ullum tempus fuisse quo mundus iste cum creaturis, quae factae sunt ad usus hominum, sic vacuus fuisset, ut nullus esset in illo ex humano genere ad hoc pertinens, propter quod factus est homo."

55. *CDH* II, 16 (S II, 119, 8–10): "Nam aliquatenus in vanum esse viderentur, quamdiu non ad hoc propter quod maxime facta essent, viderentur subsistere."

56. While Anselm's parable shows that it is conceivable for an innocent man to give recompense for sinners throughout all times and places, it is not clear how this would entail or even imply that at all times there exists at least one human that will fulfill God's intention for humanity. Whether or not this argument is sound, however, that Anselm takes it to be somehow valid is of immense interest for interpreting his arguments *ex convenientia*.

had a connection with that act of redemption, even though divine authority does not pronounce this explicitly.[57]

Anselm admits that the teaching is not pronounced by authority.
Nevertheless, he argues that we can use an argument from fittingness to demonstrate which of multiple compossible states of affairs
will obtain, so much so that we can assert its necessity. How?

Gradation arguments proceed, first, by exhaustively distinguishing all logical possibilities. Anselm does so at II, 16 by positing two
opposed propositions:

x: At some time there exists no human that will fulfill God's
intention for mankind.

$\sim x$: At no time there exists no human that will fulfill God's
intention for mankind.

Once the possibilities are exhausted, Anselm shows that one of the
two propositions is more fitting than the other. Thus, the more fitting will be true and the less fitting false.

Analysis of this gradation argument suggests three conditions
for gradation arguments in general. First, there must be multiple
logical possibilities. Second, we must be able to distinguish an exhaustive set of those logical possibilities. Third, we must be able to
establish that one is more fitting (*convenientius*) than the other(s).

Our first example of gradation arguments is very similar to a
negative limitation argument. The similarity is attributable to the
binary form of the distinction between x and $\sim x$, and the dismissal
of one of the options on the grounds of its incompossibility with
Anselm's God. Moreover, one can safely assume that Anselm has in
mind some proposition along the lines of "God is just" as a belief
with which $\sim x$ is less fitting than x.

---

57. *CDH* II, 16 (S II, 119, 14–19): "Si enim convenientius et rationabilius est
hoc, quam aliquando nullum fuisse, de quo intentio dei qua hominem fecit perficeretur, nec est aliquid quod huic obviet rationi, necesse est semper aliquem ad
praedictam reconciliationem pertinentem fuisse. Unde ADAM et EVA ad illam per-
tinuisse redemptionem dubitandum non est, quamvis hoc auctoritas divina aperte
non pronuntiet."

Other instances of gradation arguments are more complicated. These instances anticipate the series of debates over the reason for the incarnation that occupied theologians of the thirteenth century. At *CDH* II, 8 Anselm distinguishes between four possible means whereby God could create a human being: (1) from a man and woman together, (2) from neither a man nor a woman, (3) from a man alone, or (4) from a woman alone. The first three God has done apart from the incarnation. And so, Anselm argues, "in order to prove that (the fourth) method too is within his competence and that it has been kept in reserve for the very undertaking which we have in mind, it is pre-eminently fitting that he should take the man who is the object of our quest from a woman without a man."[58] This argument, Anselm insists, is not insubstantial as a cloud, but solid as a foundation. Once again, our three conditions for gradation arguments obtain: (1) there are multiple logical compossibilities, (2) Anselm distinguishes an exhaustive class of possibilities (both, neither, one, and the other), and (3) he supplies an argument for the greater fittingness of one over the others. Moreover, once again there is a similar appeal to some divine attribute, in this case to omnipotence, as in the prior gradation argument.

Thirteenth-century theologians found this argument, and others like it, rather problematic. In order to resolve these problems, many of them found it necessary to clarify fittingness, develop more sophisticated accounts of divine power, and consider more extensive implications than those treated in *CDH*. A brief comparison of Grosseteste and Bonaventure's reception of the gradation argument cited above bears this out.

In *DCL* III, Grosseteste finds Anselm's argument compelling, and supplies further warrant: "The argument that the God-man was congruously born from a virgin and without the seed of a man is clear from Anselm, to which it can be added that it should be so in

---

58. *CDH* II, 8 (S II, 104, 6–8): "Ut igitur hunc quoque modum probet suae subiacere potestati et ad hoc ipsum opus dilatum esse, nil convenientius, quam ut de femina sine viro assumat illum hominem quem quaerimus."

order that the circular period of human generation be perfectly completed."[59] Grosseteste's appeal to the fulfillment of the circular period of human generation is akin to earlier arguments in *DCL* that God "creates every kind of creature that can exist," all of which fit into Grosseteste's larger metaphysical vision.[60] For Grosseteste, a theological variant of what Lovejoy called the "principle of plenitude" (i.e., that every possible kind ought to exist) renders such gradation arguments necessary demonstrations.[61]

Bonaventure considers the same gradation argument at III *Sent.* d. 1, a. 2, q. 2, when he asks "what was the primary reason for the incarnation?" His ninth argument in support of the conclusion that redemption from sin is not the primary reason for the incarnation is Anselm's gradation argument: the God-man should be born from a woman without a man. Unlike Grosseteste, however, Bonaventure finds the argument far from compelling. Instead, he argues that Christ's birth from a woman without a man is not *de perfectione universi* (for the perfection of the universe) but *supra perfectionem universi* (beyond the perfection of the universe). The incarnation is, and here he cites Jeremiah, a *novum*, something new. And something new would not be done unless something old precedes it.[62] If something "would not be done," it cannot be necessary to the perfection of the universe. On analogy, it does not follow "that the universe would lack its perfection; just as the imperfection of the universe cannot be shown with respect to the resurrection of

59. *DCL* III.2.5: "Ratio vero quod Deum-hominem congruat nasci de virgine et sine iri semine satis evidens est apud Anselmum, cui adici potest quod sic oporteat humane generacionis circularem periodum, perfecte compleri."

60. *DCL* III.1.9: "(Deus) creat omnes species creaturarum quas possibile est esse." For a broader view of Grosseteste's metaphysics, see James McEvoy, *Robert Grosseteste*, Great Medieval Thinkers (Oxford: Oxford University Press, 2000). Further analysis of Grosseteste's arguments and concern with circularity will be treated in chapter three.

61. Arthur O. Lovejoy, *The Great Chain of Being: A Study of the History of an Idea* (Cambridge, Mass.: Harvard University Press, 1964).

62. III *Sent.* d. 1, a. 2, q. 2 (III, 27): "Et ideo Ieremias vocat illud *novum*, cum ait: *Novum faciet Dominus super terram*; hoc autem *novum* Dominus non fecisset, nisi aliqua veteratio praecessisset."

the dead, which God would not have done if humanity had remained (without sin)."[63] Finally, Bonaventure points out the possibility that God could create a human from a woman alone who was
nevertheless not God.[64]

What, then, should we make of Anselm's gradation arguments?
Three observations are in order. First, Anselm's gradation arguments express a similar concern to that expressed in the central
argument of *CDH*, which he supported with both negative limitation and embellishment arguments: the importance of God retaining order and governance over all. Fittingness plays an important
role in Anselm's argument that God's intentions are fulfilled, as
demonstrated in 2.12–19. In that argument, fittingness reflects
the internal divine obligation that is a function of both (1) the immutability of the divine will, and (2) an entirely free prior divine
determination. That is, fittingness presumes that God has the particular intention for rational creatures that God has in our world.
Were it otherwise, then, per impossibile, either God's intentions
have changed, or else God is powerless to realize those intentions.
At II, 16, we see a very similar argument: it is impossible that God
does something in vain, a Christian restatement of the Aristotelian dictum *natura nihil frustra facit*. Once again, Anselm justifies
his assertion by appeal to divine immutability and omnipotence.
It seems, then, that Anselm considers his gradation argument at
II, 16 as merely an application of his prior argument. Insofar as
that prior argument is consistent with Theses 1–3 and follows the
account of fittingness in our description of negative limitation and
embellishment arguments, we can see why Anselm might take his
argument as perfectly consistent. Second, Anselm has nevertheless
overstepped his own bounds for arguments from fittingness at this

63. III *Sent.* d. 1, a. 2, q. 2 (III, 27): "Nec ex hoc sequitur, quod universum sua
perfectione careret; sicut etiam non potest argui imperfectio universi quantum ad
suscitationem mortui, quam Deus non fecisset, si homo perstitisset."

64. III *Sent.* d. 1, a. 2, q. 2 (III, 27): "Deus posset producere hominem de mu-
liere absque viro, qui tamen non esset Deus."

point. Of course, as some have pointed out, his distinction between gradations of fittingness among the range of compossibilities might be ahead of its time, insofar as it opens the door to inductive forms of reasoning about the incarnation.[65] But Anselm takes them to be deductive and in that respect they fail. Third, and most importantly for our study, Anselm's gradation arguments impart a perplexity to future generations of theologians. To cite the relevant example, Robert Grosseteste is puzzled that so many of Anselm's arguments seem to lead to one *necessary* conclusion, which Anselm seems to deny: even if Adam had not sinned, the Son would have become incarnate.

Anselm's Theses after Anselm

I have now derived four theses on the general question (How can we determine divine reasons for divine operations *ad extra?*) from Anselm's *CDH*. They run as follows:

Thesis 1: Divine operations *ad extra* cannot be necessary.

Thesis 2: Attributes of the divine nature restrict the domain of possible divine operations *ad extra*.

Thesis 3: Prior divine operations *ad extra* and their reasons restrict the domain of possible subsequent divine operations *ad extra*.

Thesis 4: Reasons for divine operations *ad extra* possess fittingness (*convenientia*).

Anselm's contribution to subsequent debates is ambivalent. Broadly speaking, his approach to divine action and divine reasons were influential, but rarely accepted in the thirteenth century without significant revision. The theses provoked reflection, refinement,

65. David Brown finds in Anselm's arguments from *convenientia* this sort of opportunity for contemporary Christology, "'Necessary' and 'Fitting' Reasons in Christian Theology," in *The Rationality of Religious Belief: Essays in Honour of Basil Mitchell*, ed. William J. Abraham and Steven W. Holtzer (Oxford: Clarendon Press, 1987), 211–30.

and expansion on the general question. But if they were received with ambivalence, they were not received without consequence.

From the time of Alexander of Hales and Robert Grosseteste, theologians looked to Anselm for guidance in thinking about the incarnation and other divine operations *ad extra*. Several reasons can be given for why Anselm was so regularly consulted.

First, Anselm pioneers a way to address the difficulties that attend our reflection on divine operations *ad extra*. He takes up a standard theological procedure, beginning with familiar concepts (e.g., necessity and freedom), and proceeds to refine their meaning when predicated of God. As a result, Anselm develops a distinctively theological account of both necessity and freedom. Moreover, his account proved useful for further theological speculation, as it prevents a class of problematic assertions (those which entail external obligation), while allowing for rational reflection upon and speech about God's action in contingent states of affairs.

Second, Anselm extends St. Augustine's thought on freedom and rectitude, a major authority for scholastic theology in the thirteenth century. Central to Anselm's procedure is his account of the divine attributes, both positive and negative. As Robert Grosseteste makes clear, theologians were increasingly thinking alongside Augustine *and* Anselm; in the thirteenth century, the perception was that fidelity to the latter was tantamount to fidelity to the former.[66]

Finally, Anselm suggests one way in which the divine attributes might shape our understanding of divine operations *ad extra*, chiefly through his careful application of arguments from fittingness. Since divine perfection norms the way we think about divine reasons for divine operations, any assertion that entails the predication of some "lesser" property will therefore be incompossible with Anselm's God. Such assertions are unfitting and therefore false. As I have shown, this contribution was not without difficulties. It required further refinement. Nevertheless, Anselm's fittingness argu-

66. See note 6.

ments isolate a critical systematic juncture in all discussions of the hypothetical question, the primacy question, and the general question throughout the thirteenth century. That juncture, connecting divine attributes with divine action by appeal to fittingness, provoked subsequent reflections on two questions in particular. First, how should we think about the relationship between attributes of the divine nature, such as goodness and perfection, and the domain of compossible actions for a God who possesses these attributes? Second, what is the relationship between these attributes and the divine will, especially with regard to free divine determinations over contingent creatures and their divinely given ends? This systematic juncture will be *the* central locus of thirteenth-century theological reflections on the hypothetical question.

Anselm's theses provided both methodological advantages and puzzles for thirteenth-century theologians who took up the demands of supplying reasons for divine operations *ad extra,* like the incarnation. When thirteenth-century theologians came to the incarnation, they often began with a set of distinctions on the necessity and possibility of the incarnation and frequently considered the fittingness of the incarnation. Aquinas is exemplary in this regard. Earlier, in the *Scriptum* III, d. 1, Aquinas prefaces his response to the hypothetical question with two questions on the possibility and necessity of the incarnation, respectively. By the time of the *ST* III, q. 1, the two articles preceding the hypothetical question discuss the necessity and fittingness (*convenientia*) of the incarnation, respectively. And both concepts of necessity and fittingness are then considered in order to answer the hypothetical question.

All the thirteenth-century scholars who considered the reason for the incarnation at Paris evince a debt to Anselm of Canterbury and *CDH.* But no one in the thirteenth century makes their debt to Anselm on these questions so explicit as a theologian at Oxford: Robert Grosseteste.

THREE

Robert Grosseteste

In Oxford, sometime between 1230 and 1235, Robert Grosseteste produced *De cessatione legalium* (*DCL*). The argument is notoriously complex. Richard Dales and Edward King, editors of the critical edition, observe that *DCL* "is difficult to summarize because the arguments, complex in themselves, are further obfuscated by the circular and tangential conventions of the author's style."[1] Indeed, Grosseteste's method and style are sometimes obfuscating. As a result, his arguments seem disorganized.

> [Grosseteste] was not by nature a systematic thinker any more than he was by nature a tidy organizer of material from the past. His strength lay in discovering areas of knowledge to which he could make a new contribution. Having done this, he was content to leave it to others to go further if they could, while he passed on to the next problem.[2]

But instances should not be predetermined by impressions. As Stephen Hildebrand has shown, if the argument of *DCL* lacks the organizational transparency of Grosseteste's Parisian counterparts, it is not so bewildering as Dales and King suggest:

1. Grosseteste, *DCL*, xv.
2. R. W. Southern, *Robert Grosseteste: The Growth of an English Mind in Medieval Europe* (Oxford: Oxford University Press, 1986), 46.

Grosseteste's argument . . . is both coherent and comprehensive; it is not haphazard but deliberate and purposeful, even if sometimes circuitous. His great achievement is to clarify the larger theological contexts in which one must view the difficult question of the relation between the Old and New Testaments.[3]

The most commented upon arguments of *DCL* are the opening paragraphs of Book III. There Robert takes up the hypothetical question: "If humanity had not sinned, would God have become incarnate?" He gives a series of arguments for the affirmative, that God would have become human, even if humanity had not fallen. While Grosseteste was not the first to pose the hypothetical question, his *DCL* is the first extended treatment of the question.

Typically, these opening paragraphs are read as a series of loosely related arguments united by their conclusion that the incarnation would be, even if the fall were not. The analytical reading of *DCL* III.1 that follows reveals a greater unity in these passages than previously observed: Grosseteste employs two basic strategies of argumentation in *DCL* III.1.[4] Moreover, his two strategies provide one possible, and rather stark, application of the Anselmian theses to the reason for the incarnation. As a result, Grosseteste serves as a counterpoint to the Parisian debates that will be the focus of subsequent chapters. Those Parisian debates develop, in part, due to a worry about Grosselestean applications of the Anselmian theses to the reason for the incarnation. Thus, the analytical reading that follows will help bring the arguments of *DCL* into conversation both with the prior project of Anselm's *CDH* as well as the later debates at Paris.

---

3. Grosseteste, *On the Cessation*, 16–17.
4. I have developed the reading that follows, on its own terms and in greater detail, in Hunter, "Rereading Robert Grosseteste on the *Ratio Incarnationis*: Deductive Strategies in *De Cessatione Legalium* III," *The Thomist* 81, no. 2 (2017): 213–45.

De cessatione legalium

In the first chapter of *DCL* Grosseteste gives the argument he will seek to overturn: "There were many in the primitive Church who asserted that the sacraments of the Old Law together with the sacraments of the New Law must be observed and that there could be no salvation without observing them."[5] In Part I, Grosseteste recites and rebuts several arguments in support of these "many in the primitive Church." He then turns to Christology for a "slightly greater way of beginning."[6] If the assertion is cryptic, his procedure is not. Grosseteste returns to the Garden of Eden in order to narrate salvation history and to locate the law and Christ in that grand narrative.

Grosseteste first establishes the need for both natural and positive law in every state of the rational creature.[7] He then recounts the fall of both angels and humans, drawing attention to the character of their temptation and failure.[8] This brings him to an important conclusion:

It is clear, therefore, from the fact that man sinned, that there ought to be both the faith which was believed and the law which was upheld. But since man had broken the natural and positive law by sinning, and the same positive law before him, that is, of not eating the fruit, now was not law to him, because he was not in its power, another positive law would be uselessly given to him, unless first he was proven again in the observation of the natural law.[9]

5. *DCL* I.1.1: "Fuerunt plurimi in primitiva ecclesia qui astruerent sacramenta veteris legis simul cum sacramentis nove legis observanda esse nec sine illorum observacione salutem esse."

6. *DCL* I.4.1: "Paulo altius exordiendum videtur."

7. *DCL* I.4–5. As Grossesteste observes in 1.5.7, this would include a fitting reception of the positive law for angels as well as humans.

8. *DCL* I.6.

9. *DCL* I.6.19: "Liquet igitur quod ex quo homo peccavit oportuit esse et fidem que crederetur et legem que servaretur. Sed cum homo prevaricatus fuit peccando tam legem naturalem quam positivam, ipsaque lex prius illi positiva, scilicet de non edendo pomo, iam non fuit illi lex, quia non erat in eius potestate, frustra daretur ei lex aliqua alia positiva, donec prius iterum probaretur in observatione legis naturalis."

Thus, God left humanity to the natural law for some time, until the gift of the positive law might "be added for the fullness of obedience."[10] That positive law was given, initially, to Noah and Abraham. However, due to sin, ignorance, and the growing weakness of memory, by the time of Moses it was necessary for God to convert the positive law into a written law.[11]

Grosseteste revisits his narrative with a four-person headship typology at *DCL* I.8.[12] He considers "the human race, as it were, in four persons": (1) natural Adam, (2) fallen Adam, (3) Satan, and (4) Christ. All of humanity shares in the first two, insofar as they are (1) naturally begotten from Adam and (2) originally vitiated in him. The final two, however, distinguish two "races" from humanity.[13] In the third are "all the guilty and those finally great sinners," for whom Satan is and will be the head. In union with him they will all be cast into hell.[14] Conversely, Christ and his body, the church, form another race of humanity. All these together will be granted final glory.

These four persons bear four distinct relations to the various kinds of law. Thus, the headship typology allows Grosseteste to specify the nature and possibility of the cessation of (some) law in the coming of Christ. To the first person (natural Adam) was given the natural law and the positive law ("Do not eat"), but not the written law. To the second person (fallen Adam), the natural

10. *DCL* I.7.1: "Ad plenitudinem obediencie adderetur lex positiva."

11. *DCL* I.7.

12. Grosseteste's four persons appear later in the fourteenth century in John Wyclif's *De veritate Sacrae Scripturae*, ed. R. Buddensieg, 3 vols. (London: Trübner for the Wyclif Society, 1905–7), III, 28. Wyclif lauds the *dominus Lincolniensis* on the question of the cessation of the law, and follows Grosseteste in treating standard Christological *quaestiones* in this context, albeit admittedly in a way distinctive to Wyclif: "Nam ex dictis de veritate scripture occasionaliter tractatur de cessacione legalium, quam materiam post autores scripture et specialiter apostolum ad Romanos, Galatas et Hebreos dominus Lincolniensis in quodam libello istius materie tractavit egregie."

13. Augustine's *De civitate Dei* is apparently in Grosseteste's mind here.

14. *DCL* I.8.1: "Tercia vero persona est omnes criminosi et maxime finaliter peccatores cum capite suo diabolo."

law remains and the positive law stands until that obligation is removed, and now the written law is conferred in order to overcome ignorance. The third person (Satan) remains under the natural, positive, and written laws, although they are given in vain as Satan and those united to him as their head do not fulfill the obligations of the law. Finally, those who are united to Christ as their head receive Christ's liberation and redemption, whereby they are freed from the obligation to the positive law as well as the (former) written law. Instead, they are given a new written law. For Grosseteste, it is worth noting that liberation and redemption are effected, specifically, through Christ's passion:

> Redemption and liberation through the Passion of Christ was rightly given to the person whom we call Adam the transgressor, that is fallen Adam, with the human race sinning in him originally. This redemption and liberation were so given that, freed from the pit of sin Adam may pass over into the person whose head is Christ.[15]

The four-person typology demonstrates the prominence the unitive effects of the incarnation have in Grosseteste's theology. As we will see, these unitive effects are central to Grosseteste's reflection on the reason for the incarnation in *DCL* III.

The remainder of *DCL* I supplies scriptural evidence for the cessation of the ritual law—the positive, written law of the Old Testament (I.11). Satisfied with his case for the cessation of the ritual law of the Old Testament, Grosseteste shows that Jesus is the Christ promised by that law in *DCL* II. The text moves through a series of topics in Christology, insofar as those topics are anticipated in the Old Testament. The particular time of the incarnation is treated as an extended reflection on Daniel 9. The passion is considered in connection with Isaiah 52–53. In this way, Part II produces a familiar description of the coming Messiah: the Messiah brings blessing by

---

15. *DCL* I.8.4: "Redemptio vero et liberacio per Christi passionem proprie data est illi persone quam nominavimus Adam prevaricatorem, id est Ade lapso, cum humano genere in eo originaliter peccante, ut per redempcionem liberata a peccati fovea, transeat in personam cuius capud est Christus."

freedom from sin and guilt (II.2.1, 3.1–2); is both divine and human
(II.2.2–6, 3.3); is free from the stain of sin (II.3.4–6); descends from
Abraham, Isaac, Jacob, Judah, Jesse, and David (II.3.7–13); born of
a virgin in Bethlehem (II.3.13–14); and suffers insult, injury, and a
violent death to free people from sin and punishment (II.4–6) in the
time of Herod (II.7). Grosseteste sums up in one paragraph:

> [Christ] should be the greatest and best man, without any sin or lie, de-
> scending from Abraham through Isaac, Jacob, Judah, Jesse, and David, uni-
> fying all the nations in one harmonious manner by a most equitable justice,
> ruling over all and having dominion without end, conceived and born of a
> virgin, perfect from conception in wisdom and virtue, born in Bethlehem
> when the authorities and principate of the Jews were failing, affected by
> insults and despised, suffering and being killed in the way described by Isa-
> iah and the Psalmist, at the time in which the angel Gabriel announced to
> the prophet Daniel, a time which according to history proved to be when
> Tiberius Caesar was reigning. But it is impossible that all these things come
> together in any other man than the Lord Jesus, son of Mary.[16]

This is the context for Grosseteste's famous reflection on the
ratio incarnationis. DCL III takes up a parallel set of Christological
issues, but now Grosseteste supplies rational demonstrations. For
instance, he supplies five arguments to prove the appropriate place
of Christ's ministry was Jerusalem (III.3.1–4). Likewise, *DCL* III.4
gives a litany of arguments for the timing of Christ's advent, all
from reason.

The parallelism between *DCL* II and III, distinguished by the
kinds of demonstration supplied (the former from the text of the

---

16. *DCL* II.9.3: "Illum Deum, saltim concedet quod sit maximus et optimus hominum, sine omni peccato et mendacio, descendens de Abraham per Ysaac et Iacob
et Iudam et Iesse et David, adunans omnes naciones in unam morum concordiam
equissima iusticia, super omnes regnans et dominans sine termino, conceptus et
natus de virgine, perfectus a conceptu sapientia et virtute, natus in Bethlehem de-
ficiente ducatu et principatu Iudeorum contumeliis affectus et despectus, passus et
occisus per modum quem describunt Ysayas et psalmista, et illo tempore quo Gabriel
angelus nunciavit Danieli prophete quod tempus secundum hystorias convincitur
esse, regnante Tiberio Cesare. Sed hec omnia impossibile est convenire in alio homine quam in Domino Ihesu, filio Marie."

Old Testament, the latter from reason), supports Hildebrand's assertion that *DCL* "is not haphazard but deliberate and purposeful."[17] Grosseteste's extended reflection on the reason for the incarnation, therefore, serves the larger argument of *DCL* as a rational demonstration of the appropriateness of Christ's incarnation to fulfill the divine will from eternity. Accordingly, Book III's reflection on the incarnation extends Grosseteste's argument, begun in Book II, that Jesus is the Christ promised in the Old Testament. Moreover, it exhibits the many unions effected by the incarnation, in keeping with the four-person, headship typology of *DCL* I. It is at this juncture that the *ratio incarnationis* arises, as a means for Grosseteste to expand his argument for Christ as the one who brings to cessation the positive law and the former written law.

"That God would have become human, even if humanity had not fallen"

The opening paragraphs of *DCL* III, on "whether God would have become human, even if humanity had not fallen," are notably obscure. Grosseteste presents a series of arguments which are "numerous (he gives nineteen in all), extensive, and often interconnected."[18] At points Grosseteste briefly sketches an argument, proceeds to another, more detailed argument, only to return to the initial argument. The peculiarity of the organization has led Grosseteste's modern interpreters to group and synthesize the various arguments. Several proposals emerge. Where James McEvoy finds five "considerations," Dominic Unger sees ten arguments.[19] James

---

17. Grosseteste, *On the Cessation*, 16–17.

18. James McEvoy, "The Absolute Predestination of Christ in the Theology of Robert Grosseteste," in *Robert Grosseteste: Exegete and Philosopher* (Aldershot, Hampshire: Variorum, 1994), IV, 213.

19. McEvoy, "Absolute Predestination," 213–17; Dominic Unger, "Robert Grosseteste, Bishop of Lincoln (1235–1253) on the Reasons for the Incarnation," *Franciscan Studies* 16, no. 1 (1956): 26–34. Technically, Unger finds nine arguments in *DCL*, and a tenth in the sermon *Exiit Edictum*.

Ginther, like McEvoy, rehearses five arguments, although there are important differences in the details.[20]

As these readers observe, Grosseteste's arguments "that God would have become human, even if humanity had not fallen" are diverse, if not random. *DCL* III.1 gives one the impression that Grosseteste was collating a litany of arguments as they occurred to him, or as he recalled them, with little concern for their interrelationship. This characteristic of the text leads many to conclude that *DCL* III.1 is a loosely related series of arguments: "[Grosseteste] presents [his arguments] in no particular order."[21] Lest this be considered a weakness, James McEvoy insists that "[the arguments] can, however, be synthesized ... indeed they gain thereby in intelligibility and cumulative force."[22] Thus, several readings of *DCL* III.1 have emerged that reorganize and group the various elements into more consistent, developed, and distinct arguments.

James McEvoy's reading has been the most influential. He groups the twenty or so arguments into five thematic "considerations." For example, the first "consideration" runs as follows: since God is the highest good, and the highest good would actualize the best possible created effect, and since the incarnation is the best possible created effect, then God, in virtue of being the highest good, would actualize the incarnation in a world without sin. Let's call this the "highest good" consideration. McEvoy derives this "consideration" by synthesizing the arguments at paragraphs 3 and 4 with paragraphs 8 and 9. Paragraphs 5 through 7, on the other hand, express another "consideration" for McEvoy. Here Grosseteste argues that humanity's capacity for union with God cannot be contingent upon the existence of sin. Let's call this the "independent of sin" consideration. Thus, there are two "considerations" distinguished according to their primary themes—the highest good theme and dependence upon sin theme, respectively.

20. James R. Ginther, *Master of the Sacred Page: A Study of the Theology of Robert Grosseteste, ca. 1229/30–1235* (Burlington, Vt.: Ashgate, 2004), 130–37.

21. McEvoy, "Absolute Predestination," 213.

22. McEvoy, "Absolute Predestination," 213.

Dominic Unger and James Ginther diverge from McEvoy's reading on the organization of paragraphs 3–9. Both Unger and Ginther recognize that across paragraphs 5–7 Grosseteste does not consider an independent thematic consideration. Rather, paragraphs 5–7 develop an objection that contributes to the argument begun in paragraphs 3–4. However, both Unger and Ginther find other thematic groupings in paragraphs 8 and 9. For Unger, paragraphs 3–8 form a single argument, but paragraph 9 presents a second argument, grounded in divine generosity rather than divine goodness. Ginther, on the other hand, distinguishes paragraphs 3–7 from paragraphs 8 and 9; the former focuses upon the divine goodness, the latter upon the glory granted creation by the incarnation.

Ginther, McEvoy, and Unger present a variety of approaches to *DCL* III.1. No doubt, there are merits to each. The reading that follows is more analytic than those currently offered. One merit of this analytic reading is that it reveals greater unity in Grosseteste's text, although not in terms of themes. Rather, it reveals strategic unity; it shows that Grosseteste utilizes two strategies for arguing to his conclusion that God would be incarnate even if humanity had not sinned. Moreover, it is this strategic unity that provides us with a clear expression of Grosseteste's reception and application of the Anselmian theses to the reason for the incarnation.

The Divine Attributes Strategy

Grosseteste thinks we can supply reasons for the incarnation prior to the redemption from sin. That is, those reasons would still obtain in possible worlds without the fall.[23] The analysis that follows

23. "Prior" here means priority of the divine volition for incarnation over the divine volition for redemption, such that the former volition would be elicited whether or not the latter volition were. I am not the first person to introduce possible worlds semantics into analysis of the *ratio incarnationis*; see R. Trent Pomplun, "The Immaculate World," and Marshner, "Critique of Marian Counterfactual Formulae," for similar approaches.

will take up chapter one's distinction between several sets of possible worlds. To wit, I will distinguish between four sets of possible
worlds: *W, F, I,* and *X.* The set of *W*-worlds are all possible worlds
(including our own) with both a fall and an incarnation. The set of
F-worlds are all possible worlds with a fall but no incarnation. The
set of *I*-worlds are all possible worlds with an incarnation but no
fall. The set of *X*-worlds are all possible worlds with neither a fall
nor an incarnation. I will also be utilizing the account of theological compossibility developed in the first chapter. So, we are concerned with the set of possible worlds that are "compossible with
Grosseteste's God," that could be created by a God who possesses
the character Grosseteste assumes or ascribes to Him.

Having stated the hypothetical question and the conclusion
for which he will be arguing in paragraphs 1 and 2, Grosseteste
proceeds with a litany of arguments in *DCL* III.1.3. The first argument begins with several assertions likely derived from Anselm's
Proslogion: "God is supreme power, wisdom, and goodness, and He
is better than can be thought."[24] Grosseteste infers that God's su-
premacy requires that any created potency for good must be actualized, lest God be less-than-supremely good and generous: "For
if the universe were capable of some quantity of goodness which
He did not pour into it, He would not be supremely generous and
therefore not supremely good."[25]

Grosseteste draws a further, comparative implication; goodness
exerts itself not only for benefit, but also for the *greater* benefit.
Hence, he reiterates, "supreme goodness pours in as great a good
as it is able."[26] We can restate the principle as follows: if *x* is some
good, and our *W*-world is capable of *x*, then *x* will be actualized.
While Grosseteste is consistent in applying this principle, he astute-

---

24. *DCL* III.1.3; p. 120, 2–3: "Deus est summa potentia et sapientia et bonitas et
magis bonus quam etiam possit excogitari."
25. *DCL* III.1.3; p. 120, 5–7: "Si enim ipsa esset capabilis aliquante bonitatis
quam ipse illi non influeret, non esset summe largus et ita nec summe bonus."
26. *DCL* III.1.4; p. 120, 11–12: "Summa igitur bonitas tantum bonum influit
universitati quanti boni ipsa est capax."

ly observes a relevant distinction between two classes of capacity: capacity *simpliciter* and conditional capacity. If our *W*-world's capacity for incarnation has the fall as a necessary condition (a conditional capacity for incarnation), then possible worlds in which there is no fall will lack an incarnation. *I*-worlds will then be incompossible with Grosseste's God. If, on the other hand, our *W*-world has a capacity *simpliciter* for the incarnation, then an incarnation might still occur in worlds without a fall. *I*-worlds will then be compossible with Grosseteste's God. In fact, given Grosseteste's application of the aforementioned supreme goodness premise, it seems necessary that worlds without a fall will be *I*-worlds.

In the four paragraphs that follow (paragraphs 5–8), Robert gives a series of arguments in favor of our *W*-world's capacity for incarnation *simpliciter*. He begins by clarifying that the capacity at stake is a capacity of human nature for personal (i.e., hypostatic) union with the divine nature.[27] Next, he distinguishes human nature prior to the fall from human nature subsequent to the fall in terms of corruption: prior to the fall was an incorrupt human nature, subsequent to the fall a corrupt human nature. Grosseteste then takes from Lombard an account of the hypostatic union as union "to the flesh through the medium of the intellect."[28] Having clarified the relevant capacity, he then specifies what it would mean for that capacity to be conditional upon the fall: either (a) the soul is more assumable given the corruption of sin, or (b) the intellect is more united to the flesh given the corruption of sin. Grosseteste argues that (b) is impossible insofar as the union of intellect with flesh is greater preceding the corruption of sin, since the intellect shares its eternity (i.e., possibility for not dying) with the flesh.[29]

Paragraphs 5 and 6 refute option (a). Beginning from the meta-

---

27. *DCL* III.1.5; p. 120, 21–22: "Quomodo enim non ita unibilis fuit humana natura divine nature in unitatem persone ante corrupcionem humane nature, ut post?"

28. *DCL* III.1.5; p. 120, 27–28: "Unitum est carni per medium intellectum Verbum Dei." Peter Lombard, *Sentences,* 3.2.

29. *DCL* III.1.5; p. 121, 3–4: "Sed tanto fortiorem habuit unicionem quanto possibilitas non moriendi distat a necessitate moriendi."

physical premise that "everything understood is either essence or the defection or negation of essence," Grosseteste further clarifies the corruption of sin: it is a defection, or privation, of essence.[30] Moreover, given the same premise, it must be that the capacity for personal union with the divine nature is an essence (rather than a defection of essence). Thus, by substitution:

the corruption of sin → our W-world has a capacity for incarnation[31]

a defect of essence → our W-world has a capacity for incarnation

a defect of essence → an essence (capacity for incarnation)

This conclusion, Grosseteste contends, is absurd, and so it must be that our W-world's capacity for incarnation is a capacity *simpliciter*. Since our W-world's capacity for incarnation *simpliciter* is (by definition) independent of the fall, and the capacity for incarnation *simpliciter* is a good, then the incarnation must be actualized in all possible worlds, lest God be less than supremely good per *DCL* III.1.3. Thus, the set of worlds compossible with Grosseteste's God that are without a fall will include an incarnation, and so X-worlds (without a fall or an incarnation) are impossible.

Robert produces a second, related argument in support of our W-world's capacity for incarnation *simpliciter*, this time in the form of a *reductio*. Suppose that our W-world's capacity for the incarnation has the fall as a necessary condition. It follows that if humanity had not fallen, God would not have become incarnate.[32] Possible X-worlds (without a fall or an incarnation) will obtain. But our W-world is a more glorious, and therefore better, world than any X-world because our W-world contains a creature worthy of adoration while all X-worlds possess no such creature. Since (1) "the glory

30. *DCL* III.1.6; p. 121, 7–8: "Preterea, utraque corrupcio tam culpe quam pene non est essentia, sed essentie defectio."

31. That is, the capacity for incarnation is conditional upon the fall.

32. *DCL* III.1.8; p. 121, 19–20: "Ad hec ponamus quod homo lapsus non esset neque Deus homo esset."

of being worshipped incomparably exceeds every created glory," and (2) "the whole of creation was glorified in the flesh assumed by the Word; it was . . . on fire with the divinity of the Word that assumed it," our *W*-world is inestimably better than any *X*-world: *universitatem nunc supra estimacionem esse meliorem quam fuisset nisi homo lapsus esset.*[33] However, given the premise at *DCL* III.1.4 that "supreme goodness pours in as great a good as it is able," if we continue to hold that *X*-worlds are possible, we reach the absurd conclusion that *X*-worlds are possible worlds that are impossibly actual because they are inestimably worse than our *W*-world, which is to say a possible world is impossible.[34] *Reductio ad absurdum.*

In paragraph 9, Grosseteste gives a parallel argument to that formulated in paragraphs 3 and 4 and defended in paragraphs 5–8. God is supremely generous, and therefore supremely lacking in envy.[35] Thus, God "creates every kind of creature that can exist."[36] In support of this latter principle, we are given the aforementioned deductive argument from the divine generosity as well as an a posteriori argument from the evidence of creation: we see that God has actualized even the most insignificant of possible things, such as insects or reptiles.[37] In light of this empirical observation,

33. *DCL* III.1.8; p. 121, 33–p. 122, 1, 8–10: "gloriositas adorabilitatis incomparabiliter excedit omnem aliam gloriositatem creature ... sic est universitas creature magis glorificata in carne assumpta a Verbo, ut ita dicam, ignita divinitate Verbi assumentis."

34. This is a slight expansion of Grosseteste's argument, which simply concludes that one must either accept (1) that God would have become human even if humanity had not fallen, or (2) this world is inestimably better as a result of the fall. However, the latter option must be an impossibility for the reasons adumbrated above.

35. Grosseteste's argument recalls Plato's *Timaeus*, 29E: "Now why did he who framed this whole universe of becoming frame it? Let us state the reason why: He was good, and one who is good can never become jealous of anything. And so, being free of jealousy, he wanted everything to become as much like himself as was possible." Plato, "Timaeus," in *Plato: Complete Works*, ed. John M. Cooper, trans. Donald J. Zeyl (Indianapolis, Ind.: Hackett Publishing Company, 1997), 12–24, 91.

36. *DCL* III.1.9; p. 122, 19: "[Deus] creat omnes species creaturarum quas possibile est esse."

37. *DCL* III.1.9; p. 122, 21–22: "Nec etiam naturam vermiculi aut alicuiusmodi muscarum vel reptilium relinquit non creatam."

Grosseteste then poses the question: "If (God) does not omit the nature of the insect lest creation be imperfect and less beautiful, would He omit Christ, the greatest beauty of the universe?"[38] The answer is, of course, no.

These arguments all deploy a common strategy; they move from the attribution of some divine perfection to the conclusion that a particular effect would be necessary in possible worlds without the fall. The basic strategy can be expressed in four propositions:

1 Incarnation is possible.

2 Incarnation does not have sin as a necessary condition (a capacity *simpliciter*).

3 There is some divine attribute *y* that supplies a reason for the incarnation.

4 Even in possible worlds without sin, *y* supplies a reason for the incarnation.[39]

Grosseteste's arguments across *DCL* III.1, 3–9 utilize this basic strategy. Different values are substituted for *y*—goodness, glory, and generosity—but all variants are deductive arguments for the same conclusion: even in a possible world without sin, God has a reason for the incarnation, and so there is incarnation. Or, in terms of possible worlds, *X*-worlds are incompossible with Grosseteste's God. This, in Grosseteste's idiom, is sufficient to guarantee the conclusion that "if Adam had not sinned, God would become incarnate."[40] Let us call this argumentative strategy the divine attributes strategy.

---

38. *DCL* III.1.9; p. 122, 25–27: "Non omittit naturam vermiculi ne sit universitas imperfecta et minus decora, et omitteret Christum, universitatis decus maximum?"

39. It should be noted that there is an unstated assumption along the following lines: "If God has a reason for actualizing *x*, then *x*." Grosseteste seems to assume this to be the case, but this assumption is queried by theologians at Paris in the thirteenth century.

40. I have intentionally left this inference open in my analysis of the argument, as Grosseteste's presumption will be the very point at which St. Thomas and others will object.

The Created Effects Strategy

Paragraphs 10–30 present a greater challenge to my analysis of Grosseteste's argumentative strategies in *DCL* III.1. These sections of *DCL* are the primary locus of disagreement in the secondary literature on Grosseteste's organization of his various themes.[41]

James McEvoy's treatment, the most influential, passes over paragraph 10 and moves directly into paragraphs 11–15. Unger connects paragraph 10 with paragraphs 18 and 19 on the unity of the church in Christ's headship. McEvoy observes that paragraphs 11–15 are linked to paragraphs 16–17 and 22–24 as arguments for justification and redemption as "independent needs of man."[42] James Ginther, who gives the most unified treatment of *DCL* III.1, links 10–15 with 16–19 (and presumably 20–21, although this is not explicit), all of which are unified under the themes of justification and sanctification (or adoption). And yet, while all are in agreement that paragraphs 22–24 form a unit, as do 25–29, these are treated as two distinct arguments, both of which are distinct from the preceding arguments of paragraphs 10–21. Only James Ginther suggests an overarching unity amongst Grosseteste's treatise, although the nature of that unity is not apparent.[43]

In sum, paragraphs 10–30 have largely been read as a reflection of the unsystematic character of Grosseteste's mind. And yet, several textual clues suggest such a strategic unity across these paragraphs.

First, in paragraph 10 Grosseteste states: "If there were no [incarnation] ... the Church would be headless and so would humanity." This twofold division of Christ's headship (of the church and of humanity) is underscored by the iteration of Christ's dual headship in paragraphs 16, 17, 22, and 25. If we follow this suggestion,

---

41. Ginther, *Master of the Sacred Page*, 132–41; McEvoy, "Absolute Predestination," 214–17; Unger, "Grosseteste on the Reasons for the Incarnation," 25–32.

42. McEvoy, "Absolute Predestination," 214.

43. Ginther, *Master of the Sacred Page*, esp. 135–36.

we discover that the ensuing arguments can be divided into two groups: those having to do with Christ's headship of the church, which I will call "goods of supernatural headship," and those having to do with Christ's headship of humanity (and by extension all of creation), which I will call "goods of natural headship." And, it turns out, we have two subdivisions in the text: paragraphs 11–24 on the goods of supernatural headship achieved by the incarnation, and paragraphs 25–29 on the goods of natural headship achieved by the incarnation.

Second, there are movements internal to the subdivisions into goods of supernatural and natural headship. Among the supernatural goods, Grosseteste moves with the order of salvation from justification in paragraphs 11–15, to adoption in paragraphs 16–17, to union with the church in paragraphs 18–21, and finally to beatitude in paragraphs 22–24. Among the natural goods, he moves through elevating degrees of union, from an argument for humanity as the microcosmic principle of the unity of creation in paragraphs 25–27, to the God-man as the union between creature and Creator in paragraph 28.

Third, in paragraphs 11–15, Grosseteste analyzes the sentence "The suffering God-man justifies fallen humanity." These paragraphs are the longest argument Grosseteste gives for a particular created effect as a reason for the incarnation. But the logic of that argument is transferable to all the goods specified in ensuing arguments, both for goods of supernatural and natural headship.

In keeping with these textual clues, the subsequent analysis will follow the division suggested at paragraph 10: (1) paragraphs 11–24 on the goods of supernatural headship, and (2) paragraphs 25–29 on the goods of natural headship.[44]

---

44. Paragraph 30 is a bit oddly located, insofar as it returns to the order of grace and the union effected in the sacrament of the Eucharist. However, this can be attributed to the fact that the paragraph is chiefly comprised of an extended citation from Radbertus, which reiterates several key arguments from paragraphs 16–21. The passage is unique in form as an extended citation, and therefore is something of an addendum.

Paragraphs 11–24: Goods of Supernatural Headship

Grosseteste gives a semantic analysis, in paragraphs 11–15, of the proposition:

3.1 The suffering God-man justifies fallen humanity.[45]

Grosseteste supplies two axioms: "The cause is precisely proportionate to the effect,"[46] and "There is always a single cause."[47] The implication for 3.1 is twofold. First, there exists some perfect correspondence between each term in the subject and object of 3.1. Second, the cause of a particular good (i.e., justification) in our world will be the cause of that good in other possible worlds. Given these rules, Grosseteste poses the following question: if we are seeking to reformulate 3.1 for those possible worlds in which the fall does not obtain, what is precisely proportionate to "fallen"? He considers two options: either (A) "suffering" is precisely proportionate to "fallen," or else (B) "suffering man" is precisely proportionate to "fallen." If option A is correct, then 3.1 must be revised for worlds without the fall as follows:

3.2 The God-man justifies humanity.

Alternatively, on option B, 3.1 is revised to:

3.3 God justifies humanity.

Now that he has clarified the possible analyses of 3.1 without "fallen" to 3.2 (option A) or 3.3 (option B), Grosseteste proceeds to supply an argument in support of 3.2 and against 3.3 in paragraphs 13–15. In support of 3.2 over against 3.3, Grosseteste begins with appeals to authority. First, he cites 1 Corinthians 1:30:

---

45. *DCL* III.1.11; p. 123, 13–14: "Deus-homo passus per se jusficat hominem lapsum."

46. *DCL* III.1.11; p. 123, 14: "Est hec precise conproportionata causa huic effectui."

47. *DCL* III.1.12.

"[Jesus Christ] became [*factus est*] for us wisdom from God, justice to you and holiness and redemption." As Grosseteste notes, Christ confers justice "by his becoming," which is to say by his humanity. Second, Romans 5:19 asserts, "by one (man's) obedience, the many will be made righteous." As obedience can only be said of Christ's human will, it must be that Christ's humanity is involved in the justification of humanity.

Having made his case that 3.2 is warranted by Scripture, Grosseteste expands the object of the assertion:

3.4 The God-man justifies rational creatures.

Once again, he turns first to authority, in this case to Dionysius the Areopagite's *Celestial Hierarchies* 7. Dionysius's text itself is rather convoluted:

(The superior intelligences) are contemplative also because they have been allowed to enter into communion with Jesus not by means of the holy images, reflecting the likeness of God's working in forms, but by truly coming close to him in a primary participation in the knowledge of the divine lights working out of him. To be like God is their special gift and, to the extent that it is allowed them, they share, with a primordial power, in his divine activities and his loving virtue.[48]

Grosseteste, following the *versio Eriugena*, renders the final passage "because the likeness of God has been given to them substantially, these kind communicate, as much as is possible in their preoperative power, in the same deiformity and human virtues."[49] While the *Hierarchy* is obscure, Grosseteste's conclusion could not be clearer. Even the superior intelligences, the highest rational creatures— *cherubim* and *seraphim*—who surround the throne of God in endless praise and contemplation, are justified by the God-man. Their

48. *The Celestial Hierarchy* 7, 208C, 32–40; text taken from Pseudo-Dionysius, *Pseudo-Dionysius: The Complete Works*, trans. Colm Luibheid and Paul Rorem, The Classics of Western Spirituality (New York: Paulist Press, 1987).

49. *DCL* III.1.13; p. 124, 21–23: "Et quia Deosimile ipsis substancialiter donatum est, communicant huiusmodi ut possibile in preoperatrice virtute deificis ipsius et humanis virtutibus."

God-likeness is given in virtue of their sharing in the "deiformity *and human virtues*" of Christ, the God-man. Thus, on authority, we conclude 3.4, and, a fortiori, affirm 3.2 and deny 3.3.

Immediately, however, there is a problem with assertion 3.4: "The God-man justifies rational creatures." While Grosseteste takes it that he has established that Christ's humanity is in some manner the cause of justification in every justified rational creature, two questions remain: How does Christ's humanity cause justification? And how does it relate to God's causality in justification? If "the formation in justice always happens in one way, because the cause of one thing is always one,"[50] it remains to be shown how the two (divinity and humanity) are involved in producing the single effect. This, Grosseteste holds, is given in the formula "justice always and simply descends from God through Christ, the God-man, into every rational creature who is made just."[51] Thus, in two ways over the course of paragraphs 13 and 14 Grosseteste refines 3.2 (Option A): (1) the God-man justifies not only humanity, but all rational creatures, and (2) the God-man is involved in this justification, "always and simply," as the one *through* whom justice descends to rational creatures, while God is the one *from* whom justice descends. So, we can finally render Grosseteste's overarching assertion as follows:

3.5 Always and simply, God justifies rational creatures *through* the God-man.

Grosseteste returns to his original semantic analysis of 3.1: "The suffering God-man justifies fallen humanity." He has offered support of his position that "suffering" corresponds to "fallen" such that, in those possible worlds in which there is no fall, proposition 3.2 "The God-man justifies humanity" remains true. If so, for these worlds that resemble our own insofar as God wills the justification

---

50. *DCL* III.1.14; p. 124, 26–27: "Quapropter si iusticie informacio uno modo semper fit, quia unius semper una est causa."

51.*DCL* III.1.14; p. 124, 27–28: "In omnem creaturam rationalem iustam factam simpliciter et semper descendit iusticia a Deo per Christum, hominem-Deum."

of humanity, there must be a God-man. Therefore, they will be *I*-worlds—with incarnation and without fall. But the entire argument will dissolve if Grosseteste cannot supply an account of his position that "suffering" corresponds to "fallen" (which I have called Option A) and, conversely, that "suffering man" cannot correspond to "fallen" (or Option B.)

Paragraph 15 works out this final issue of the semantic analysis of 3.1. Grosseteste's argument is extremely terse, but the basic strategy is a kind of *reductio*. Assuming Option B and 3.3 are true, without any mediation (*absque mediacione*) through the God-man, then we must tell a story about the incarnation in the de facto order that does not violate 3.3: "God justifies humanity." If not for justification, why did God become incarnate? Grosseteste considers one alternative: to satisfy by passion. "The Passion of Jesus Christ is satisfaction for our tresspasses."[52] For the sake of simplicity:

3.11 Jesus Christ satisfies by Passion (i.e., suffering).[53]

By "Jesus Christ," Grosseteste designates the humanity assumed by the Son in the incarnation, distinct from the divinity that is the sole cause of justification (there is no *through*-ness involved). This analysis provides an account of what it means for "suffering man" to correspond to "fallen" in 3.1.

Grosseteste's *reductio* runs as follows. If the passion of Jesus Christ is the proper and proportionate cause of satisfaction, and God the proper and proportionate cause of justification, then it seems to follow that "the humanity of Jesus Christ would only be materially necessary for the Passion; and so it would exist only so that God the Son could suffer in it and by his Passion satisfy for the transgression of humanity. But this does not seem fitting."[54]

---

52. *DCL* III.1.15; p. 124, 9: "Item, passio Ihesu Christi est satisfactio pro nostro delicto."

53. Presumably, underlying the assertion is Grosseteste's acceptance of Anselm's argument that only the God-man can offer satisfaction in *CDH*. In this case, the Son would take on humanity only in order to die to give satisfaction for our offenses.

54. *DCL* III.1.15; p. 125, 12–17: "Si igitur ponamus Deum precisam causam

Once again, Grosseteste is terse, but the argument is not difficult to tease out. If the only purpose we can assign to the Son's assumption of a human nature is to suffer and die, then, it seems, God creates some creature (Christ's human nature) for the sole purpose of its suffering. This result, "God creates some creature only so that it can suffer," Grosseteste deems *inconvenientia*.

Paragraphs 11–15 develop a semantic analysis that sketches a form of argument Grosseteste will reuse in subsequent paragraphs. Some good x (e.g., the infusion of justice) has for its cause the God-man as the means of mediation: "x is *from* God *through* the God-man." That is, the incarnation is a necessary condition of x. Moreover, since x is not conditional upon the fall (lest *inconvenientia* ensue), then the assertion holds in possible worlds without fall, and so I-worlds are compossible with Grosseteste's God, and X-worlds (without a fall or an incarnation) are not.

What follows in paragraphs 16–29 are a series of arguments that work from the premises and strategies outlined in both paragraphs 3–9 and 11–15. The arguments all gather around a concern over various "unitive" aims of the incarnation intimated by paragraph ten's language of "headship" and hearkening back to the four-person headship typology of Book I. Moreover, they follow the arc of topics summarized in paragraph 10: they move from the order of grace (between Christ and the church, in the sacrament of marriage, and in beatitude) to the order of nature (among all creatures and between Creator and creation). The way in which the two preceding strategies (in paragraphs 3–9 and 11–15) are together applied to the subsequent "unitive aims" arguments is rather complicated. Thus, I will withhold analysis of these two strategies and their interrelation in the later arguments until I have given an analytic description of those arguments.

---

et comproporcionatam absque mediacione aliqua iustificationi, et passionem satisfactioni, humanitas Ihesu Christi solumodo erit materialis necessitas ad passionem, ideo videlicet solum existens ut Deus Filius in ea posset pati, et passione sua pro delicto humani generis satisfacere. Quod non videtur conveniens."

Grosseteste argues, in paragraph 16, that the incarnation obtains in possible worlds without a fall because, even without sin,
"humanity would have been adopted children of God through
grace."[55] Unity of will, the greatest possible union without incarnation, is insufficient for adoption. "But with our conformity of
will there is the unity of nature in which we communicate with
Christ."[56] This unity of nature requires the Son taking on a human
nature; that is, it is effected by the incarnation. "Unless the Son
of God were a participant in our nature, we would not be partici-
pants in his divinity by adoption, nor would we be his brothers, nor
the adopted sons of God the Father."[57] Grosseteste returns to this
point later when, considering the Eucharist, he cites Radbertus:[58]

And Christ is in us today not only by an agreement of wills, but he is also
in us by nature, just as we are rightly said to remain in him. For if the Word
was made flesh, and we truly receive the Word as flesh in the food of the
Lord, how is Christ not rightly thought to remain in us naturally, who assumed the nature of our flesh and made it inseparable from himself, God-
made-man, and who admixed the nature of his own flesh to the nature of
eternity under this sacrament of the flesh being communicated by us?[59]

---

55. *DCL* III.1.16; p. 125, 18–19: "Homines, ut videtur, fuissent filii Dei adoptivi
et per gratiam."

56. *DCL* III.1.16; p. 125, 22–25: "Sed hanc unitatem qua sumus unum vel unus
in Christo non facit solum conformitas voluntatis nostre cum voluntate Christi, sed
cum hoc etiam unitas nature in qua communicamus cum Christo."

57. *DCL* III.1.17; p. 126, 5–7: "Igitur nisi Filius Dei esset particeps nature nostre, nos non essemus per adopcionem participes divinitatis sue, neque fratres eius,
neque filii adopcionis Dei Patris."

58. Grosseteste mistakenly attributes the position to Rabanus. Pascasius Radbertus, *De corpore et sanguine Domini: cum appendice Epistola ad Fredugardum*, ed. Bedae Paulus, Corpus christianorum, continuatio mediaevalis 16 (Turnholt: Brepols,
1969), *De corpore* 9.4.

59. *DCL* III.1.30; p. 132, 24–133, 3: "Necnon et Christus hodie in nobis non
solum per concordiam voluntatis sed etiam per naturam in nobis, sicut et nos in illo
recte manere dicitur. Nam si Verbum caro factum est, et nos vere Verbum carnem in
cibo dominico sumimus, quomodo Christus in nobis manere naturaliter iure non es-
timatur, qui et naturam carnis nostre inseparabilem sibi homo natus Deus assumpsit,
et naturam carnis sue ad naturam eternitatis sub sacramento hoc nobis communi-
cande carnis admiscuit?"

It must be, then, that even in those possible worlds without a fall, an incarnation obtains.

Once again, a *reductio* is offered in support of the conclusion. If there were no incarnation in possible worlds without a fall, then the unity between God and humanity would simply be the conformity of wills, which only brings friendship or servitude.[60] Since this unity is inferior to the unity of adoption, the state of humanity in a sinless world would be worse than in a world with sin. Thus, some possible world with sin is better than a sinless possible world, which is absurd. Moreover, we would have to attribute sin as the cause of adoption, which is to derive an essence from a privation, to use the earlier logic from paragraph 6.

Moreover, if there were no incarnation in possible worlds without the fall, then the church, as the communion of adopted children, would lack its unity with Christ. "Unless humanity had sinned, the church would lack the greatest good, for it would not be one with Christ the Son of God."[61] In this case, these worlds would be worse than possible worlds with sin. So, the argument of paragraphs 16–17 is applied in this parallel instance: some possible world with sin is better than a sinless possible world, which is absurd.

God's unitive aims for Christ and the church are further buttressed by an appeal to Paul's interpretation of Genesis 2:24 in Ephesians 5:32:

Adam prophesied, before his fall, the marriage of Christ and the church, saying, "Therefore a man shall leave his father and mother and will cleave to his wife, and there will be two in one flesh." About this the Apostle said, "This great mystery is of Christ and the church."[62]

60. *DCL* III.1.30; p. 126, 10–12: "Sola namque conformitas voluntatum non facit aliquam filiacionem, sed inter pares facit amicitiam et societatem; inter impares vero servitutem obedientem."

61. *DCL* III.1.18; p. 126, 24–26: "Maximo itaque bono careret ecclesia nisi peccasset homo, non enim esset unus Christus cum Dei Filio."

62. *DCL* III.1.20; p. 127, 3–6: "Item, Adam ante lapsum suum prophetavit matrimonium Christi et ecclesie, dicens: *Quamobrem relinquet homo patrem et matrem et adherebit uxori sue; et erunt duo in carne una.* De quo dicit apostolus: *Sacramentum est hoc magnum in Christo et ecclesia.*"

What appears to be a straightforward application of scriptural warrant turns out to express a sacramental argument that inverts a temporal objection Grosseteste raised in paragraph 14. In paragraph 20, he begins with an argument for Adam's prophetic knowledge of the union of Christ and the church, which antedated the fall. According to Genesis 2, Adam held the belief that Christ would be married to the church, and therefore believed that Christ would *be*. Thus, "while knowing and believing nothing about the sin of the human race, which was to come, he believed in the marriage of Christ and the church."[63]

This leads into a second argument from the sacrament of marriage. Grosseteste distinguishes between three "indissoluble unions" (*indivisibilis unionis*): (1) the hypostatic union of humanity and divinity in Christ, (2) the sacramental union of Christ and the church, which is a marital union, and (3) the marital union between a husband and wife.[64] Grosseteste reasons that the first is a condition of the latter two. Unless there is a hypostatic union between humanity and divinity in Christ—unless there is incarnation—neither the union of Christ and the church nor of marriage will exist. Since the union between a husband and wife would have existed indissolubly even if there were no fall (lest the sacrament of marriage would have less dignity in a sinless world than it would have in a fallen world), it must be that even in possible worlds without a fall the incarnation would occur both (1) for the union of Christ and the church, which is the church's greatest good, as well as (2) for the indissolubility of marriage.

A minor transition arises in paragraphs 22–24. Formally, the passage shares with the three arguments immediately preceding (in paragraphs 16–17, 18–19, and 20–21) an opening by appeal to authority, in this case to Pseudo-Augustine. Pseudo-Augustine, in *On*

---

63. *DCL* III.1.20; p. 127, 13–15: "Nichil igitur de peccato humani generis quod esset futurum sciens vel credens, credidit matromonium Christi et ecclesie."

64. The three "indissoluble unions" of paragraph 21 indicate further conceptual scaffolding underlying *DCL* III, 1.15–21.

the Spirit and the Soul, argues that the interior and exterior senses of humanity each have their own distinct objects, which bring about their perfection in beatitude. The incarnation perfects both senses in a single object: the God-man.

Therefore God became man in order that the whole human might be beatified in him and the whole conversion of humanity might be to him, and the whole delight might be in him, because he was seen by the sense of the flesh through flesh, and by the sense of the mind through the contemplation of God.[65]

The existence of the God-man, then, is a necessary condition of the final perfection of humanity in the beatific vision.

Unity remains central to the argument. Grosseteste considers the possibility that a human could be beatified by the mind's contemplation of God (interior sense) while sensing something else with the flesh.[66] Perfect beatitude cannot be had in this way, he argues, insofar as perfect beatitude requires "the conversion of the whole attention of the soul to the highest good."[67] Since perfected humans in a world without an incarnation would direct the attention of their rational soul to God, the highest good, and their sensitive soul to another, lesser good, it will be a less perfect world than one in which final beatitude has a single object.

Grosseteste extends his argument by appeal to a scriptural vision of the eschaton, at which time:

The flesh of the Lord Jesus Christ will be manifested after the resurrection more splendid and more beautiful than the sun and every corporeal creature, because in comparison with the splendor of the Christ's flesh, the sun will seem not to shine. But when our eyes will be glorified, it will be possible see the splendor and beauty of Christ's flesh.[68]

---

65. *DCL* III.1.22; p. 128, 10–13: "Propterea enim Deus homo factus est ut totum hominem in se beatificaret et tota conversio hominis esset ad ipsum, et tota dileccio esset in ipso, cum a sensu carnis videretur per carnem, et a sensu mentis per divinitatis contemplacionem."

66. *DCL* III.1.23.

67. *DCL* III.1.23; p. 128, 30–129, 1: "Nec posset esse sic beatitudo perfecta que exigit tocius intencionis anime in summum bonum conversionem."

68. *DCL* III.1.24; p. 129, 4–7: "Ad hec caro Domini Ihesu Christi manifestabitur

Two consequences follow for possible worlds without an incarnation. First, for the human creature, beatitude would be a state of unceasing misery. The creature *must* obtain every natural good in its final state, otherwise the creature's final state will retain an unceasing desire for something lacking and will not be at rest. In this case, the exterior sense of the human being must perceive God, otherwise it will desire something greater than that which it obtains. Perception of God by exterior sense is only possible if God is united to a creature possessing a sensible body, a condition satisfied by the God-man.

Moreover, creation itself obtains an aesthetic perfection by the presence of the God-man. Drawing upon his earlier recitation of John Damascene in *DCL* III.1.8, Grosseteste argues that all of creation is perfected in beauty by the presence of the God-man, just as wood enflamed by its union with fire becomes more beautiful in the form of charcoal than it was otherwise. And, if a possible world is more beautiful, just as if it has more goodness, then it will be actualized by a perfectly good and beautiful God (per paragraphs 3–9).

Paragraphs 25–29: Goods of Natural Headship

The transition to the aesthetic good of creation precedes a final transition in Grosseteste's argument. Whereas the other unitive aims of the incarnation are goods of supernatural headship—justification, adoption, sacramental union, and beatitude—the unitive aims treated in paragraphs 25–29 are goods of natural headship.

The foundational premise is given at paragraph 26. Grosseteste argues that "since perfection and beauty consist in unity, in greater unity there is greater perfection and beauty."[69] And since, according to Grosseteste, God would actualize the greatest possible

---

post resurrectionem splendidior et pulcrior sole et omni corporali creatura, quia camparacione splendoris carnis Christi, nec sol splendere videbitur. Possibilis est autem oculus noster carnalis cum glorificabitur ad visionem splendoris et pulcritudinis carnis Christi."

69. *DCL* III.1.26; p. 130, 7–8: "Cum perfeccio et pulchritudo in unitate consistat, et in maiori unitate perfeccio et pulchritudo maior."

perfection, it must be that the greatest possible unity obtains in this world and any other possible worlds that God would choose to actualize (all worlds compossible with Grosseteste's God).

The question is, what is the greatest possible unity that God could actualize in creation? Grosseteste distinguishes three kinds of unity: numerical, natural (having the same nature), and generic (occupying the same genus). Some unities are "stronger" than others, and generic unity is the weakest. Although all created things, which together comprise the universe, occupy the single genus of creatures, they have "the least true unity."[70] So while generic unity would (and does) satisfy the unity-requirement that is a condition of a "universe," if it is not the greatest possible unity the universe *could* possess, then the universe would be deprived by its Creator of some possible good, which is unbefitting a perfect Creator.

Moreover, the unity of the created universe itself is only part of the unity that Grosseteste is seeking. There is another unity: that of Creator with creation. And in this case, generic unity does not obtain, since God does not occupy a common genus with creation.[71] Of course, neither does numerical unity.

If, however, there possibly exists some single principle in which both the aforementioned "strongest possible unity of creation" conditions are met, and the union of Creator with creation is effected, then it must be that a perfect God would actualize that possible principle of unity. The God-man, Grosseteste argues, is such a principle of unity. As to the first issue (the unity of the universe itself), Grosseteste advances a microcosmic argument for a natural unity between humans and every other creature. Unlike the angels, humans possess a natural unity with all corporeal natures in virtue of

---

70. *DCL* III.1.26; p. 130, 1–2: "Unitas que secundum genus est unitas est debilissima et minimum habens vere unitatis."

71. *DCL* III.1.27; p. 130, 9–12: "Pretera, si connumeremus Deum, qui est principium omnium in universitate, cum ipse non possit communicare cum creatura aliqua in genere vel specie, non possumus dicere quod universitas participat unitate secundum genus." To this point I might add, God is not in any genus, as there is no genus-species composition in God if God is perfectly simple. See Thomas Aquinas, *ST* I, q. 3, a. 5.

the human body's composition of the elements (i.e., light, heat, humidity, and coldness): "[The human body] is united, consequently, with all the elemental natures united with the elements themselves."[72] Thus, humanity possesses a natural unity with all corporeal creatures, both those composed of multiple elements and those which are simply one element, such as light. Additionally, because humanity possesses a rational soul, together with the lower powers (sensitive and vegetative), humans are naturally united to all animate creatures: "The rational soul is also united with the sensible soul of brute animals in the sensitive power, and with the vegetative soul of plants in the vegetative power."[73] To this we can add the human creature's natural union with all intelligent creatures, in virtue of the rational soul. Thus, given humanity's unity with all corporeality and animate beings, a human nature is apt for service as the unifying principle of the universe.

If a human *nature* can unite creation, it cannot serve as the unifying principle of the Creator and creature. As there is no generic unity between the Creator and creature, neither is there any natural unity. Either, then, only the creation of *some* human creature is necessary for Grosseteste's God, or else there must be some principle in which both Creator and creation are united. If the latter is possible, it must be actualized by Grosseteste's God. And if the creature in which Creator is united to creation is a human being, in whom all of creation is naturally united, then the greatest possible unity will obtain.[74] This is possible, not by natural union, but by personal (hypostatic) union. As Grosseteste puts it:

---

72. *DCL* III.1.27; p. 130, 31–p. 131, 2: "Communicat etiam per consequens cum omnibus naturis elementatis communicantibus cum ipsis elementis."

73. *DCL* III.1.27; p. 131, 2–4: "Communicat quoque anima rationalis cum anima sensibili brutorum in potentia sensitiva, et cum anima vegetabili plantarum in potentia vegetativa."

74. Technically, it could be that two distinct principles effect each of these unities—one between Creator and creature, and the other between all of creation. If both of these are possibly actualized by Grosseteste's God, then they would be independent of one another given one condition: they could not possibly be actualized in a single principle. If they could be actualized in a single principle, then the same

If, then, God assumed man in a unity of person, creation is reduced to the fullness of unity; but if he should not assume, creation has not been drawn to the fullness of unity possible for it. Therefore, leaving aside the fall of man, it is nonetheless fitting that God assume man in a unity of person, because he could do it and it would not be inappropriate for him to do it; but it would be much more appropriate, because without this the universe would lack unity.[75]

Thus, in possible worlds without a fall, God could assume man (because He has in our world), and it would be appropriate for all the reasons Grosseteste has supplied. And so we should conclude that He would. *Potuit, decuit, ergo facit.*

Grosseteste gives another rendition of these unitive aims arguments, in this case from the "circular fulfillment" of creation: "If (the incarnation) were truly done, creation would have the fullest and most fitting unity, and through this all natures would be led back into a circular fulfillment."[76] Not only does Christ unite all creation in a natural unity in virtue of being truly human, and the Creator to the creature by a unity of assumption, but Christ further unites the series of human generation in a circular unity. "Seth is from Adam, and Enosh is from Seth ... and so on in a line descending all the way to Jesus. And I can reflect and say, Adam is from Jesus, for this man, referring to Jesus, created Adam."[77] Thus, Christ unites all of humanity in a circle of human generation. By now the argument for the actualization of this possibility in those worlds will be familiar:

---

logic that demanded the actualization of two distinct principles will lead to the necessary actualization of the single principle instead.

75. *DCL* III.1.28; p. 131, 9–15: "Si igitur assumat Deus hominem in unitatem persone, reducta est universitas ad unitatis complementum. Si vero non assumat, nec universitas ad unitatis complementum sibi possibile deducta est. Circumscripto igitur hominis lapsu, nichilominus convenit Deum assumere hominem in unitatem persone, cum et hoc possit facere nec dedeceat ipsum hoc facere; sed multo magis deceat, cum sine hoc careat universitas unitate."

76. *DCL* III.1.28; p. 131, 16–18: "Hoc vero facto, habeat universitas plenissimam et decentissimam unitatem, redacteque sint per hoc omnes nature in complementum circulare."

77. *DCL* III.1.29; p. 131, 27–30: "Possum enim sic dicere: ex Adam est Seth et ex Seth Enos et ex Enos Cainan, et ita linealiter descendendo usque ad Ihesum.

Since, therefore, it is better for the creation of things that the series of human generation be united in such a circular period than that they be deprived of this union, it would be possible for God to perfect them in this way. And that these things are perfected in this way seems to be manifest, because the perfection of the circular period in this way needs to exist.[78]

This time, however, he introduces a new theological premise into his argument by appeal to John Damascene's *De fide orthodoxa* II, 29, which Grosseteste renders as follows:

Providence is the will of God, according to which everything that exists receives fitting direction. But if the will of God is providence, it is altogether necessary for everything that happens by providence to be what is best and what most befits God, according to right reason, so that it could not turn out better.[79]

Here we reach a critical juncture: the intersection of will (providence) and nature, in this case implied by reference to the attribute of perfection. This issue will emerge as a critical point of debate for subsequent theologians.

Recalling the sweep of the argument extending across paragraphs 11–30, we can now express a second general strategy:

(a) God actualizes some created effect *x* in our world.

(b) *x* does not have the fall as a necessary condition.

(c) If there were no fall, God would actualize *x*.

(d) *x* has a human nature hypostatically united to a divine person as a necessary condition.

Possumque reflectere et dicere: ex Ihesu Adam; iste enim homo, demonstrato Ihesu, creavit Adam."

78. *DCL* III.1.29; p. 131, 30–132, 2: "Cum igitur melius sit tam rerum universitatem quam humane generacionis seriem tali circulacionis periodo uniri quam ista unicione privari, possibile quoque sit et Deum sic perficere. Et ista sic perfici manifestum videtur esse quod huiusmodi circularis periodi perfeccionem necesse sit esse."

79. *DCL* III.1.29; p. 132, 2–7: "Ait namque Iohannes Damascenus: 'Providentia est voluntas Dei, propter quam omnia que sunt convenientem deduccionem suscipiunt. Si autem Dei voluntas est providentia, omnino necesse est omnia que providentia fiunt, secundum rectam rationem et optima et Deo decentissima fieri, et ut non est melius fieri.'"

(e) If there were no fall, there would be a human nature hypostatically united to a divine person (for the sake of *x*).

Let us call this argumentative strategy the created effects strategy.

Questioning Hypotheticals

History has not been kind to the hypothetical question and
responses of Grosseteste and others. The form of the question, a
subjunctive conditional, raises the spectre of counterfactual speculation, a controversial domain of speculative theology. Recent treatments of *DCL* III.1 reflect a particular worry about counterfactual
speculation. Is it not too proud to inquire into the mind of God?
Could any god whose mind we could investigate to the point of
knowledge of other possible states of affairs be anything other than
an idol? Is not the hypothetical question yet another, perhaps *the*,
instance of scholastic *superbia*? To entertain the question might be
to gaze upon some god other than the God revealed in Jesus Christ.

Recent commentators on *DCL* III are deeply vexed by this pos-
sibility. In light of these worries, James McEvoy suggests Grosseteste's arguments should be read inductively, rather than deductively.
Another strategy has been to distinguish between two classes of
worlds—actual and possible. Putatively, the worry can be resolved
so long as the hypothetical question does not wander too far into
speculation about other possible worlds, but retains its focus upon
our actual world. So Dominic Unger insists that "the hypothesis
of no sin and yet an Incarnation is not outside the present world
order," distinguishing between (1) responses to the hypothetical
question and (2) arguments for the absolute existence of Christ.[80]

Criticisms of the hypothetical question are not only directed at
Robert Grosseteste. Juniper Carol, in *Why Jesus Christ?*, refers to the
hypothetical question as an "insoluble pseudo-question."[81] While

---

80. Unger, "Grosseteste on the Reasons for the Incarnation," 26.
81. Carol, *Why Jesus Christ?* 132.

articulating what Carol terms "the Scotistic thesis" on the motive for the incarnation, he pauses to consider whether Scotus's position is concerned with what God would have done "in the hypothetical order of things ... the world of the unreal," or rather with the de facto world in which we find ourselves. That is, Carol asks whether Scotus's various comments on the hypothetical question are concerned with a counterfactual or actual state of affairs. This interpretive issue arises as a result of Scotus's aside on the hypothetical question in his larger treatment of Christ's predestination in *Reportatio* III, d. 7, q. 4, in which Scotus speculates that if Adam had not sinned, Christ would have become incarnate, but his flesh would have been glorified immediately. Though we are not yet concerned with Scotus, it is worth noting the line of defense Carol advances for Scotus's speculations on the hypothetical question simply in order to clarify (1) potential problems with the putatively insoluble pseudo-question, and (2) which applications of the hypothetical question might be retained. Clarifying these questions will help in evaluating Grosseteste's developments of the Anselmian theses.

Carol recognizes that Scotus's speculative comments on the hypothetical question are somehow concerned with a counterfactual state of affairs. So, he cannot entirely avoid conditional speculation. But Carol also issues normative claims as to how one ought to think about responses (at least Scotus's response) to the hypothetical question. "Regardless of Scotus' true position, we ourselves believe that the theory of an Incarnation in any hypothesis cannot be proved with apodictic arguments."[82] This assertion stands against the "standard Scotist" position, of Adolpho Martini and others, who, according to Carol, hold that "If Adam had not sinned, God *certainly* would have become man."[83] The problem is the tendency of theologians, in response to the hypothetical question, to formu-

82. Carol, *Why Jesus Christ?* 132.

83. Carol, *Why Jesus Christ?* 133. Of course, Carol likewise inveighs against the "standard Thomist" position that "If Adam had not sinned, God certainly would *not* have become man."

late assertions concerning the divine will and intentions that arrive at certainty.

Carol proposes the following rules for avoiding this problem. First, we cannot obtain certainty about divine actions in counterfactual states of affairs except on one condition: that God reveals to us what God would do in that counterfactual state of affairs. Absent that condition (which is the case in our de facto order, Carol seems to imply), we cannot say with certainty what God would do in that counterfactual world. Second, while we cannot arrive at certainty, we can speculate as to "some rather plausible reasons why Christ (and Mary) should have existed even if Adam had not fallen, but our speculations would yield only an argument from fittingness."[84] These speculations are acceptable, so long as they are recognized to arrive merely at fittingness, *convenientia*. The danger of the hypothetical question, then, and the reason for which it is dubbed an "insoluble pseudo-question," is that it invites overly confident responses. For Carol, so long as that qualification is recognized, it would seem, we can continue to speculate as to the fittingness of the incarnation in other possible worlds, while avoiding idolatry.

Does Grosseteste's treatment avoid the problem isolated by Carol? Part of the difficulty in answering the question is the underdeveloped concept of *convenientia* in Grosseteste's writings. As we saw in the previous chapter, Anselm deploys the concept of *convenientia* in a variety of ways, some more perspicuous than others. Grosseteste prefers to present a series of deductive arguments in support of the affirmative response to the hypothetical question. Prima facie, at least, this tendency suggests that Grosseteste takes an overweeningly confident position in response to the hypothetical question.

Grosseteste's commentators have observed this tendency and potential danger. Two strategies have been presented in an attempt to redeem Grosseteste's arguments: (1) highlighting Grosseteste's

84. Carol, *Why Jesus Christ?* 133. Most intriguingly, immediately following the aforementioned swipe at the Thomists, Carol asserts almost verbatim the position of Thomas at *ST* III, q. 1, a. 3.

ambivalence about the results of his arguments, and (2) refining his arguments away from any overweening tendencies. The former strategy seems warranted by Grosseteste's ruminations in *DCL* III.2:

> These and similar arguments seem to be able to show that God would become man, even if man had never sinned. Nevertheless, I know that I do not know whether this is true, and I am not mildly sorrowful at my ignorance about this. For, as I said above, I do not recall seeing anything from our authorities about this determination. Neither do I wish or dare to assert anything on such an arduous question without express authority, because a verisimilitudinous argument can quickly deceive my small mind and knowledge.[85]

The halting admission of ignorance renders plausible an interpretation of Grosseteste's comment in *DCL* III.1.1 that there "seem to be efficacious reasons" in support of the affirmative response to the hypothetical question as an indication of ambivalence.[86] And, if his ambivalence reflects caution, then we might have warrant to suspect that Grosseteste is less than overweeningly confident in his conclusions. He may be, in spite of the form of his arguments, properly cautious.

But we may not be able to infer much from Grosseteste's hesitations. After all, the point remains that he produces, for several pages, a series of deductive arguments, giving no indication that any of the objections he considers are successful against his argument. At best, we might conclude that Grosseteste simply formulates the arguments, reckoning them to be rationally persuasive, and registers concern about the tenability of rational arguments unaccompanied by authoritative teaching of the "expositors of sacred Scripture."

85. *DCL* III.2.1; p. 133, 20–27: "Hiis et huiusmodi raciocinacionibus videtur posse astrui Deum esse hominem licet numquam peccasset homo. Quod tamen an verum sit me ignorare scio, et meam in hac parte ignorantiam non mediocriter doleo. Nichil enim, ut supradiximus, a nostris auctoribus super hoc determinatum me vidisse recolo. Nec sine expressa auctoritate aliquid in tam ardua questione asserere volo vel audeo, quia parvitatem ingenii mei et scientie mee cito potest fallere verisimilis ratiocinacio."

86. *DCL* III.1.2; p. 119, 16–18: "Videntur tamen esse raciones efficaces ad ostendendum simpliciter quod Deus esset homo etiam si numquam lapsus fuisset homo."

This reading is consistent with the larger structure of *DCL*, as Grosseteste argues from Scripture (specifically the Old Testament) in Part II, and from reason in Part III. In any event, the lack of authoritative teaching in no way detracts from the rational efficacy of his arguments. So long as those deductive arguments stand, it would be irrational not to assign them certainty. Thus, to accept the arguments as they stand, one must either grant them certainty or else deny the arguments and face irrationality.

Dominic Unger gives the most insightful evaluation of Grosseteste's confidence in *DCL* III. He asks, "How certain was the Bishop of his opinion?"[87] Recognizing the deductive form of Grosseteste's arguments, Unger grants that they are "not doubtful." Nevertheless, he is careful to specify *which* argument is indubitable. Unger refines Grosseteste's arguments in order to avoid problematic entailments for counterfactual states of affair, introducing a similar distinction to Carol's distinction between an actual and hypothetical world. Unger's distinguishes two plans: a present plan and a hypothetical one.[88] Whatever Grosseteste intended, we can accept his argument with respect to the present plan, and leave off worry about any hypothetical one. In this way, Unger seeks to retain the rationality of Grosseteste's arguments while avoiding any excessive confidence in hypothetical speculation. In order to clarify such a reading of Grosseteste's arguments, let us return to Anselm, and note how Grosseteste applies the Anselmian theses.

Grosseteste and Anselm

In the prior chapter, I distinguished four Anselmian theses on the general question, "How can we determine divine reasons for divine operations *ad extra*?":

---

87. Unger, "Grosseteste on the Reasons for the Incarnation," 35.

88. Unger, "Grosseteste on the Reasons for the Incarnation," 25–26, 35–36.

Thesis 1: Divine operations *ad extra* cannot be necessary.

Thesis 2: Attributes of the divine nature restrict the domain of possible divine operations *ad extra.*

Thesis 3: Prior divine operations *ad extra* and their reasons restrict the domain of possible subsequent divine operations *ad extra.*

Thesis 4: Reasons for divine operations *ad extra* possess fittingness (*convenientia*).

Robert Grosseteste performs one application of the Anselmian theses to the reason for the incarnation in *DCL* III. Where Anselm gives theses, Grosseteste produces strategies for determining divine reasons for divine operations *ad extra.* Grosseteste's myriad arguments reduce to two strategies: the divine attributes strategy and the created effects strategy.

Let us consider, first, Grosseteste's development of theses 1 and 2. As we noted with Anselm, theses one and two are consistent. To use Anselm's language, "necessary" in thesis one is necessity *proprie,* necessity without external constraint. But this does not prevent the restriction of the domain of possible states of affairs to those compossible with the attributes of the divine nature. These constraints are internal and therefore offer no threat to divine freedom, according to Anselm. Thus, thesis two does not undermine thesis one.

Grosseteste's strategies accept Anselm's account of necessity. Robert repeatedly applies parallel arguments: divine goodness restricts the domain of possible states of affairs to those actualizing maximally good creatures, such as a human nature hypostatically united to a divine person. For Grosseteste, as for Anselm, the class of possible reasons for divine operations *ad extra* will be restricted by their respective accounts of the divine attributes. As we saw, Grosseteste's account of divine goodness significantly restricts the domain of worlds compossible with Grosseteste's God.

Not only do attributes of the divine nature restrict the domain of possible worlds to those compossible with Grosseteste's God, but Grosseteste further restricts the set of compossible worlds to those which resemble our actual *W*-world (with a fall and an incarnation) along the lines of Anselm's third thesis. For Anselm, divine reasons for divine operations *ad extra* restrict the domain of possible subsequent divine operations. So in our world, creatures will retain both their natural ends as well as those supernatural ends granted to them by God. Otherwise, Anselm argues, God is either unable to accomplish his purpose, or the divine will is mutable.

Grosseteste seems to expand this rule across all possible worlds. Divine immutability played an essential role for Anselm in deriving thesis three from theses one and two. It is notable that, for Grosseteste, immutability goes without mention. In his applications of the divine attributes strategy, his emphasis remains upon the divine perfections: goodness, beauty, and generosity. Those perfections supply reasons for God's determination to become incarnate. The created effects strategy hinges upon the same set of divine attributes, especially divine goodness.

Interestingly, Grosseteste's arguments often reduce to *inconvenientia*. These reductions are executed by positing two sets of counterfactual worlds, those distinct from our own insofar as neither sin nor incarnation obtain, and those distinct from our own insofar as sin does not obtain, and showing the former is "less good" than the latter (e.g., *DCL* III.1.17, 18) and therefore unfitting for God. Once again divine goodness—not immutability—is the key attribute. The argument requires the premise from *DCL* III.1.4 that "the supreme good pours in great a good as possible" to complete the *reductio,* and so the attribute of goodness supplies a key premise in satisfying the second condition for the values of *y* in the created effects strategy.

In the analysis of the fourth Anselmian thesis, I distinguished three instantiations of arguments *ex convenientia*: negative limitation, embellishment, and gradation arguments. In *DCL* III.1, Grosseteste uses *convenientia* on seven occasions. None of them occur in the divine attributes strategy of the early paragraphs. There is an important *reductio ad inconvenientiam* in the semantic argument of paragraph 15. There is also the refusal that the human race could be in a better condition with sin than without in paragraph 17, as well as the parallel argument concerning marriage at paragraph 21. The rational soul is "fit" to the body in paragraph 27. In paragraph 28, Grosseteste speaks of God's assumption of a human nature as "fitting" for the fullness and decorousness of the universe, on account of the circular concatenation thereby completed. In that case he connects the parallel concept of appropriateness (*decens*). Finally, the citation from Damascene in paragraph 29 attaches "fittingness" to providence, which "is the will of God," granting to everything its order.

Every instance of *convenientia* and *inconvenientia* in *DCL* is synonymous with "compossible" and "incompossible." Grosseteste's most significant use is in the *reductio ad inconvenientiam* for the semantic analysis at *DCL* III.1.15, a clear instance of a negative limitation argument *ex convenientia*. It is *inconvenientia* for God to create some creature (i.e., Christ's human nature) merely for the sake of its suffering. At this juncture, the created effects strategy redounds to the divine attributes strategy; the fundamental premises are the assertions of divine perfections, which guard against such unfitting consequences. In short, *inconvenientia* is incompossible with Grosseteste's God.

Otherwise, the observation of *convenientia* is followed by a deduction that God would, ought, or must actualize that "fitting" good. Even in the domain of embellishment, we seem to arrive at rational necessity, as the universe is more beautiful or decorous than it would be without the incarnation. Consider, for instance, the circular concatenation of the universe, necessary in its fullest extent, including the union of God and humanity in a person for the sake of the maximal unity of the universe. A similar conclusion follows Grosseteste's argument from the circle of human generation, which he says is both congruous and necessary.

In light of these arguments, we can see that gradation arguments *ex convenientia* will always eventuate in necessity for Grosseteste. When, in DCL III.1.28, he distinguishes two worlds, which differ only insofar as one lacks the circular fulfillment of all natures back into one by the assumption of a human by God, Grosseteste argues that it would only be appropriate for God to actualize the circularly fulfilled world. The other is unfitting. More precisely, only maximally circularly fulfilled worlds are compossible with Grosseteste's God, because they are better than the others.

Grosseteste, then, presses all of Anselm's *convenientia* arguments toward necessity. Integral to this process are the deductive strategies, both of which derive from divine perfections like goodness and beauty. "Fitting," for Grosseteste, drifts toward "necessary."

An alternative, more cautious reading of Grosseteste's arguments could develop along the lines suggested by Unger's appeal to the de facto order. The created effects arguments seem to assume resemblance relations between the worlds under consideration. They begin by assuming some created good x actualized in our W-world. On a cautious reading, these arguments are successful if the possible worlds under consideration resemble our W-world as far as excepting sin permits. Most significantly, this resemblance must include God having a divine reason for actualizing the particular created good under consideration.

Such a cautious reading of Grosseteste would preserve the possibility of God creating other possible worlds that do not bear the relevant resemblances with our own. Of course, God's reasons would be different in those worlds than in the ones for which these arguments obtain. This revision would permit Grosseteste's arguments to have purchase across a specific domain of possible worlds (those that resemble our W-world in the relevant sense), without demanding that God have the same reasons in every possible world.

A "cautious" reading can be distinguished from a "confident" reading of Grosseteste, which holds that the only possible worlds compossible with Grosseteste's God are those sharing the same reasons. This would be a strong application of the divine perfections, and inclines towards Leibniz's best of all possible worlds.

Grosseteste's modern interpreters have this "cautious" reading in mind when they focus on the de facto order. According to Dominic Unger, "it is quite probable that [Robert] would hold what most scholars held later, that the hypothesis of no sin and yet an Incarnation is not outside the present world order."[89] Of course, this is a line of interpretation—even Unger's preferred interpretation, by his own admission, is at best "probable."

For Unger, it is of primary importance to maintain a unified Franciscan tradition of reflection on the question, arriving at a summative achievement in John Duns Scotus. For our sake, however, Unger's strategy obscures the series of developments across the discourse of the thirteenth century. For these purposes, the apparently confident reading of *DCL* outlined above, with full hypothetical implications and a necessary interpretation of *convenientia*, grants us an opportunity to observe the profound internal tensions in the search for divine reasons for divine operations *ad extra*. Thus, I have pursued Grosseteste on his own terms, first and primarily, rather than with any late-thirteenth-century revisions, which develop and deploy more sophisticated and apt strategies for determining divine reasons for divine operations *ad extra*. As we will see in the next chapter, it was arguments along the lines of the "confident" reading of Grosseteste that were the impetus for the significant advances on the reason for the incarnation at Paris over the course of the thirteenth century.

89. Unger, "Grosseteste on the Reasons for the Incarnation," 26.

FOUR

The Dominicans at Paris

We have, to this point, been tracking a conversation that originated and developed in the British Isles.[1] As is well documented, Paris was *the* center of theological education in the West in the thirteenth century. Already by the time of Grosseteste, receiving an au courant theological formation meant traveling to Paris. The lengthy modern debates over whether Robert's own theological formation took place at Paris attest to the relative importance of the *studia* surrounding the cathedral at Notre Dame. The presumption, until the latter half of the twentieth century, was that Robert's formation was too advanced to have developed elsewhere.[2]

Whether and how the arguments of Grosseteste's *DCL* were received in the debates at Paris is difficult to discern. Like Robert's legacy more broadly, there is no strong evidence that his in-

---

1. There has been some analysis of the debates over the motive for the incarnation in the latter half of the thirteenth century at Oxford. See, for instance, R. James Long, "The Cosmic Christ: The Christology of Richard Fishacre, OP," in *Christ among the Medieval Dominicans: Representations of Christ in the Texts and Images of the Order of Preachers*, ed. Kent Emery and Joseph Wawrykow, 332–43, Notre Dame Conferences in Medieval Studies 7 (Notre Dame, Ind.: University of Notre Dame Press, 1998); Peter Raedts, *Richard Rufus of Cornwall and the Tradition of Oxford Theology* (New York: Clarendon Press, 1987).

2. For a summary of the debates and the seminal argument for the now-dominant position that Grosseteste was educated in England, see chapter 3, "Two Patterns of Education," in Southern, *Robert Grosseteste*.

fluence was significant in either Paris or Oxford.[3] As we will see, there are notable similarities between recurring arguments for the affirmative response to the hypothetical question at Paris and the arguments from *DCL*. But the Parisian arguments could have developed independently of Grosseteste; the sources cited in support of the arguments suggest as much. Even Duns Scotus, whose position some suggest was anticipated by Grosseteste, does not cite Robert at any point in his reflections on the incarnation, nor in his Christology more broadly. This is in spite of his apparent familiarity with Grosseteste's work.[4] The thirteenth-century debates over the motive for the incarnation at Paris descend, not from Grosseteste, but from the Masters who occupied the Dominican and Franciscan

3. Southern, *Robert Grosseteste*, 296: "At his death ... [Grosseteste's] name was revered, but his influence on the main stream of even Franciscan theology was small. The meagerness of his influence even in Oxford becomes very conspicuous with John Duns Scotus. Scotus had access to all Grosseteste's literary remains, and it is clear that he had looked at them with care but without admiration. He quoted from Grosseteste's commentary on the *Posterior Analytics*, which was the most widely quoted of all his works; also from his *Hexaemeron* and *Dicta* and from his notes on the *Ethics* and his translations of Ps.-Denys, and from other notes, sermons, and memoranda preserved in the Franciscan library. These quotations are widely distributed in his works, but they are seldom important. They formed no part of the structure of Grosseteste's thought. Grosseteste pointed towards an integration of science and theology, and of Greek and Latin thought, on generous lines; Scotus initiated a new stage of scholastic refinement." Daniel Horan's speculation of Grosseteste's influence on Scotus is unpersuasive; see Horan, "How Original Was Scotus on the Incarnation?" I have found no clear evidence that Scotus, or anyone else in thirteenth-century Paris, ever directly encountered *De cessatione legalium*. Any influence seems to be indirect, and can be explained often enough with reference to common sources: Augustine, Damascene, and Lombard. The possible exception is Bonaventure, but the evidence, as it stands at present, is inconclusive. I will, however, note marked similarities between arguments cited by Grosseteste and those circulating at Paris. Even at Oxford, where Grosseteste's influence would have been most natural, it is difficult to discern whether there was a direct impact on such figures as Richard Fishacre; see Long, "The Cosmic Christ," 335.

4. Scotus explicitly references Robert (*Lincolniensis*) on three occasions in the *Ordinatio*. First, in his discussion of the *filioque* in Book I, Scotus cites Robert's *Notula super epistolam Ioannis Damascene "De trisagion"* (*Ord.* I, d. 11, q. 1). Later, in his discussion of angelic cognition in Book II, Scotus cites Robert's translations and notes on both Aristotle's *Nicomachean Ethics* (*Ord.* II, d. 3, p. 2, q. 1) and Pseudo-Dionysius's *Celestial Hierarchies* (*Ord.* II, d. 3, p. 2, q. 3). Book III makes no explicit reference to *Lincolniensis*.

Chairs at the University of Paris. While they isolate a similar set of issues, raise similar concerns, and draw upon resources similar to Grosseteste's, the theologians at Paris finally reject the Grosseteste-an strategies and arguments. And in rejecting Grosseteste's strategies, they reject Grosseteste's reception of Anselm, charting their own path, equally deferential to Anselm and *CDH*.

Two developments are increasingly relevant to the texts, figures, and arguments on the reason for the incarnation at Paris. First, the occupation of chairs by the Dominican and Franciscan orders, beginning with the installation of Roland of Cremona in St. Boniface's Chair in 1229, established new, formidable schools of theological inquiry that would flourish throughout the remainder of the thirteenth century. Roland's chair would become the Dominican Chair for Interns. Shortly after Roland's entry into the Order of Preachers, a second chair was gained for the Dominicans (the Chair for Externs) when John of St. Gilles entered the Order in 1230. The Franciscan Chair was gained with the entry of Alexander of Hales into the Order of the Friars Minor in 1236 or 1237.[5]

The analysis of the motive for the incarnation at Paris in this chapter and the next will focus on the occupants of two of these three mendicant chairs: the Dominican Chair for Externs (chapter four) and the Franciscan Chair (chapter five). The focus on the mendicants is justified both by the relative importance of these chairs in thirteenth-century theology and the exceeding importance that two occupants would take in subsequent debates over the motive for the incarnation: Thomas Aquinas and John Duns Scotus. It should be noted, though, that Dominican and Franciscan thought on the motive for the incarnation crossed the boundaries of the orders. Often, we will see Dominican theologians influenc-

---

5. The standard text on the Parisian masters in the thirteenth century remains Palémon Glorieux, *Répertoire des Maîtres en théologie de Paris au XIIIe siècle*, Etudes de philosophie médiévale 17–18 (Paris: J. Vrin, 1933). A summary of the attainment of the chairs by the mendicant orders can be found in James A. Weisheipl, *Friar Thomas D'Aquino: His Life, Thought, and Work*, 1st ed. (Garden City, N.Y.: Doubleday, 1974), 54–67.

ing Franciscans, and vice versa. But we will also see that the preponderance of evidence suggests that the mendicants were most directly engaged with prior occupants of their respective chairs. Thus, the chapters will divide according to the orders, and the points of influence across the orders will be highlighted along the way.

Many theologians discuss Thomas and Scotus on the motive for the incarnation. The analysis that follows is distinct insofar as it reads the classic texts of the Angelic and Subtle Doctors in conversation with those who preceded them in their chairs at the University of Paris. This strategy allows for the individual contributions to be viewed within the larger context of thirteenth-century debates over the motive for the incarnation.

A second development, which will take on increasing importance as the argument proceeds, is the rise of the commentary tradition on Peter Lombard's *Sentences* from the time of Alexander of Hales. Much of the debate over the motive for the incarnation subsequent to Alexander is located within the larger project of commentary on the *Sentences*. Neither too much nor too little should be made of this point. It would be too much to infer that the motive for the incarnation was subsumed under another theological project by thirteenth-century theologians. Especially as the thirteenth century moved along, the *Sentences* simply provided an outline of Christian doctrine, which helped to organize debates and provoke developments. Accordingly, many of the various issues treated in the commentaries on the *Sentences* can be considered independently of the larger argument of those commentaries. By the time of Scotus, in particular, distinctions and articles often mark discrete and increasingly subtle debates. But it would be too little to suggest that Peter Lombard's seminal text provided *merely* an outline for organizing discrete debates. The *Sentences* commentaries, like scholastic theology in general, prized coherence across theological loci. Locating questions like the hypothetical one within the various distinctions into which Alexander divided the *Sentences* often signals substantive proposals on the question itself. Moreover, Lombard offers substantive proposals in his own right, many of which are reflected in his organizing principles.[6] It is therefore worth a brief examination of Lombard's organization of the opening distinctions of Book III of his *Sentences*, where the Parisian theologians generally located their treatment of the reason for the incarnation.

Peter Lombard (d. 1160)

Peter does not treat either the primacy question or the hypothetical question in the *Sentences*. Nevertheless, two features of his text shape the debates over the motive for the incarnation among the Masters in thirteenth-century Paris. Both bear upon the general question. First, Lombard provides a catalogue of modal questions related to the incarnation and passion in Book III of the *Sentences*. Those questions became a standard sequence for scholastic reflection on the incarnation, where the discussion of the motive for the incarnation found its home. Second, in Book I, Peter makes influential, original contributions to the doctrine of divine omnipotence. In response to the teaching of Abelard, Lombard develops a distinction between divine will and power that would prove highly influential for counterfactual speculations, like those provoked by the hypothetical question, throughout the thirteenth century.

In the first distinction of *Sentences* Book III, Peter raises a series of questions: Why did the Son take on flesh, and not the Father or Holy Spirit?[7] Was it possible for the Father or Holy Spirit to become incarnate? Can they now?[8] Following this delicate series of questions, Peter proceeds to clarify the concept of incarnation. These clarifications, many of them metaphysical, all substantiate the claim that the incarnation is *possible*. Among this tangle of issues, Lombard's most significant contribution to medieval Christology was

6. For analysis of these contributions, see Marcia L. Colish, *Peter Lombard*, 2 vols, Brill's Studies in Intellectual History 41 (Leiden: Brill, 1994); Philipp W. Rosemann, *Peter Lombard*, Great Medieval Thinkers (Oxford: Oxford University Press, 2004).

7. *Sentences* III, d. 1, ch. 1.

8. *Sentences* III, d. 1, ch. 2.

formulated. In distinctions six and seven, Peter distinguishes and analyzes three theories (or models) of the hypostatic union: (1) the *assumptus homo* theory, (2) the *subsistentia* theory, and (3) the *habitus* theory.[9] These three positions would form the landscape of subsequent debates over the metaphysics of the incarnation. However, it is notable that these influential metaphysical considerations are all oriented to a larger concern: the modal status of the incarnation. In variously modeling the metaphysics of the incarnation, theologians were interrogating the incarnation's *possibility*.

A parallel series of modal topics arises in and around distinction twenty, when Peter considers whether it was necessary that God liberate humanity by passion. There he concludes that "it was possible (for God) to liberate (us) by another way." He cites Book XIII of Augustine's *De Trinitate*: "Another way was possible for God, to whose power all things are subject, however there would not have been, nor ought there to be, another way more convenient (*convenientiorem*) healing of our misery."[10] Continuing with *De Trinitate* XIII, Lombard clarifies the distinction between what is possible and what is fitting; while it was possible for humanity to be liberated by power alone, it was more fitting that humanity be liberated "by the righteousness of [Christ's] humility."[11]

Peter's ruminations on the possibility and fittingness of the incarnation and passion recall his doctrine of divine omnipotence, developed across the concluding distinctions of Book I. His position is advanced in opposition to Peter Abelard's. In Book I, distinction 43, Lombard summarizes Abelard's account of the divine

9. Marcia Colish gives a nice overview of the context of Lombard's presentation, as well as the immediate reception of Lombard's three theories. She argues that Lombard did not express a preference for any position (including the *habitus* theory), but saw the issue in the domain of the *diversi, sed non adversi*; Colish, *Peter Lombard*, 399–438.

10. *Sentences* III, d. 20, c. 1: "Alium modum fuisse possibilem Deo, cuius potestati cuncta subiacent, sed nostrae miseriae sanandae convenientiorem modum alium non fuisse, nec esse oportuisse."

11. *Sentences* III, d. 20, c. 3: "Iustitia ergo humilitatis hominem liberavit, quem sola potentia aequissime liberare potuit."

will and power as follows: "God is not able to do other than what he does, nor to do better than that which he does, nor to omit something which he does."[12] In support of the claim, Peter Lombard recites the following argument:

They say: God is not able to do anything other than what it is good and just to do. But it is not just and good for him to do other than what he does. For if there were something good and just for him to do other than what he does, then he does not do all that is just and good for him to do. But who would dare to say this?[13]

The argument parallels Grosseteste's deductive strategies, in particular the gradation arguments *ex convenientia.*

Lombard addresses the argument directly in distinction 44, when he considers "whether God can do anything better than he does."[14] Here, Lombard gives a summary of the position propounded by the *scrutatores;* he surely has in mind Abelard.[15] The *scrutatores* state, "that which God does, is not possible to do better, because if [better things] were possible to do and were not done, God would be envious and not the greatest good."[16] Ivan Boh refers to this Abelardian commitment as "axiological necessitarianism." That is, the domain of God's activity is restricted "by some a priori axiological consideration."[17]

---

12. *Sentences* I, d. 43, c. 1: "Aiunt enim: Non potest Deus aliud facere quam facit, nec melius facere id quod facit, nec aliquid praetermittere de his quae facit."

13. *Sentences* I, d. 43, c. 1: "Non potest Deus facere nisi quod bonum est et iustum fieri; non est autem iustum et bonum fieri ab eo nisi quod facit. Si enim aliud iustum est et bonum eum facere quam facit, non ergo facit omne quod iustum est et bonum est eum facere? Sed quis hoc adeat dicere?" A second argument is also supplied, but the former is sufficient for our point above.

14. *Sentences* I, d. 44, c. 1: "An Deus possit facere aliquid melius quam facit."

15. Colish, *Peter Lombard*, 299; William J. Courtenay, *Capacity and Volition*, 53–55; Ivan Boh, "Divine Omnipotence in the Early *Sentences*," in *Divine Omniscience and Omnipotence in Medieval Philosophy: Islamic, Jewish, and Christian Perspectives*, ed. Tamar Rudavsky, 185–211, Synthese Historical Library 25 (Dordrecht: D. Reidel, 1985), 198.

16. *Sentences* I, d. 44, c. 2: "Solent enim illi scrutatores dicere quod ea quae facit Deus, non potest meliora facere, quia si posset facere et non faceret, invidus esset et non summe bonus."

17. Boh, "Divine Omnipotence in the Early *Sentences*," 197.

Lombard responds to Abelard's axiological necessitarianism in two steps, one critical and one constructive. First, he distinguishes two possible reasons as to why God could not create a universe of things better than it is. Either (1) the universe is the highest good (*summum bonum est*), or else (2) some great good is lacking from it, which it is not capable of having.[18] The former, which I will call AN1 (axiological necessitarianism 1), will not do. God is the *summum bonum*, and the creature, by definition, is not. On AN1, there will be no distinction between the Creator and the creature.

While this seems a rather obvious problem, Peter points out that it is more difficult to stave off than his opponents suspect. In the paragraph preceding his distinction between AN1 and AN2, Lombard objects to his opponents' interpretation of Augustine's statement:

God could not generate something better than himself, for there is nothing better than God; and so he was obliged to generate his equal. For if he willed and could not, then he is weak; if he could and did not will, he is envious. From which we conclude that he generated the Son as his equal.[19]

As Lombard points out, the appeal to Augustine in support of the assertion that "God cannot do better than he does" confuses the generation of the Son with creation. Of course, that which is generated from God's own substance cannot be better, because it is divine. In this case, AN1 obtains. However, those things that are not generated from God's own substance, but issue from the divine will, could be better; they could be divine! AN1, then, confuses creature and Creator.

18. *Sentences* I, d. 44, c. 3: "Verum hic ab eis responderi deposco, cur dicunt rem aliquam, sive etiam rerum universitatem, in qua maior consummatio expressa est, non posse esse meliorem quam est: sive ideo, quia summe bona est, ita ut nulla omnino boni perfectio ei desit; sive ideo, quia maius bonum quod ei deest, capere ipsa non valeat."

19. *Sentences* I, d. 44, c. 2: "Ait enim Augustinus in libro *Quaestionum 84*: 'Deus quem genuit, quoniam meliorem se generare non potuit: nihil enim Deo melius, debuit aequalem. Si enim voluit et non potuit, infirmus est; si potuit et noluit, invidus. Ex quo conficitur aequalem genuisse Filium.'"

AN2, on the other hand, holds that God cannot do anything greater even if some great good is lacking because it is beyond the capacity of the creature. If AN1 violates the distinction between the Creator and creature, axiological necessity will still hold so long as nothing better could be simply in virtue of creaturely limitations. If AN2 holds, the Abelardian account of divine omnipotence is sound, and Grosseteste's deductive strategies, assuming the other premises are sound, will win the day. In response, Lombard appeals to Augustine's commentary on Genesis 11, "God could have made man such that he would have been neither able nor willing to sin; and if he had made him such, who doubts that he would have been better?"[20] While the argument is a bit thin, Lombard's substantive position on God's capacity for doing otherwise, and even better, is perfectly perspicuous. There must be some distinction between what God *can do* and what God *does*. "Power, or capacity, exceeds volition."[21]

Peter Lombard's wrangling with Abelard and the *scrutatores* over divine omnipotence anticipates subsequent counterfactual speculation. While Lombard's distinction between divine power and divine will was not immediately applied to the motive for the incarnation, over time it came to shape reflection on the necessity, possibility, and suitability of the incarnation and passion. As William Courtenay has shown, Lombard's distinction between will and power was fundamental to the thirteenth-century development of the distinction between God's absolute and ordained power, a distinction that would come to have increasing importance in the debates over the motive for the incarnation in the thirteenth century. Among his other influential developments, Peter Lombard's distinction marks a significant divergence from the account of necessity *proprie* and necessity *improprie* and the attendant notions of capacity and inca-

---

20. *Sentences* I, d. 44, c. 3: "Unde Augustinus, *Super Genesim*: 'Talem potuit Deus hominem fecisse, qui nec peccare posset nec vellet; et si talem fecisset, quis dubitat eum meliorem fuisse?'"

21. Courtenay, *Capacity and Volition*, 55.

pacity, as we saw in Anselm. Courtenay describes the new perspective as follows:

There is a sphere of potentiality open to God by reason of his power that need never be realized, a sphere of potentiality larger than those things which God has in fact chosen to do. Through the influence of Lombard's *Libri sententiarum* more than any other work, the gloss on divine *impotentia* that sufficed for Desiderius and Anselm, namely that *non potuit* should be understood as *noluit*, was replaced by the Augustinian *potuit, sed noluit*.[22]

As we will see, the Dominicans at Paris were eager to apply Peter's account of divine power to the motive for the incarnation.

Guerric of Saint-Quentin (d. 1245)

The first Parisian Dominican response to the motive for the incarnation comes from an occupant of the Dominican Chair for Externs.[23] Guerric of Saint-Quentin considers the question "whether the Son of God would have become incarnate if humanity had not sinned" in his *Quaestiones de quodlibet* VII, a. 1, composed sometime around 1240.[24] Guerric was a Doctor of Medicine and Master of Arts at the University of Paris, and he served as Regent Master

22. For an overview of the development of the absolute-ordained power distinction, from the widespread acceptance of Augustine's *potuit, sed noluit* to the distinction's systematic formulation in Paris by 1245, see Courtenay, *Capacity and Volition*, 68–74. Courtenay, in pointing out the significance of Lombard for the development of the absolute-ordained power distinction, stands against Lovejoy and with Boh. See Lovejoy, *The Great Chain of Being: A Study of the History of an Idea*, 73, and Boh, "Divine Omnipotence in the Early *Sentences*."

23. Guerric's *Quaestiones de quolibet* are antedated by Alexander of Hales's *Glossa* and *Quaestiones disputatae*, which will be treated in the subsequent chapter on the Franciscans at Paris.

24. Walter H. Principe, "Guerric of Saint-Quentin, OP, on the Question: *Utrum Filius Dei esset incarnatus si homo non peccasset?*" in *Ordo sapientiae et amoris: Image et message de Saint Thomas d'Aquin à travers les récentes études historiques, herméneutiques et doctrinales*, ed. Carlos-Josaphat Pinto de Oliveira (Fribourg: Studia Friburgensia, 1993), 510. Further text-critical information, with commentary, can be found in Jonathan Black's "Preface" to Guerric, *Guerric of Saint-Quentin: Quaestiones de quolibet*, ed. J. Black and W. H. Principe, Studies and Texts 143 (Toronto: Pontifical Institute of Mediaeval Studies, 2002).

from 1233 to 1242 in what would become the Dominican Chair for Externs. That Chair was later occupied by Albert the Great and Thomas Aquinas.

Walter Principe and John-Pierre Torrell have produced excellent summaries of *Quodlibet* VII, noting the significant variants between the Prague and Vatican manuscripts (VG), which appear to be *reportationes,* and the Assisi manuscript (A), the origins of which are less clear.[25] In what follows, I will give a brief description of Guerric's argument in conversation with Principe and Torrell. As interesting as Guerric's comments are in their own right, they chiefly serve as a starting point for analysis of the subsequent, more influential contributions to the question developed by Albert the Great and Thomas Aquinas. Most importantly, Guerric's arguments, viewed in light of the Grossetestean strategies, illumine the tensions internal to the state of the hypothetical question as it began to circulate among the Parisian Masters.

Article one of Guerric's seventh quodlibetal question asks the hypothetical question, which Guerric states as follows: "Whether the Son of God would have become incarnate if humanity had not sinned."[26] In support of the negative response to the hypothetical, Guerric cites Psalm 68:3 (69:3), "I descend into the deep mud," together with Augustine's Christological *Gloss*: "If humanity had remained in that which God gave him, the Son would not have been descending into mud."[27] While Guerric favors the negative response, he is more emphatic that his position is merely probable.

25. Jean-Pierre Torrell, "Guerric de Saint-Quentin et ses quodlibet: Introduction historique et theologique," in *Guerric of Saint-Quentin,* 84–91; Principe, "Guerric of Saint-Quentin, OP."

26. *Quodl.* 7, a. 1, 2 (A): "Quaesitum est primo utrum Filius Dei esset incarnatus si non peccaset homo." When merely trivial variance is noted, the Assisi Manuscript (A) will be cited rather than the Prague and Vatican manuscripts (VG). Otherwise, disparities will be indicated.

27. *Quodl.* 7, a. 1, 2 (VG): "Videtur quod non: dicit enim super illud Ps, *Infixus sum in limo profundi* etc., *Glossa:* 'Si maneret homo in eo quod Deus ei dedit, Filius non esset infixus in limo.'" Reference to *limo* recalls the creation of Adam *de limo terrae* in Genesis 2:7.

The Psalm and its *Gloss* are indeterminate, so it is only possible to opine rather than determine.[28] After all, Guerric observes, the *Gloss* on Psalm 68:3 could be understood to mean, simply, that the incarnation would be less fitting in a possible world without sin than it is in our world. Presumably, since less fitting is a kind of fittingness, the incarnation remains possible in a world without sin.

Guerric gives two arguments in support of his opinion that the Son would not become incarnate in a possible world without sin, both of which are of interest in light of Grosseteste's *DCL*. The first argument shows the centerpiece of Guerric's thought on the motive for the incarnation. Guerric's chief concern is that arguments to the contrary (that the Son would be incarnate in a world without a fall) should not restrict the domain of divine power. Principe puts it nicely: "[Guerric's] reason is the transcendence of God—God's power is not bound to anything. God *would* be bound to the creature if the need for the completion or beauty of the universe were imposed on God as a necessity."[29] The transcendence of God is Guerric's most insistent commitment on the motive for the incarnation; it simply cannot be the case that God is required to become incarnate for the sake of the beauty or completion of the universe.[30] Otherwise, as Guerric puts it, the Creator would be in servitude to the creature. I will call this the divine transcendence argument.

Guerric supplies and refutes a series of arguments that violate divine transcendence. They derive from needs for the perfection, beauty, and unity of the universe. Resonances from Grosseteste abound. The arguments Guerric considers can be summarized as follows:

---

28. *Quodl.* 7, a. 1, 11 (A): "Dicendum quod quia hoc parum determinatum est in Scripturis, licet ad utramque partem opinari."

29. Principe, "Guerric of Saint-Quentin, OP," 513.

30. *Quodl.* 7, a. 1, 11 (A): "Et ideo propter complementum universi vel decorem non oportuit ponere Incarnationem."

ARGUMENT A

4.1 The perfection of the universe requires a person who cannot sin.

4.2 Only a person united to God cannot sin.

4.3 The perfection of the universe requires a person united to God.[31]

ARGUMENT B

4.4 The beauty of the universe requires everything be united into one.

4.5 Only the union of some creature with Creator would unite everything into one.

4.6 The beauty of the universe requires the union of some creature with the Creator.[32]

ARGUMENT C

4.7 It is necessary that everything in a genus reduce to some optimal in that genus.

4.8 A human body united to God is the optimal in the genus of body.

4.9 If there are bodies, there must be some human body united to God.

4.10 There are bodies.

4.11 There must be some human body united to God.[33]

Guerric's commitment to divine transcendence requires rebuttal for each of these arguments, which he supplies in paragraphs 15–20 of article one. Against (4.1), he argues that a creature who necessarily cannot sin (that is, by nature) is impossible. To be a spiritual crea-

---

31. *Quodl.* 7, a. 1, 4–5.

32. *Quodl.* 7, a. 1, 6. The argument in (A) is given two renditions, the first appealing to the unity of the universe, the latter to its beauty. To this is attached an argument that the creature united to Creator ought to be a human, since a human being is the microcosm of creation. *Quodl.* 7, a. 1, 7, gives a similar argument for the reduction of the multitude to some one from the premise "omnis multitudo ad unitatem reducitur."

33. *Quodl.* 7, a. 1, 8.

ture is to have free will, and therefore to be capable of sin by nature and confirmed to sinlessness only by grace.[34] Against (4.5), Guerric insists that unity in some creature is sufficient for the beauty of the universe. The unity of creation in a human being, who is the microcosm of creation, satisfies that requirement. The unity of some creature with God is owed to the power of love in the Creator and the creature's need for reparation, not to the beauty of the universe.[35] The third argument unravels along similar lines.[36]

By now, the point is clear: whatever argument is supplied for the fittingness of incarnation in a world without sin—and Guerric remains open to those fittingness arguments—the incarnation in our world cannot be necessitated by the reasons expressed in 4.1– 4.11. If such reasons necessitated the incarnation, then God would be bound to act necessarily for some created good, and therefore the domain of divine power would be restricted and divine transcendence depleted.

Manuscripts V and G intertwine these arguments with further arguments from Paul's Epistle to the Romans. Manuscript A, on the other hand, considers first and only the arguments above (paragraphs 1–20), before moving on to the arguments from Romans in paragraphs 21–24. But, before I consider those Pauline arguments, let us return to paragraph 11 and the second argument (along with the divine transcendence argument) that Guerric gives in support of his "probable opinion."

Guerric asks, "What gratitude do I owe someone for that which he necessarily had to do for me?"[37] Were God required to become

34. *Quodl.* 7, a. 1, 16 (VG): "Immo ad integritatem creaturarum est quod sit creatura spiritualis separata non confirmata per liberum arbitrium, confirmanda per gratiam. Unde ad integritatem universi exigebatur quod esset spiritualis creatura separata a corpore et spiritualis unita corpori et utraque habens liberum arbitrium, et ex eo (exigebatur) quod creatura vertibilis esset per naturam et comfirmanda per gratiam, et ita quod omnis posset peccare eo quod creatura de nihilo facta (est)." (A) puts it rather industriously: "Sed necessario non peccare: hoc non est de ratione creaturae."

35. *Quodl.* 7, a. 1, 17.

36. *Quodl.* 7, a. 1, 18.

37. *Quodl.* 7, a. 1, 11 (VG): "Quam enim gratiam debeo alicui de hoc quod necesse habet facere propter me?"

incarnate, it would detract from the gratuity of the incarnation. Necessary incarnation would be less worthy of our gratitude and therefore less attractive to the sinner. I will call this the spiritual attraction argument. Spiritually, the necessity of the incarnation for reasons other than the fall renders the incarnation less attractive to sinners than it would be otherwise, an implication Guerric calls "most unfitting (*magnum inconveniens*)."

The attractive power of the incarnation's incongruity is a constant theme in Guerric's Christology. In *Quodlibet* 5, pondering whether there was another way possible for Christ to liberate us, Guerric accepts Augustine's view that another way was possible but none was more fitting (*convenientior*).[38] Why? Because it is maximally fitting that enemies be attracted by the greatest beneficence.[39] In fact, Guerric is perfectly content with incongruity, so long as that incongruity is between the extent of divine grace and the degree of human fallenness. He straightforwardly admits that the humility of the incarnation is greater than the pride of Adam.[40] This incongruity is not problematic for Guerric, as it increases the spiritual attraction of the incarnation. Alternatively, necessary unitive and aesthetic goods, which require incarnation in sinless possible worlds, detract from the alluringly incongruous divine beneficence manifest in the incarnation of the Son in our fallen world.

Guerric does worry that his arguments imply that sin is the cause of the incarnation, which would have the negative implication that sin is most laudable.[41] But, he avers, sin is not the cause of the incarnation. The cause of so great a good as the incarnation is God's knowledge, capacity, and volition for it *for the sake of*

38. *Quodl.* 5, a. 1, 14.

39. *Quodl.* 5, a. 1, 14 (P): "Verum est quod dicit Augustinus quod 'alius modus fuit possibilis, sed nullus convenientior,' quia inimicus maxime convenienter attrahitur summo beneficio."

40. *Quodl.* 5, a. 1, 15.

41. While he makes no mention of it, Guerric's concern here recalls the "happy fault" arguments that arise later on as theologians of the thirteenth century increasingly turn to the *praechonium paschale* as an authoritative source for positions akin to Guerric's.

sin.[42] That is, the cause is most fundamentally a free divine volition, which wills the incarnation as a beneficent response to the
problem of sin.

Guerric's spiritual attraction argument introduces two issues
that will recur in the subsequent debates. First, Guerric introduces
into the debates an argument from piety: Which position attracts
the sinner to God? Which elicits the most gratitude? A transcen-
dent God, who is not bound by a creature, turns out to be the most
attractive God who elicits the most gratitude. A decrease of divine
beneficence, entailed by certain affirmative responses to the hypothetical question, issues in Guerric's strongest rejection: *magnum
inconveniens.* Second, Guerric raises the question of divine power,
capacity, and volition. Whereas Grosseteste sought reasons for the
incarnation in the perfections of the divine nature (e.g., goodness
and unity), Guerric turns to divine power.[43]

Guerric's Pauline arguments derive from Romans 1:4, "[Christ
Jesus] was predestined in power to be the Son of God," and the
Glossa ordinaria on Romans 5:19: "Another way of being saved is
impossible except by faith in the incarnation."[44] Romans 1:4 was
a standard text in the debates over Christ's predestination in the
thirteenth century, a topic that frequently followed questions on
the modal status and motive for the incarnation. Guerric applies,
for the first time, a distinction still made today, between a succession of (1) divine prevision of sin, and (2) the subsequent predestination of Christ for redemption. This sequence is commonly de-
nominated the supralapsarian position in Reformed scholasticism
and contemporary theology; it resolves both Romans 1:4 and the

---

42. *Quodl.* 7, a. 1, 13 (VG): "Unde ille solus laudandus est qui tantum bonum
scivit et potuit et voluit elicere de peccato."

43. As I will observe later, this commitment may not be entirely consistent with
the spiritual attraction argument, since that argument can be developed from the
divine attribute of beneficence to a necessary negative response to the hypothetical
question—a kind of inverted application of Grosseteste's divine attributes strategy.

44. *Glossa Ordinaria*, Patrologia Latina 114, ed. Jacques-Paul Migne (Paris: Garnier, 1852), 486.

Gloss on Romans 5:19 in support of Guerric's response to the hypothetical question: both texts concern humanity in the postlapsarian
state, subsequent to the prevision of sin.

Finally, Guerric's gloss of Pseudo-Augustine's argument—that
the perfection of humanity's exterior sense requires a sensible object—is similar to Guerric's gloss of Romans.[45] Pseudo-Augustine's
argument pertains only to the state of humanity after the fall.[46]
Manuscript *A* puts it more directly: the God-man is not necessary
for beatitude. Rather, "[humanity] would have been perfected otherwise if Adam had not fallen."[47]

Walter Principe observes that Guerric's arguments appear to
have impacted the Franciscan school more than his Dominican suc-
cessors, Albert and Thomas. Both Odo Rigaldi and Bonaventure
supply arguments from piety and spiritual attraction arguments
resembling Guerric's in *Quodlibet* 7, a. 1, 12.[48] As we will see momentarily, however, Albert takes seriously Guerric's spiritual attraction argument, and, more significantly, Albert advances Guerric's
stance on divine transcendence more rigorously and consistently
than Guerric himself. On this latter point, Thomas, while he favors the opposite opinion in response to the hypothetical question,
preserves the priority of divine transcendence, as did Guerric and
Albert.

45. N.b., Grosseteste considers the same argument from *De spiritu et anima* 9 at
DCL III.1.22. In *DCL*, the argument is given in support of Grosseteste's affirmative
response to the hypothetical question.

46. *Quodl.* 7, a. 1, 14 (VG): "Respondeo quod loquitur ibi Augustinus et omnes
tales secundum statum hominis post lapsum."

47. *Quodl.* 7, a. 1, 14 (A): "Nec oportuisset sic beatificari, sed aliter perficeretur
si non cecidisset."

48. Principe, "Guerric of Saint-Quentin, OP," 514–16. See also Bonaventure,
III *Sent.* d. 1, a. 2, q. 2 (III, 25): "Plus enim excitat devotionem animae fidelis, quod
Deus sit incarnatus ad delenda scelera sua quam propter consummanda opera in-
choata."

Albert the Great (d. 1280)

The successor of John of Saint-Giles, Guerric of Saint-Quentin was the second occupant of the Dominican Chair for Externs, which he held from 1233 to 1245. Guerric's successor, Albert the Great, held the chair until 1248, before passing it down to Elie Brunet, Thomas Aquinas's Master and predecessor.[49] Albert came to Paris in 1243 or 1244, if not earlier. Shortly thereafter, under the Regency of Guerric, Albert lectured on the *Sentences*.[50] By 1249, when at Cologne, he had completed his *ordinatio* of those lectures. His comments on the motive for the incarnation at *In Sententiarum* reflect the influence of Master Guerric on the young Albert.[51]

Albert raises the hypothetical question at *In Sententiarum* d. 20, a. 4.[52] Whereas the *Summa Halensis,* Aquinas's *Scriptum* and *Summa Theologiae,* and Bonaventure's *Commentarius* raise the hypothetical question in distinction one, on the incarnation, Albert locates his reflection in distinction twenty, on the passion. The most explicit justification he gives for his preferred affirmative response to the

49. James A. Weisheipl, "The Life and Works of St. Albert the Great," in *Albertus Magnus and the Sciences,* ed. James A. Weisheipl, 13–51, Studies and Texts 49 (Toronto: Pontifical Institute of Mediaeval Studies, 1980), 24. Note the discrepancy between these dates and those given in Weisheipl, *Friar Thomas D'Aquino,* 66–67. In the latter text, Weisheipl retains the designation of 1245 for Albert's installation as Regent Master, but concludes Guerric's regency in 1242. This is, likely, in imitation of Glorieux's dating; see Glorieux, *Répertoire des Maîtres.*

50. Weisheipl, "The Life and Works of St. Albert the Great," 23.

51. Principe suggests a lack of influence of Guerric's position on Albert, relative to Odo and Bonaventure. This is due to Odo and Bonaventure's explicit reference to Guerric's spiritual attraction argument. Admittedly, Albert does not reflect the clear debt as does Odo. Nevertheless, Albert reflects Guerric's first concern admirably—the "divine transcendence" argument—and it is possible that Albert's cryptic appeal to the *pietati fidei* reflects Guerric's spiritual concerns. Principe, "Guerric of Saint-Quentin." The most extended reflection on Albert on the motive for the incarnation that is available is by Donald Goergen, who considers Albert in connection to his student, Thomas; see Goergen, "Albert the Great and Thomas Aquinas on the Motive of the Incarnation," *The Thomist* 44, no. 4 (1980): 523–38.

52. Albert the Great, *Commentarii in III Sententiarum,* vol. 28, *Opera omnia,* ed. A. Borgnet (Paris: Vivès, 1894), d. 20, a. 4 (hereafter, *In Sententiarum*).

hypothetical question is that it is more concordant with the piety of the faithful (*pietati fidei*).

Albert's chief conviction is that his solution is uncertain. He presents no substantial defense of his preferred response. He calls his view opinion (*possum opinari*), and he consistently uses the language of "belief" (*credere*). Guerric rebutted some arguments for his own position, as in his gloss on Psalm 68:3. But Albert is most striking in that he rebuts *all* the arguments he supplies that support his own preferred response to the hypothetical question.

Albert recites and refutes four arguments in support of Guerric's preferred negative response to the hypothetical question. The first two arguments appeal to sacred hymnody: the first to the *Sequentiae* of Abbot Notker of St. Gall (Notker Balbulus), the second to the *praechonium paschale*.[53] The argument is the same; both hymns praise sin for its role in bringing about the incarnation. "O greatly blessed sin, by which nature is redeemed. God, who created all, is born of a woman." "O happy fault, that merits so great and excellent a redeemer."[54] Albert's summation of Notker's *Sequentia* makes his point concisely: "Sin is finished by this very thing, that God was made man."[55]

Albert glosses the hymns. The phrases "sin is blessed" and "sin is felicitous" are most inappropriate (*valde improprie*) unless they are distinguished. "Blessed and felicitous" are not said of sin in itself (*in se*), but as a consequence (*ex consequenti*). Sin is "blessed" or "happy" as a consequence of the redemptive work of Christ's labor, passion, and death. The significance of Albert's gloss is twofold. First, it clarifies the improper ascription of blessedness to sin *simpliciter*. Sin is only blessed or felicitous as a consequence of Christ's

---

53. Notker Balbulus, *Sequentiae*, c. 1, *Eia recolamus*, Patrologia Latina 131, ed. Jacques-Paul Migne (Paris: Garnier, 1853), 1005. Also available in Guido Maria Dreves, *Ein jahrtausend lateinischer hymnendichtung : Eine blütenlese aus den analecta hymnica mit literarhistorischen erläuterungen* (Leipzig: O.R. Reisland, 1909), 103–4.

54. *Commentarii in* III *Sententiarum* d. 20, a. 4 (28, 360): "O culpa nimium beata, qua redempta est natura. Deus qui creavit omnia, nascitur ex foemina." "O felix culpa, quae tantum ac talem meruit habere redemptorem."

55. *In Sententiarum* d. 20, a. 4 (28, 360): "Hoc ipso quod culpa peracta est, Deus homo factus est."

redemptive work. In itself, sin remains wretched. Second, the incarnation itself is independent of sin. That is, while sin may be a condition of the work of redemption by labor, passion, and death, it cannot be a condition of the incarnation.

Albert considers two further arguments for the negative response to the hypothetical question. The first recalls Guerric's spiritual attraction argument. Albert appeals to Romans 8:28: "Since we know for those who love God all things work together for the good, for those holy ones who are called according to His purpose," to which, Albert observes, the *Glossa ordinaria* adds the claim, "even sin." Given the extent of original sin, any good elicited from it must be similarly extensive, which "does not come about easily except by the incarnate Christ."[56] So, it seems, the incarnation is the means of God's working all things, including original sin, for the good.

To this argument, Albert objects that sin does not, in fact, cooperate in the good, "unless accidentally."[57] Intriguingly, Albert's clarification of his claim looks to be an appropriation of Guerric's spiritual attraction argument. Sin cooperates in the good *per accidens* in the way that anything lost, once found, issues in more fervent and expansive gratitude, greater humility, and circumspection.[58]

Albert's emphasis is distinguishable from Guerric's. For Guerric, the incongruity of divine beneficence in response to sin renders the incarnation for sin more attractive than if the incarnation was both for redemptive goods as well as some necessary good of creation (e.g., beauty or unity). Those necessary goods detract from the beneficence of the gift of redemptive incarnation. Albert, on the other hand, while noting that redemption from sin by the work, passion, and death of the incarnate Christ elicits greater grat-

---

56. *In Sententiarum* d. 20, a. 4 (28, 361): "Autem peccatum originale est quod omnes trahunt ab Adam: ergo aliquod bonum potest elicit ex illo: hoc autem non de facili invenitur nisi incarnato Christo."

57. *In Sententiarum* d. 20, a. 4 (28, 361): "Peccatum non cooperatur in bonum nisi per accidens."

58. *In Sententiarum* d. 20, a. 4 (28, 361): "Scilicet quia ferventior et magis gratus aliquis quandoque resurgit, quam cecidit, et magis efficitur humilis et cautus."

itude, does not take this to entail that the incarnation has sin for a condition. Only redemption through death has sin for a condition. Guerric's arguments, then, apply to the redemptive death of Christ; that God willed the incarnate Christ to redeem by death manifests a most attractive divine beneficence. But that argument need not apply to the incarnation itself.[59]

Albert gives a fourth and final argument for the negative response to the hypothetical question. The Son became incarnate because we needed a teacher, liberator, and redeemer. But there would be no need for such things without sin, and so God's charity would not have been so excited as it was as a result of the fall. To this argument, Albert simply objects that the incarnation accomplished multiple enticements for humanity, who now gaze upon the Son in flesh like their own. One hears resonance with Guerric's concerns over the spiritual attraction of the incarnation. In these two arguments, we can perceive the alternative spiritual emphases animating Albert's preference for the affirmative response to the hypothetical question. That response, Albert insists, is more concordant with the piety of the faithful.

Although Albert prefers the affirmative, he is more insistent that his position is mere opinion. No certainty is to be found. Just as he refutes the arguments for the position he opposes, Albert also refutes the arguments in favor of his preferred response to the hypothetical question in the *sed contra*. We need not consider all six arguments and objections in detail, but can simply focus on the key issues and most illuminating arguments and objections.

Grossetestean arguments populate the *sed contra*. Both the first and last argument cited by Albert recall Grosseteste's divine attributes strategy. In the former, Albert begins from the premise "The Good is diffusive of itself and being." Since the best possible diffusion of God in creation is by incarnation, and angelic incarnation is

---

59. *In Sententiarum* d. 20, a. 4 (28, 361): "Si autem et Christi incarnatio secuta est, nescio: sed hoc certum est, quod redemptio per mortem est secuta." Guerric's argument, then, is given an Anselmian revision; it works for the passion of Christ.

impossible, it must be that God becomes incarnate in human flesh. Similarly, in the final argument for the affirmative, Albert takes for his premise, "Maximal love communicates itself in a maximal way." The maximal way of loving is to unite something to oneself. If God loves humanity maximally, then God and a human will be united if possible. Neither argument is contingent upon sin, because they both derive from perfections of the divine nature: goodness and love.

For Albert, the former argument fails by neglecting an important qualification: the good will only share itself according to the capacity of that which receives it. But the capacity of human nature cannot merit a gift such as the incarnation. That is a gift of grace and therefore, by definition, unmerited by nature. Hence there is no obligation for God to be so diffused.[60] Albert's rebuttal to the latter argument is sparser, but relies upon a similar principle. The union of humanity with God in glorification is a sufficient expression of God's great love, and so there is no obligation to express that great love by way of incarnation. To drive the point home, he states: "It is not necessary that God show every kind of love."[61] As Goergen puts it, "Albert appeals to God's freedom."[62] Here we see Guerric's central commitment to divine transcendence repeated by Albert.

This transition from divine nature to divine freedom, and the correlated distinction between that which is *ex natura* and *ex gratia*, are developed throughout the remainder of Albert's objections to the arguments for the affirmative position. Those remaining arguments bear a marked resemblance to Grosseteste's created effects arguments. Albert isolates some need or capacity of creation, and argues from that need to the conclusion that God would satisfy it in a world without sin. Like Grosseteste, he attaches these arguments to

60. *In Sententiarum* d. 20, a. 4 (28, 362): "Bonum non diffundit se secundum ordinem naturae, sed capicitatem eorum qui capiunt illud: non autem cadit in capacitatem aliquam naturae vel meriti unio deitatis ad carnem."

61. *In Sententiarum* d. 20, a. 4 (28, 362): "Non oportuit Deum omnem modum amoris ostendere."

62. Goergen, "Albert the Great and Thomas Aquinas," 529–30.

attributes of the divine nature; God will fulfill any natural capacity in virtue of his goodness or justice.[63] And like Grosseteste, he considers fittingness arguments.[64] He even recites the same circular generation argument from Anselm's *CDH* II, 8, which Grosseteste developed in *DCL* III.2.5.[65] In rebuttal, Albert marks his critical divergence from Grosseteste's position, thereby displaying his debt to Guerric.

Albert's rebuttal of the circular generation argument is the first thorough and direct rebuttal of the axiological necessitarianism of Grosseteste's position. From Albert's day forward, we have no record of a theologian who accepts Grosseteste's arguments without significant revisions along Albertian lines.[66] Albert distinguishes between that which is from nature and that which is from grace. He contends that there is nothing problematic about God not creating a human from a woman alone, even if it would be optimal with regard to grace. "It is not necessary that God do each thing in the optimal manner which is possible for God to do *if he wills*, but it suffices that God does as he wills, so long as he does not negate anything to them of their nature."[67] The only condition for God producing a graced effect, such as the assumption of a human nature, is that God wills it. Notably, however, Albert retains this prin-

63. Albert variously expresses these premises: in the second and fifth arguments, he states "Cum Dei perfectus sunt opera"; in the third, "Nulla aptitude frustra sit creata a Deo."

64. *In Sententiarum* d. 20, a. 4 (28, 361): "Ergo similior Deo sit sine peccato, quam post peccatum, videtur etiam unibilior: et sic Deo magis conveniebat ei uniri, ut videtur."

65. Since there is a human from neither man nor woman (or, as Albert puts it, from the earth, "de terra"), a human from a man alone (Eve), and humans from a man and a woman, there ought to be a human born from a woman alone in order to perfect the order of generation.

66. That is, until recent proposals on the motive for the incarnation, which come perilously close to Grosseteste's axiological necessitarianism. At least, it is not apparent that Edwin Chr. van Driel or Marilyn McCord Adams have not redeveloped Grosseteste's strategies for today. See van Driel, *Incarnation Anyway*; Adams, *Christ and Horrors*; Adams, "Primacy of Christ."

67. *In Sententiarum* d. 20, a. 4 (28, 362): "Nec oportet hoc quod Deus faciat unumquodque in optimo esse quo posset ipsum facere si vellet: sed sufficit ut faciat sicut vult, dummodo nihil neget eis de naturalibus."

ciple alongside his theological application of Aristotle's principle "nature does nothing in vain." Albert is delicate; he does not refute the principle, but rather shows that no *natural* capacity is fulfilled by the incarnation, such that it could be said to be required by created nature. Neither does he allow any other divine attribute to entail the incarnation, as did Grosseteste.

Albert's other objections develop from this key insight. The aptitude of humanity for assumption by the Son of God is not from nature, but from grace, and therefore God is free to give it if God so wills.[68] Humanity is not made more unitable by sin, and so there is no natural necessity for incarnation. Sin simply renders humanity in need of a redeemer, and while that need provokes the mercy of God to become incarnate, the incarnation remains a free decision of divine mercy.

What about Albert's decision to locate the question at distinction twenty rather than distinction one? As noted above, Albert considers the motive for the incarnation amid questions on the possibility and appropriateness of the passion as the means for redemption. The articles preceding the hypothetical question ask whether it was possible for humanity to be redeemed in any way other than the passion. In those pages, Albert evaluates the argument of Anselm's *CDH.* Apparently, Albert thinks of the reason for the incarnation as a means to clarify the position developed in those articles on the kinds of possibilities open to God and how the fall determines the ways in which God acts to meet the need of fallen humanity.[69]

Later in life, Albert returns to the hypothetical question with a new set of arguments in article four of his *Quaestio de conceptione Christi,* composed sometime between 1260 and 1265.[70] Here he re-

---

68. *In Sententiarum* d. 20, a. 4 (28, 362): "Illa aptitudo non est ex natura, sed ex gratia electionis, ut supra saepe habitum est: quia homo ille ut in unitatem Filii Dei assumeretur, non meritis, vel natura, sed gratia habuit."

69. See, for instance, the discussion of divine power treated in *In Sententiarum* d. 20, a. 2.

70. Albert the Great, *Quaestio de conceptione Christi,* vol. 25, bk. 2, *Opera omnia,* ed. Henryk Anzulewicz, Wilhelm Kübel (Münster: Aschendorff, 1993), xliv.

peats his preference for the affirmative response to the hypothetical question. He also reiterates his judgment that certainty cannot be obtained. As he puts it, "nothing of the truth is possible to know" unless the answer were found in revelation.[71] The appeal to the piety of the faithful is lost, however. But Albert reasserts that it is not possible to know "from necessity," hence it is possible to hold multiple opinions.[72]

Notably, Albert considers 1 Timothy 1:15, "Jesus Christ came into this world to save sinners," which is Thomas Aquinas's favorite passage in support of the negative response to the hypothetical question.[73] Albert notes the *Gloss*: "There was no cause for the coming of Christ the Lord unless to save sinners."[74] However, Albert draws attention to the definite article *hunc* in the Vulgate: Jesus Christ came into *this* world, *in hunc mundum*. He proceeds to distinguish between the cause of Christ coming "into a world" (*in mundum*) and the cause of Christ's coming "into this world" (*in hunc mundum*).[75] In the case of this world (*in hunc mundum*), in which humanity is fallen, the cause of Christ's coming is the redemption from sin through passion and death. In the case of a world (*in mundum*), on the other hand, the cause of Christ's coming is "the love of humanity and the unitability of human nature."[76] Albert therefore distinguishes between two causes, or reasons: one for Christ coming as redeemer (*ut redemptor*), and the other for Christ com-

71. *Quaestio*, a. 4, p. 263, 34–37.

72. *Quaestio*, a. 4, p. 263, 53–55.

73. It is worth noting that, whereas Albert does not mention 1 Timothy 1:15 in his earlier *In Sententiarum*, he does consider it in this later work. This is interesting, given the importance his student, Thomas Aquinas, consistently gives to the text in his treatment of the motive for the incarnation. Perhaps the student and teacher disagreed in their application of the text to this disputed question.

74. *Quaestio*, a. 4, p. 263, 17–18: "Nulla causa veniendi fuit Christo domino nisi peccatores salvos facere."

75. *Quaestio*, a. 4, p. 263, 41–42: "Unde alia est causa veniendi in mundum et alia veniendi in hunc mundum."

76. *Quaestio*, a. 4, p. 263, 42–45: "Causa veniendi in mundum est amor hominum et unibilitas naturae humanae; sed causa veniendi in hunc mundum est redemptio a peccato per passionem et mortem."

ing simply (*simpliciter*). Albert glosses both 1 Timothy 1:15 and the *praechonium paschale*, "Our birth would be no gain, if we were not redeemed," a passage cited by Aquinas in support of the negative response in the same way: these reasons hold in this world, but not necessarily for every world.[77]

This raises a question: Is Albert's appeal to the "love of humanity and unitability of human nature" an acceptance of the earlier argument from divine attribute of love to the necessity of the greatest possible union? Does Albert accept Grosseteste's divine attributes strategy? Albert rearticulates the argument concisely:

Human nature in itself is unitable with divinity, but it is imperfect to be unitable while remaining un-united. But "the works of God are perfect," as it is said in Deuteronomy 32:4. Therefore that which is potentially unitable ought to be actually united, even if humanity had not sinned.[78]

His response is equally concise; the argument does not establish necessity. Why? The only way to know the truth about the hypothetical question is through revelation. Albert's emphasis on revelation in *Quaestio de conceptione Christi* marks a significant development in his thought. It is only possible to opine about the reason for the incarnation, because God is free to act as God wills with regard to that which is in the order of grace. In the order of grace, the reason for which God acts in any possible world is simply the wisdom of divine ordination, which exceeds our creaturely wisdom.[79] Thus,

---

77. *Quaestio*, a. 4, p. 263, 48–52: "Opus incarnationis ordinatur ad opus redemptionis in adventu in hunc mundum, sicut dicitur in benedictione cerei paschalis: 'Nihil nobis nasci profuit, nisi redimi profuisset'; sed si simpliciter venisset, non esset talis ordo." It is notable that, around the time that Aquinas is preparing the *tertia pars* of the *Summa Theologiae*, Albert reflects on the two central authorities that Thomas will cite in support of his preference for the negative response.

78. *Quaestio*, a. 4, p. 263, 25–29: "Humana natura de se est unibilis divinae; unibile autem non-unitum remanet imperfectum; sed 'dei opera perfecta sunt,' sicut dicitur Deut. XXXII (4); ergo unibile secundum potentiam oportuit uniri secundum actum, etiam si homo non peccasset."

79. This language, *sapientia ordinationem*, is also used by Albert in the *solutio* of *In Sententiarum* d. 20, a. 2, in a passage that suggests the relevance of the absolute-ordained power distinction to the discussion of the possibility of the incarnation.

to know the reason for God's acts of grace, we must be given access to that wise ordination through revelation. When we consider God's reason for the incarnation, which has not been explicitly revealed, our best answers are only probable. Thanks to those merely probable reasons, Albert continues to favor the positive response to the hypothetical question: if man had not sinned, Christ would have become incarnate.

Throughout his writings, Albert's insistence that answers to the hypothetical question are merely opinion is more fundamental than his preference for an affirmative response. In this, he shares much in common with his finest student, Thomas Aquinas, even while Thomas inclines toward the alternative response.

Thomas Aquinas (d. 1274)

No doubt, Thomas Aquinas is one of the most influential figures in the history of debates over the motive for the incarnation. To this day, it is common to describe the debate as one between the Thomists and the Scotists. As Gerhard Ludwig Müller writes, "medieval discussions [of the incarnation] centered on whether God had become human only because of the redemption [per the Thomists] or whether God would have done so regardless of human sin [per the Scotists]."[80] In the early decades of the twentieth century, there was no shortage of Thomists to defend the "Thomist" position against the "Scotists" or "Suarezians." Reginald Garrigou-Lagrange, in trenchant essays, such as *Motivum incarnationis fuit motivum misericordiae*, reflects the spirit of the early twentieth-century debates.[81]

---

80. Gerhard Ludwig Müller, "Incarnation," in *Handbook of Catholic Theology*, ed. Wolfgang Beinert and Francis Schussler Fiorenza, 377–80, (New York: Crossroad, 1995), 378.

81. Reginald Garrigou-Lagrange, "*Motivum incarnationis fuit motivum misericordiae*," *Angelicum* 7 (1930): 289–302. Garrigou devotes a remarkable amount of space to the question in *Christ the Savior: A Commentary on the Third Part of St. Thomas' Theological Summa*, trans. Dom Bede Rose (London: B. Herder Book, 1950), 76–104. In the

On the whole, however, the twentieth century was a time of waning interest in the motive for the incarnation. Whether from virtue or weariness, by the mid-twentieth century defenses of the "true Thomist position" of "one efficacious decree concerning the redemptive Incarnation in passible flesh," as Garrigou puts it, were difficult to find.[82] Increasingly rare are vigorous defenses of Thomism against the Scotists who, as Audet put it in 1962, "implicitly liquidate of the entire history of salvation in the Bible."[83] In spite of Audet's anxieties, Thomism in the latter half of the twentieth century became increasingly conciliatory. In fact, Frederick Christian Bauerschmidt detects a larger transition in Catholic theology toward Scotism:

> In the last century theology seems to be tilting in the Scotist direction; there seems to be a growing agreement that one ought to think of the Incarnation first in terms of perfecting creation for the glory of God rather than repairing it.[84]

Juniper Carol has produced a helpful, if subversive, collation of the history of debates over the motive for the incarnation.[85] From Carol's collation, and Bauerschmidt's observation, we can observe two developments in the twentieth-century considerations of the motive for the incarnation. First, Thomists became increasingly generous in their evaluation of Scotist reflections on the motive

---

1920s and 1930s, Garrigou was embroiled in a debate with Fr. Chrysostom, OFM, on the motive for the incarnation. See, for instance, "La redemption est-elle le motif de l'incarnation?" *La France Franciscain* 14 (1931): 113–67.

82. Garrigou, *Christ the Savior*, 104.

83. Th. A. Audet, OP, "Approches historiques de la Summa Theologiae," in *Etudes d'histoire litteraire et doctrinale*, Universite de Montreal publications de l'institut d'etudes medievales 17 (Montreal: J. Vrin, 1962), 28. Audet is cited in Carol, *Why Jesus Christ?* 104.

84. Frederick Christian Bauerschmidt, "Incarnation, Redemption, and the Character of God," 459. It should be noted that this way of characterizing things is rhetorically effective for Bauerschmidt's argument. Nevertheless, it is consistent with Carol's findings in *Why Jesus Christ?* Bauerschmidt gives a more concise and similar treatment of the question in *Thomas Aquinas: Faith, Reason, and Following Christ*, 183–86.

85. Carol, *Why Jesus Christ?*

for the incarnation.[86] Second, the twentieth century saw a dramatic increase in supporters of the Scotist position, often in light of its perceived Christocentrism.[87] Although it is difficult to say *why*, precisely, Catholic theology moved in this direction—Bauerschmidt suggests it was due to a "more general shift in Catholic theology toward a closer integration between the order of nature and the order of grace"—it will suffice for our purposes here to note simply *that* the shift transpired.[88]

The drift toward Scotus, or at least toward conciliatory evaluations of Scotus, leaves intact the characterization of the issue as one between "Thomists" and "Scotists." These two schools, it is presumed, divide along the lines demarcated by Thomas and Scotus themselves. One of the ironies of the piece by Bauerschmidt, which sketches an intriguing, informed, and novel modern Thomistic argument on the motive for the incarnation, is that it eventuates in the same narration of the thirteenth-century figures and their respective positions. Perhaps because he never investigates Scotus's own arguments, Bauerschmidt reinstitutes the rather thin claim that Scotus's approach is excessively hypothetical, and that only Thomas's solution preserves God's freedom by retaining a redemptive incarnation in a non-hypothetical world.[89]

Our focus remains on the thirteenth century, before there were Thomists and Scotists. Our focus on the thirteenth-century developments allows us to clarify the teaching of Thomas and Scotus in their theological context. By returning to the sources, I hope to extricate Thomas and Scotus from their reception as precursors of the schools of the Thomists and the Scotists.[90] While he does not manage to fully

86. Carol, *Why Jesus Christ?* 119.

87. Carol, *Why Jesus Christ?* 392. It should be noted that Carol, while presenting his final overview of the "embarrassingly numerous witnesses" who support the Scotist position in the twentieth century (which numbers 622), is admittedly loose in his ascription of the term "Scotistic."

88. Bauerschmidt, "Incarnation, Redemption, and the Character of God," 460.

89. See, in particular, Bauerschmidt's analysis of John Paul II in these terms in "Incarnation, Redemption, and the Character of God," 469–70.

90. To be clear, our aims for extrication in no way entail a condemnation of the

extricate his reading of Thomas from the Thomist-Scotist paradigm, Bauerschmidt makes considerable progress in doing so by his own return to the primary sources.[91] What follows is an extension of that project, which will both utilize the conceptual apparatus I have been assembling and ground Thomas and Scotus's teachings in the larger context of the debates of the thirteenth century.

The following section presents a historical overview of Thomas's various treatments of the motive for the incarnation. Thomas considers the topic explicitly on three occasions: in his *Scriptum super Sententiis* (*Scriptum*) III, in the *Summa Theologiae* (*ST*) III, and in his *Super Primam Epistolam ad Thimotheum lecturam*. Moreover, several of Thomas's central concepts and arguments on the motive for the incarnation in those texts also appear in the *Summa contra Gentiles* (*SCG*) and *De rationibus fidei*, during the middle period of Aquinas's work. Minor comments are also to be found in *De veritate*. With this in mind, the subsequent analysis is divided into three periods, distinguished by Thomas's primary *summae*: (1) the *Scriptum* period, (2) the *SCG* period, and (3) the *ST* period. By proceeding in this manner, we will be able to observe any developments in Aquinas's thought, and track the relation between Thomas's position on the motive for the incarnation and the positions developed by Guerric, Albert, and others.

Scriptum super Sententiis et cetera

Like Albert before him, Aquinas supplies several arguments for both responses to the hypothetical question in the *Scriptum*: seven for the affirmative and four for the negative. Unlike Albert, Thom-

---

issue as formulated between the schools of Thomas and Scotus over the centuries. Many novel, compelling, and singular contributions to the motive for the incarnation are developed by the Thomists and Scotists across the centuries. However, even for our understanding of that later history, it will be advantageous to disentangle the arguments of Thomas and Scotus themselves from the ensuing debates and later characterizations of the issues.

91. Bauerschmidt, "Incarnation, Redemption, and the Character of God," 465–68.

as only rebuts the arguments for the affirmative position. Nevertheless, the influence of Albert can be seen in Thomas's argument.

Aquinas makes three key assertions in the *responsio* of *Scriptum* III, d. 1, q. 1, a. 3, that summarize his early position. (1) The only way to know the will of God is for God to reveal it. Aquinas is clear, "the only one able to answer (the hypothetical question) truly is the one who was born and poured out (i.e., Christ), because he willed it."[92] Thus, the authority of Scripture and the holy expositors of Scripture are the only means of access we have to the motive for the incarnation. (2) The only cause given for the incarnation by those sacred authorities is redemption from sin.[93] Aquinas cites a chorus of authorities in the *sed contra,* including Augustine's comment on Matthew 18:2 and *Gloss* on 1 Timothy 1:15; Hebrews 2:14; and the *praechonium paschale.* (3) Both the negative and the positive responses to the hypothetical question can be held *probabiliter.* Thomas concludes the passage as follows:

> Since not only liberation from sin, but also the exaltation of human nature and consummation of the entire universe was accomplished by the incarnation of the Son of God, even if sin had not existed, for those reasons the incarnation would have been. This also can be sustained with probability.[94]

And so, while he favors the negative response to the hypothetical question, he does not "know truly" (*veritatem scire*), since truth can only be given by God. Rather, his answer is only "said with probability" (*probabiliter dicunt*). The positive response "can be sustained" as well, presumably with less probability in Thomas's estimation.[95]

---

92. *Scriptum* III, d. 1, q. 1, a. 3, *corpus*: "Hujus quaestionis veritatem solus ille scire potest qui natus et oblatus est, quia voluit."

93. *Scriptum* III, d. 1, q. 1, a. 3, *corpus*: "Et quia in canone Scripturae et dictis sanctorum expositorum, haec sola assignatur causa incarnationis, redemptio scilicet hominis a servitute peccati."

94. *Scriptum* III, d. 1, q. 1, a. 3, *corpus*: "Alii vero dicunt, quod cum per incarnationem Filii Dei non solum liberatio a peccato, sed etiam humanae naturae exaltatio, et totius universi consummatio facta sit; etiam peccato non existente, propter has causas incarnatio fuisset: et hoc etiam probabiliter sustineri potest."

95. Thomas's use of *probabiliter* in these passages of the *Scriptum* should not be taken in a particularly rigorous fashion. Thomas also says that both positions can

And he suggests the kinds of created effects that would explain an incarnation without a fall: the exaltation of human nature and the consummation of the entire universe.

Assertions (1) and (2) may appear inconsistent with the moderate, probabilistic cognitive attitude taken by Aquinas in (3). Greater clarity can be gained from the two preceding articles treating the possibility (a.1) and congruence (a.2) of the incarnation. Together with the third article on the hypothetical question, these articles present Aquinas's full position on the motive for the incarnation at the time of the *Scriptum*.[96] Articles one and two give Aquinas's response to the general question, while article three gives Aquinas's response to the hypothetical question.

Aquinas is explicit about his intentions when he states, in article two, that since it is impossible to demonstratively prove the incarnation, "it suffices to defend that it is not impossible for the incarnation to be, as was said in article one."[97] Sans demonstration, which is to say sans certainty, possibility is all that can be rationally defended. And, as article one argues, it ought be defended.

While article one defends the possibility of incarnation, article two aims "to show a certain congruence to the incarnation."[98] Thomas's arguments, however, all suppose the fall. Supposing the fall, congruence is manifest in three ways: from the plenitude of divine mercy, from the immobility of divine justice, and from the decorous order of divine wisdom.[99] Thomas proceeds to develop

---

be held *probabiliter* while preferring one position. The simplest explanation is that Thomas uses *probabiliter* with varied senses; *probabiliter* is less rigorously applied here than *convenientia* in the *ST*.

96. N.b., both articles three and four are extensions of the topic of article two on the congruence of the incarnation, insofar as the issue in article four on the time of the incarnation concerns the congruence (rather than necessity) of the time of the incarnation.

97. *Scriptum* III, d. 1, q. 1, a. 2, *corpus*: "Et ideo sufficit defendere quod non est impossibile incarnationem esse, quod in 1 art. ex parte dictum est."

98. *Scriptum* III, d. 1, q. 1, a. 2, *corpus*: "Ostendere aliquam congruentiam ad incarnationem, quod ad hunc articulum pertinet."

99. *Scriptum* III, d. 1, q. 1, a. 2, *corpus*: "Sciendum ergo, quod supposito lapsu humanae naturae, congruentia incarnationis apparet ex tribus: scilicet ex plenitudine

each of these themes, showing thereby that the mode of reparation chosen by God is the most fitting (*convenientissimum*). Thus, while no rational demonstration can be given because the incarnation proceeds from the divine will alone, possibility can be rationally defended and congruence can be shown. Notably, the arguments for congruence derive from the same divine attributes developed by Grosseteste: goodness (*summum bonum*), immutability and justice (*immutabilitate justitiae*), and decorous wisdom. Moreover, Aquinas utilizes comparative and superlative forms of *convenientia*, forms that Grosseteste used to develop demonstrations arriving at necessity. For Thomas, however, they simply arrive at congruity—congruity between divine attributes and contingent divine operations.

Most importantly, the goods specified in article two that render the incarnation congruous all have the fall as a necessary condition. It was congruent with divine goodness and mercy that God repair humanity, if humanity was capable of reparation subsequent to the fall. It was congruent with immutable divine justice for God not to leave human nature without satisfaction, so long as any means remained possible for satisfaction. Finally, it was congruent with divine wisdom that the most fitting way of reparation obtain, which, given humanity's current state of misery, is achieved by God's becoming visible and moving us to love God thereby. In all three cases Aquinas includes the fall as a condition, and so his congruent reasons in article two are consistent with his three assertions in article three.

The objections of article three bear this out. The third argument asserts that God, being infinitely powerful, wise, and good, would manifest those properties through created effects of infinite power, wisdom, and goodness, even if humanity had not sinned. The relevant effect is, of course, the hypostatic union. Thomas responds that these natural goods, which lack the fall as a necessary condition, are sufficient to account for the gracious gift of incar-

---

divinae misericordiae, et ex immobilitate justitiae ipsius, et ex decenti ordine sapientiae ejus."

nation. The idea is similar to Albert's distinction between goods of nature and of grace. Thomas argues that other created effects suffice to manifest God's infinite power, goodness, and wisdom; "The infinite power, wisdom, and goodness of God is manifest in the production of the smallest creatures."[100] That God gives bountifully according to God's infinite capacity sufficiently reveals the infinite power, wisdom, and goodness of God.[101] In this way, Thomas circumvents the Grossetestean deductions from divine perfections to the necessity of the incarnation.

Thomas further reinforces his position in article three by refuting a series of arguments for the affirmative response to the hypothetical question. Argument one, drawing upon the now familiar premise at Deut. 32:4 (the works of God are perfect), argues for the circular perfection of the universe by the conjoining of God (the first) and a human (the last). Aquinas responds that such a conjunction need not be of personal union, but can obtain by the ordination of the last to the first as an end. The fourth argument for the affirmative derives from divine love. Since God, who is infinite love, loves each thing as much as possible, God would not withhold any good (including incarnation) from a creature capable of receiving it. In response, Aquinas distinguishes two senses of "creaturely capacity": those said according to natural power (*secundum potentiam naturalem*) and those said according to the power of obedience (*secundum potentiam obedientiae*). The capacity for personal assumption belongs to the latter. Here, Thomas's famed obediential potency functions along the lines of Albert's *ex gratia*. God is under no obligation to fulfill such capacities, but only to fulfill them "if God wills."[102]

These arguments demonstrate Thomas's general strategy of response to Grosseteste's divine attributes strategy. It is notable, how-

100. *Scriptum* III, d. 1, q. 1, a. 3, *ad* 3: "Ad tertium dicendum, quod in productione minimae creaturae manifestatur potentia infinita et sapientia et bonitas Dei."

101. *Scriptum* III, d. 1, q. 1, a. 3, *ad* 3: "Sufficit ad ostendendam bonitatem infinitam hoc quod unicuique secundum suam capacitatem largitur."

102. The resonance with Albert's *ex natura* and *ex gratia* are apparent.

ever, that Aquinas considers an original divine attributes argument. Since "humility is perfect strength," and all perfections are attributed to God, then God will have the most perfect humility. But the most perfect humility will be manifest in subjection to or conjunction with that which is inferior. The former is impossible. Thus, a perfectly humble God would be conjoined to some creature, even if humanity had not fallen.

In response, Aquinas refutes the attribution of perfect humility to God. Not all creaturely virtues are pure perfections because God cannot fall under their proper concept. Pride is impossible for God, since it is impossible to overestimate God's own worth. So is humility, the virtue opposed to the vice.

Along with the aforementioned speculative arguments, Thomas considers two authoritative arguments for the affirmative response to the hypothetical question. The first is a standard authority: Pseudo-Augustine's assertion in De spiritu et anima that the incarnation was necessary to unify the beatific vision in a single object.[103] Thomas finds the argument unpersuasive. In the beatific vision, glory redounds from the intellectual soul into all the inferior parts of the soul and body. The second argument from authority derives from Bernard of Clairvaux's famous argument that Satan fell out of resentment over the Son's union with a human, as opposed to an angelic, nature. Bernard's statement implies Satan foresaw the incarnation before his own, primordial fall.[104] Here, Thomas posits that foreseeing the incarnation without knowledge of the fall does not entail that the fall was not a condition of the incarnation. Satan's foreknowledge could lack certain features of the incarnation, such as the conditional fall. After all, Satan could foresee incarnation without foreseeing his own fall.[105] In short, Aquinas finds no satisfactory argument from authority for the affirmative response in

---

103. *Scriptum* III, d. 1, q. 1, a. 3, *arg.* 6.

104. *Scriptum* III, d. 1, q. 1, a. 3, *arg.* 7.

105. Grosseteste, speaking of Adam's foreknowledge of the marriage of Christ and the church, takes the opposite view at *DCL* III.1.20.

the *Scriptum*; the only ones to which he gives assent are the speculative arguments deriving from the divine attributes specified in the *responsio* as possible "causes" of the incarnation in a world without sin.

Thomas's final argument for the affirmative response to the
hypothetical question recalls his central commitments concerning
the motive for the incarnation in the *Scriptum*. His rebuttal sounds
similar to Guerric's spiritual argument, and refers for the second
time in article three to the *praechonium paschale*. If the fall is a necessary condition of that which is "for the maximal dignity of human
nature" (i.e., assumption into personal union with the Son), then
humanity is rendered more suitable for assumption by the fall. But
this is absurd; sin cannot increase human dignity. Yet this seems to
be implied by the negative response to the hypothetical question.[106]

Thomas's response is very precise: "Non est inconveniens ut aliquod bonum Deus ex peccato eliciat quod sine peccato non fuisset." It is not unfitting. The negative response to the hypothetical
question is possible. Why? He cites, first, Romans 5:20: "Where sin
abounded, grace super-abounded." He continues:

> Hence it was not unfitting that God elicit some good from sin that would
> not have been without sin, as is seen in many virtues, such as patience, pen-
> itence, and the like. And therefore God is able to elicit even this great good
> from the sin of humanity, for the sake of which the Son of God became
> incarnate. On account of this Gregory said, "O happy fault, which merited
> so great and glorious a Redeemer."[107]

Thomas's argument recalls Guerric's appeal to spiritual attraction.
Importantly, even in his own rendition of Guerric, Thomas deli-
cately chooses his language. He connects fittingness with possibility
and divine power: "Deus potuit elicere." God is able to elicit these

---

106. *Scriptum* III, d. 1, q. 1, a. 3, *arg.* 5: "Non est credendum quod homo ex peccato aliquod commodum reportaverit. Sed maxima dignitas humana naturae est in
hoc quod assumpta est in unitatem personae divinae."

107. *Scriptum* III, d. 1, q. 1, a. 3, *ad* 5: "Ut patet in multis virtutibus, ut in patien-
tia, poenitentia, et hujusmodi. Et ita etiam ex peccato hominis hoc optimum bonum
Deus potuit elicere, ut Filius Dei incarnaretur. Propter quod dicit Gregorius: 'O Felix
culpa, quae talem ac tantum meruit habere Redemptorem.'"

goods from the sin of humanity, although there is no necessity to do so. In this way, Thomas, like Guerric and Albert before him, retains the commitment that any response to the hypothetical question can only be held *probabiliter*.

The *Scriptum*, viewed in light of Albert and Guerric, is notable for its interest in the kinds of arguments supplied for both conclusions. An important feature of Thomas's mature position, its emphasis upon arguments from revelation and attention to classes of arguments (from authority and from reason), is already reflected in this early text. Indeed, distinctions as to the quantity and relative weight of different kinds of arguments characterize Thomas's generation of debates over the motive for the incarnation.

We said earlier that Thomas is convinced that authority favors the negative response to the hypothetical question. However, in keeping with his conclusion that any response can be held *probabiliter*, he concludes his treatment of the hypothetical question in the *Scriptum* with a gloss on his own preferred authorities. Not only does Thomas assert the possibility of the alternative conclusion, but he also provides a means of rebuttal against his own arguments from authority:

It could be responded according to another opinion, that these authorities (cited in support of my position) are said in reference to the coming in passible flesh for the sake of redemption—for redemption would not have been unless it were preceded by servitude to sin—and not the coming in the flesh simply.[108]

The paragraph presents text-critical problems. There appear to be two recensions of Book 3, d. 1, one including the paragraph, the other lacking it. The latter recension, which lacks the paragraph, comes from a fragment found in *Vat. Lat. 9851*. It was most certainly authorized by Thomas himself; his handwriting is found in

---

108. *Scriptum* III, d. 1, q. 1, a. 3, *ad sed contra*: "Ad ea vero quae in contrarium objiciuntur, potest responderi secundum aliam opinionem, quod auctoritates illae loquuntur de adventu in carnem passibilem ad redimendum—redemptio enim non fuisset nisi servitus peccati praecessisset—et non de adventu in carnem simpliciter."

the margins. It is unclear whether the first recension was authorized, but it includes the full text of Book III, d. 1, and serves as the basis for the Parma edition.[109] By the time of John Capreolus, the paragraph was accepted as Thomas's teaching; Capreolus, after all, deems the argument worthy of rebuttal.[110] Moreover, the paragraph is very similar to Bonaventure's description of "a certain opinion held by some of the Masters."[111]

The most striking feature of the paragraph, a feature counting against the likelihood that the paragraph was Thomas's own teaching, is the mention of Christ's possible coming *in carnem passibilem*—in passible flesh. Until the mid-twentieth century, Scotists were vigilant in developing and defending John Duns Scotus's famous speculation of an incarnation in impassible flesh in worlds without fall.[112] Moreover, Thomas makes no mention of the possibility for incarnation in passible flesh in later treatments of the question. This might suggest that the paragraph is a later addition, added by theologians after Thomas's treatment began to be read in light of Scotus's arguments. However, Thomas's contemporary, Bonaventure, who lectured on the *Sentences* in close proximity to Thomas, mentions the same position. Bonaventure speaks of two opinions on the "chief reason for the incarnation."[113] The first opinion, which entails an affirmative response to the hypothetical question, distinguishes between two ways of speaking of the flesh

109. For a full treatment of these issues, see the commentary of P. M. Gils in "Textes inédits de St. Thomas. Les premières rédactions du Scriptum super Tertio Sententiarum," *Revue des sciences philosophiques et théologiques* 45 (1961), 201–28; "S. Thomas écrivain," vol. 50, *Opera omnia iussu Leonis XIII*, 173–209 (Rome: Cerf, 1992).

110. John Capreolus, *Defensiones theologiae Divi Thomae Aquinatis*, ed. C. Paban and T. Pègues, vol. 5 (Tours: Alfred Cattier, 1904), III, d. 1, q. 1, a. 3, *ad* 1.

111. III *Sent.* d. 1, a. 2, q. 3, *respondeo.*

112. While recent Scotists downplay this part of the Scotist tradition, Trent Pomplun has demonstrated and defended its historic importance to Scotism; "The Immaculate World: Predestination and Passibility in Contemporary Scotism," *Modern Theology* 30, no. 4 (2014): 525–51.

113. III *Sent.* d. 1, a. 2, q. 2 (III, 21): "Quae fuerit incarnationis ratio praecipua." Bonaventure does not ask the hypothetical question directly, but focuses upon the primacy question and priority (*praecipua*) among reasons for the incarnation.

assumed in the incarnation: (1) with respect to substance, and (2) with respect to the defect of passibility.[114] This line of reasoning, while lacking the explicit reference to the passible flesh in Bonaventure and Aquinas, is suggested by many prior theologians.[115] Recall Robert Grosseteste's analysis of "the suffering Godman justifies fallen humanity."[116] Grosseteste aligns "fallen" with "suffering," implying that the humanity would be of a kind that does not suffer. As we will see in the next chapter, Odo Rigaldi also alludes to the connection between Christ's passible flesh and incarnation in a fallen world.[117] In light of the evidence, we can say with some confidence that Scotus received the idea of impassible flesh from prior Masters. It also seems clear that speculation on Christ's impassible flesh was circulating by the time of Thomas's *Scriptum*. The paragraph seems therefore possibly authentic to St. Thomas.

Even if the final paragraph is not Thomas's authorized teaching in the *Scriptum*, it was certainly received as such. John Capreolus, for instance, took it to be Thomas's early teaching, even if Capreolus found the overall position of the *Scriptum* presumptuous and happily rejected in the *ST*.[118] And we can see why it was received as Thomas's teaching; the paragraph fits nicely with Thomas's central commitments in the *Scriptum*.

Another early text is consistent with Aquinas's position on the

114. III *Sent.* d. 1, a. 2, q. 2, *respondeo* (III, 23): "Est enim incarnatio carnis assumtio; de carne autem assumta est loqui dupliciter: aut quantum ad *substantiam*, aut quantum ad *defectum passibilitatis.*" While the sentence has textual variants, they are additions; some codices and the Vatican edition add "*et mortalitatis*" (and mortality) to the end of the sentence. The reference to passibility is included in all.

115. Trent Pomplun nicely cites the early and most suggestive instances: "The Immaculate World," 530.

116. *DCL* III.1, 11–12.

117. Johannes Bissen, "De motivo incarnationis," *Antonianum* 7 (1932): 336: "Illi autem qui volunt dicere quod fuisset unitus creaturae, dicunt quod nihilominus debemus ei gratiarum actiones, quia tunc assumpsisset naturam passibilem et mortalem, sicut fecit post peccatum; et ideo nihilominus tenetur ad gratiarum actiones, sed non tamen ad tot." This passage will be treated at length in the subsequent chapter.

118. See note 110 above.

hypothetical question in the *Scriptum*. Thomas concludes an early set of disputed questions (1256–1259), entitled *De veritate*, with a question (question twenty-nine) in eight articles on the grace of Christ.[119] In the fourth article, Aquinas asks whether the grace of headship belongs to Christ according to his human nature.[120] The fifth difficulty raises an objection. Both good angels and humans comprise the one church. But Christ in his human nature is not head of the good angels who did not sin, since they are not conformed to him naturally. Thus, it seems that Christ's human nature is not necessary for his headship. Thomas replies that Christ is the head of the good angels both in his divine and human nature, appealing to Pseudo-Dionysius's *De Divinis nominibus*. But angels and humans are distinct. Angels do not share a conformity of nature with Christ, and so angels bear a different relation to Christ's humanity than do humans. Thus:

> [The incarnation] was principally for the liberation of humanity from sin, and so the humanity of Christ is ordained to the influence which it has upon humans, as the end intended; but it flows to angels not as the end of the incarnation, but as a consequence of the incarnation.[121]

Even while Thomas argues that Christ's humanity is the cause of grace for the whole church, much as did Grosseteste at *DCL* III.1.18, he nevertheless retains his commitment to the negative response to the hypothetical question; the incarnation was principally for the

119. Thomas Aquinas, *Quaestiones disputatae de veritate*, vol. 22, bk. 3/1, *Opera omnia iussu Leonis XIII P.M. edita* (Rome: Typographia Polyglotta, 1973). For background and dating, see Jean-Pierre Torrell, *L'initiation à Saint Thomas d'Aquin: Sa personne et son oeuvre* (Fribourg: Editiones Universitaires de Fribourg, 1993); *The Person and His Work*, vol. 1, *Saint Thomas Aquinas*, trans. Robert Royal (Washington, D.C.: The Catholic University of America Press, 2005), 59–67.

120. Torrell notes that, in this and the following article, Aquinas already shows signs of development from the *Scriptum* in terms of the kind of causality exercised by Christ-the-head in all grace. See *Saint Thomas*, 1:66–67.

121. *De veritate*, q. 29, a. 4, *ad* 5: "Quae quidem principaliter facta est propter hominum liberationem a peccato; et sic humanitas Christi ordinatur ad influentiam quam facit in homines, sicut ad finem intentum; influxus autem in Angelos non est ut finis incarnationis, sed ut incarnationem consequens."

liberation from sin. Here he is perfectly consistent with the *Scriptum*.

To sum up Aquinas's early phase, he is clear that no rational demonstration can be given in response to the hypothetical question. Here he follows his teacher Albert. Only God can reveal that which flows from the divine will, and the authoritative evidence is entirely on the side of the negative response to the hypothetical question. Rationally, we can (1) defend the possibility of incarnation, and (2) observe certain "congruences" in light of the fact of the incarnation. These congruences connect divine attributes to the contingent divine operation of incarnation. But he cuts off any and all deductions from divine attributes to the incarnation, Grossetestean or otherwise. Moreover, it should be noted that Thomas, very carefully, only supplies speculative arguments for the "congruity" of the negative response. He leaves open the possibility (although he terms it probability) for an affirmative response in the *responsio*, speculating as to possible reasons for which God *could* become incarnate without sin. But the comment, viewed in context, is less a concession to the affirmative position and more an elaboration of his earlier assertion that no rational demonstration can be given. Nowhere does he refer to the affirmative response as congruous or fitting. The closest he comes, apart from the *probabiliter* of the *responsio*, is in the final comment of the *Scriptum*, the authenticity of which, if possible, is not certain.

Summa contra Gentiles et cetera

Book IV of the *Summa contra Gentiles* (*SCG*) was completed sometime between 1263 and 1267.[122] The *De rationibus fidei ad Cantorem Antiochenum*, which draws frequently upon the *SCG*, is dated slightly after 1265.[123] There remains much debate as to the occasion and audience of the *SCG*.[124] For our purposes, the distinc-

---

122. Torrell, *Saint Thomas*, 1:102.
123. Torrell, *Saint Thomas*, 1:125.
124. The classic debate centers around alternative interpretations of the *SCG*

tion in the opening chapters of the *SCG* is immediately relevant, wherein Thomas speaks of the "twofold truth of divine things." For the first set of truths, "the investigation of reason is competent to reach [it]." For the second, it is not; such reasoning exceeds its power.[125] The former is approached "through demonstrative reasons, by which the adversary may be convinced." The latter, however, cannot attain to convincing, rational demonstration. Rather, "[our adversary's] arguments, which are against the truth, ought be resolved."[126] The discussion of the incarnation in Book IV falls under this latter heading. Since demonstrative reasons for the incarnation cannot be given, defense of the incarnation's possibility must be pursued.[127] Moreover, Thomas writes:

> But the only way of convincing the adversary, who is against these truths, is from the authority of Scripture divinely confirmed by miracles. For those things which are beyond human reason, we will not believe unless they are revealed by God. Nevertheless, some probable reasons should be brought forth in order to make manifest truths of this kind.[128]

This second strategy, aimed at the second class of truths, delivers what Thomas calls "probable reasons."[129]

---

developed by Thomas Hibbs and Norman Kretzmann in Hibbs, *Dialectic and Narrative in Aquinas: An Interpretation of the* Summa Contra Gentiles (Notre Dame, Ind.: University of Notre Dame Press, 1995); Kretzmann, *The Metaphysics of Theism: Aquinas's Natural Theology in* Summa Contra Gentiles *I* (Oxford: Oxford University Press, 1997).

125. Thomas Aquinas, *Summa contra Gentiles*, vols. 13–15, *Opera omnia iussu Leonis XII P.M. edita* (Rome: Typographia Polyglotta, 1918–30), I, 9.1: "Ex praemissis igitur evidenter apparet sapientis intentionem circa duplicem veritatem divinorum debere versari, et circa errores contrarios destruendos: ad quarum unam investigatio rationis pertingere potest, alia vero omnem rationis excedit industriam."

126. *SCG* I, 9.2: "Sed quia tales rationes ad secundam veritatem haberi non possunt, non debet esse ad hoc intentio ut adversarius rationibus convincatur: sed ut eius rationes, quas contra veritatem habet, solvantur."

127. *SCG* I, 9.3.

128. *SCG* I, 9.3–4: "Singularis vero modus convincendi adversarium contra huiusmodi veritatem est ex auctoritate Scripturae divinitus confirmata miraculis: quae enim supra rationem humanam sunt, non credimus nisi Deo revelante. Sunt tamen ad huiusmodi veritatem manifestandam rationes aliquae verisimiles inducendae."

129. *SCG* I, 9.5.

This twofold distinction recalls Thomas's earlier treatment of the motive for the incarnation in the *Scriptum*. Once again Thomas rejects the possibility of rational demonstration for the motive for the incarnation. As we will see, he maintains this position in the *ST*. It is therefore unsurprising that Thomas locates his treatment of the fittingness of the incarnation under the second class of truths, those things that surpass reason such that only likely arguments for the training of those who have faith can be given.

Thomas marks a similar distinction in chapter two of *De rationibus fidei*. Here he urges that in disputations "over the articles of faith" the Christian should not attempt to prove faith by rational necessity because faith is sublime. The truths of faith exceed the grasp of human and angelic minds. But any accusations of falsity must be met: "It is not possible to disprove the truth of faith by necessary reasons."[130] In short, no necessary reasons can be given for or against the truths of faith. And so, *De rationibus fidei* and *SCG* do not seek to demonstrate the truths of faith, but rather to defend their possibility.

Thomas does not treat the hypothetical question in *SCG*. He does, however, consider the fittingness (convenientia) of the incarnation in *SCG* IV, 53–55. Several of his *convenientia* arguments could easily support the affirmative response to the hypothetical question; only two of the eight arguments recited in *SCG* IV, 54, include any reference to sin. Rather, his chief focus is on the manner in which the incarnation provides the most efficacious help to humans striving for beatitude.[131] Incarnation stirs up hope for beatitude.[132] It removes obstacles to beatitude, such as doubt as to our worthiness.[133] The incarnation makes possible God's instruction

---

130. Thomas Aquinas, *De rationibus fidei ad Cantorem Antiochenum*, vol. 40, *Opera omnia iussu Leonis XIII P.M. edita* (Rome: Typographia Polyglotta, 1968), ch. 2.

131. *SCG* IV, 54.2: "Primum igitur hoc considerandum est, quod incarnatio Dei efficacissimum fuit auxilium homini ad beatitudinem tendenti."

132. *SCG* IV, 54.2.

133. *SCG* IV, 54.3.

of humanity, which gives certainty to faith.[134] It induces to divine love, garners deeper friendship with God, and exemplifies the life of virtue.[135] Finally, Aquinas supplies two fittingness arguments for the incarnation, which both have the fall as a necessary condition. Again, for the sake of beatitude, and now in light of the problem of sin, the incarnation is fitting both for the remission of sin and for the certitude of that remission of sin.[136] Moreover, Thomas recites the argument from satisfaction in Anselm's *CDH*.[137]

Are these arguments from *SCG* not *convenientia* arguments for goods independent of the fall? Could some of these arguments be read as variations on Grosseteste's created goods strategy? The parallel treatment of the same arguments in *De rationibus fidei* indicates otherwise. In the *SCG*, Thomas began his discussion of the fittingness of the incarnation with the concept of beatitude, a sensible strategy since he had already established the need for and clarified the concept of beatitude in *SCG* III, 26–63.

De rationibus fidei 5, on the other hand, moves narratively through various reasons for the incarnation, or "causes," as Thomas puts it here. The arguments of *SCG* IV, 54, are reorganized in *De rationibus fidei* according to salvation history. Following John 1, Thomas begins from the insight that the Son, the Word, is that through which everything is made. Since that through which things are made should be that by which things are repaired, creation should be repaired by the Son.[138] Aquinas then supplies several reasons for why the creature through whom the repair ought to come should be (1) an intellectual creature, and (2) not an angel. All of these reasons presuppose the fall because they concern the reparation worked by the Son.

---

134. *SCG* IV, 54.4.
135. *SCG* IV, 54.5–7.
136. *SCG* IV, 54.8.
137. *SCG* IV, 54.9.
138. *De rationibus fidei* 5: "Unaquaeque autem res per eadem fit et reparatur: si enim domus collapsa fuerit, per formam artis reparatur, per quam a principio condita fuit."

Thomas supplies another premise: "The way of reparation ought to be fitting with the nature being repaired, and the sickness."[139] He gives the same description of sickness and reparation as in his discussion of beatitude in *SCG* IV: our sickness is a perversion of will and our reparation is the call back to the love of God above all others. There is no more powerful means for this reparation, Thomas argues, than by the incarnation of the Son of God. At this point, the series of arguments in *SCG* IV, 54, is succinctly rehearsed. Aquinas is clear, in *De rationibus fidei*, that all of these arguments are ordered to the reparation of fallen humanity so that the sickness deriving from the fall might be repaired and beatitude gained. Thus, all the goods specified in *SCG* IV, 54, can be rendered consistent with his earlier negative response to the hypothetical question in the *Scriptum*.

Summa Theologiae

Among Thomas's texts on the motive for the incarnation, the *Summa Theologiae* has been commented upon most frequently.[140] Capreolus is quite insistent that only the *ST* III, q. 1, a. 3, reflects Thomas's mature position. Moreover, Capreolus insists that in the *ST* Thomas casts off the "presumptuousness" of the *Scriptum*, where he permitted probable arguments for the affirmative response.[141] The *ST*, on the other hand, delivers Thomas's mature, unequivocal, and pious defense of the negative response.

However, Thomas's response to the hypothetical question in the *ST* is remarkably consistent with his earlier views. No doubt, there is development. More consistently than before, he employs the category of *convenientia*. This development is apparent by comparison

---

139. *De rationibus fidei* 5: "Modus autem reparationis talis esse debuit qui et naturae reparandae conveniret, et morbo."

140. While there is a comment in the commentary on 1 Timothy 1:15, it is substantially reproduced in the *ST*. For the sake of brevity, I will focus on the latter, more substantial argument of the *ST*.

141. John Capreolus, *Defensiones* III, d. 1, q. 1, a. 3, *ad* 1.

of the sequence of questions considered in the opening articles of the *Scriptum* III, d. 1, q. 1, and *ST* III, q. 1. In the *Scriptum*, Thomas inquired whether the incarnation was possible (a. 1) and whether it was congruous (a. 2) before taking up the hypothetical question. In the *ST*, he asks, first, whether it was fitting (*convenientia*) for God to become incarnate, and second, whether it was necessary for the reparation of human nature. The third articles of both texts raise the hypothetical question.

Statistical analysis shows both (1) a general increase in the language of *convenientia* over the course of Thomas's career, and (2) that incarnation is a high point of *convenientia* speculation.[142] In Thomas's mature theology, *convenientia* is a weak form of necessity, and occupies a space between the possible and the necessary, much as *congruum* or *probabile* did in the *Scriptum*.[143] Early in the *tertia pars*, Thomas says that something can be said to be necessary for an end in two ways: (1) when the end cannot be without that thing, and (2) when the end is better and more fittingly (*melius et convenientius*) attained thereby.[144]

Aquinas, in *ST* III, q. 1, a. 2, supplies a list of goods achieved

142. Aidan Nichols, *Redeeming Beauty: Soundings in Sacral Aesthetics*, Ashgate Studies in Theology, Imagination, and the Arts (Burlington, Vt.: Ashgate, 2007), 15.

143. Narcisse makes this point, albeit somewhat idiosyncratically, when he states, "L'argument de convenance apparait essentiellement comme la garantie du medium entre le 'Possible Probable' et le 'Realise Necessaire.' Cette garantie, celle du propositum theologique, touche d'abord le processus rationis dans son ensemble, rendant intrinseque l'argument d'autorite dans sa vigueur speculative." Gilbert Narcisse, *Les raisons de Dieu: Argument de convenance et esthetique theologique selon Saint Thomas d'Aquin et Hans Urs von Balthasar* (Fribourg: Editions universitaires, 1997), 147. Thomas actually prefers to speak of *convenientia* as a kind of necessity, as in *ST* III, q. 46, a. 1, when he distinguishes between necessity of that which cannot be otherwise on account of its nature and that which is necessary from something exterior, such as for the convenience of some particular end. In light of Thomas's preference to think of *convenientia* as a form of necessity, scholars have sometimes distinguished between strong and weak necessity in Thomas, with *convenientia* serving as an instance of the latter. A very helpful example of this distinction is given in Barnes, "Necessary, Fitting, or Possible," 670–74.

144. In illustration of the second kind of necessity: an airplane is not the necessary means for travel to upstate New York from Texas; however, it is a more convenient means than driving, walking, or crawling. See *ST* III, q. 1, a. 2, *corpus*.

by the incarnation, many of which would seem to obtain in possible worlds without sin. Thomas supplies five goods "for the promotion of humanity in the good," as well as five goods "useful for our removal from evil." Finally, he asserts these goods are in no way exhaustive: "But there are many more advantages which follow [from the incarnation], beyond the comprehension of human understanding."[145] Does Aquinas undermine his subsequent argument, in article three, for the negative response to the hypothetical question? He does not. Recall that Thomas supplied a similar set of goods (for faith, hope, love, providing an exemplar, and stirring up virtue) in his middle phase, both in the *SCG* and *De rationibus fidei*. In that period, Thomas thought of these goods as subsequent to the fall. Or, in the language of *ST*, they are goods for the furtherance in good after the fall and for the reparation of evil from the fall. As Bauerschmidt points out, this pairing is deeply ingrained in Thomas's soteriology:

[The incarnation] fits with the end of human salvation by accomplishing both the union of human beings with God and the forgiveness of sins, necessitated by the Fall. These two effects of the incarnation form for Thomas a fundamental structure within which to think about God's saving activity: God is always perfecting and repairing created nature.[146]

So, the second article's fitting reasons for the incarnation, "for the furtherance in good," should be understood soteriologically. When Thomas addresses the hypothetical question in the third article, he considers whether the second article's arguments for the furtherance in good warrant an affirmative response to the hypothetical question. His response confirms this reading of article two. All of those goods specified are conditional upon the fall. If Adam

145. *ST* III, q. 1, a. 2, *corpus*: "Sunt autem et aliae plurimae utilitates quae consecutae sunt, supra comprehensionem sensus humani."

146. Bauerschmidt, *Thomas Aquinas*, 183. Bauerschmidt draws this insight from Romanus Cessario, *The Godly Image: Christ and Salvation in Catholic Thought from St. Anselm to Aquinas*, Studies in Historical Theology 6 (Petersham, Mass.: St. Bede's Publications, 1990).

had not fallen, "he would have been filled with the light of divine wisdom, and perfected by God in the righteousness of justice in order to know everything necessary (for beatitude)."[147] So the set of effects for the furtherance in good are likewise conditional upon the fall.

Article one, on the other hand, defends the fittingness (*convenientia*) of the incarnation with what appear to be several Grossetestean divine attributes arguments. That is, Thomas's "fitting" arguments proceed from divine attributes. Citing John Damascene in the *sed contra* of article one, Thomas argues that the goodness, wisdom, justice, and power of God make fitting the incarnation. In this vein he asserts that "for each thing, that is fitting (*conveniens*) which agrees with it according to the concept of its proper nature, just as for humanity it is fitting to reason because this agrees with humanity insofar as it is rational according to nature."[148] Aquinas then cites Pseudo-Dionysius's dictum from *De Divinis nominibus*: "It belongs to the concept (*rationem*) of the good to communicate itself to another."[149] Hence, he argues, it pertains to the greatest good to communicate itself in the greatest way. This is actualized by the Son taking a human nature into a unity of person "from three, Word, spirit, and flesh," according to Augustine.[150] Interestingly, to this point in the debates the Dionysian dictum has always been supplied in support of the Grossetestean arguments for the affirmative response![151] Howev-

147. *ST* III, q. 1, a. 3, *ad* 1.

148. *ST* III, q. 1, a. 1, *corpus*: "Respondeo dicendum quod unicuique rei conveniens est illud quod competit sibi secundum rationem propriae naturae, sicut homini conveniens est ratiocinari quia hoc convenit sibi inquantum est rationalis secundum suam naturam."

149. *ST* III, q. 1, a. 1, *corpus*.

150. *De Trinitate* 13.

151. Intriguing also are the parallels between the citation of Augustine and the argument from the *Summa Halensis* for the affirmative response to the hypothetical question; since God's power is manifest in the existence of three persons in one nature (Trinity) and three persons in three natures (three rational creatures), it ought to be that God's omnipotence manifest itself in one person in three natures, as it is in virtue of the incarnation that the Son is "divinity, soul, and body." We will encounter this argument in the subsequent chapter.

er, for Thomas these arguments pertain only to the fittingness of the incarnation. And whatever fittingness arguments for the incarnation amount to, they do not persuade Thomas to divert from his commitment to the negative response to the hypothetical question. Before he responds to the hypothetical question in article three, Thomas has already commenced a radical modal innovation in his relocation of the Grossetestean arguments into the domain of *convenientia*.

We have already encountered three of Thomas's objections in article three, which treats the hypothetical question. Like Guerric, in his third objection Thomas considers an argument from predestination based on Romans 1:14. Thomas responds that predestination presupposes foreknowledge, in this case foreknowledge of sin. Like Grosseteste, his fourth objection reflects upon Adam's prevision of Christ's marriage to the church from Ephesians 2. Here Thomas contends that nothing prevents the revelation of an effect to someone without the revelation of the cause. As in the *Scriptum*, Thomas's second objection considers the speculative argument that divine omnipotence must reveal itself in an infinite effect. In the *ST*, he responds that divine omnipotence is sufficiently revealed, not in the creation of the most minute creature as in the *Scriptum*, but in creation ex nihilo.

The third objection of article three argues that since God would not withhold from human nature any good of which it is capable, and since human nature is capable of incarnation in a possible world without a fall, God would become incarnate even if Adam had not sinned. Here, in succinct form, is Grosseteste's created goods strategy. Aquinas's response distinguishes between two kinds of capacity: (1) one concerning the order of natural power, and (2) another concerning the ordination of divine power.[152] The former power (*potentia*) is always fulfilled by God, "who gives to each thing according to their natural capacity." The latter is not. "Otherwise, God would not be able to do other than he has done in

---

152. The distinction is functionally analogous to Albert's distinction between that which is from nature and that which is from grace.

creatures."[153] Like Peter Lombard, Aquinas holds that divine power extends beyond the divine will; *potuit, non voluit*. Interestingly, Thomas apparently takes it that his distinction between two kinds of capacity renders it possible for God to raise human nature to something greater after sin than human nature would be elevated to apart from sin. So, he concludes the *ad* 3 with citations from the *praechonium paschale* and Romans 5:20. It is possible that Thomas has in mind the spiritual attraction argument of Guerric, which he earlier produced in the *Scriptum* in connection with Romans 5:20 and the *praechonium paschale*.

Thomas's treatment of the motive for the incarnation in the *ST* III is perfectly consistent with his earlier writings.[154] In the *sed contra* of *ST* III, q. 1, a. 3, Thomas appeals, once again, to Augustine's exposition on Luke 19:10—"The Son of Man came to seek and save the lost"—and the Gloss on 1 Timothy 1:15. The *corpus* delivers a concise expression of Thomas's central commitments:

Those things which proceed from the will of God, and are above all that is due to creatures, we are unable to know unless they are revealed in Sacred Scripture, through which the divine will is made known. Hence, since everywhere in Sacred Scripture the reason for the incarnation is assigned to the sin of the first man, it is more fitting to say that the incarnation is a work ordained by God for the remedy of sin, such that, had sin not existed, the incarnation would not have been. Nevertheless the power of God is not

---

153. *ST* III, q. 1, a. 3, *ad* 3: "Ad tertium dicendum quod duplex capacitas attendi potest in humana natura. Una quidem secundum ordinem potentiae naturalis. Quae a Deo semper impletur, qui dat unicuique rei secundum suam capacitatem naturalem. Alia vero secundum ordinem divinae potentiae, cui omnis creatura obedit ad nutum. Et ad hoc pertinet ista capacitas. Non autem Deus omnem talem capacitatem naturae replet, alioquin, Deus non posset facere in creatura nisi quod facit; quod falsum est, ut in primo habitum est."

154. Here our findings are consistent with those of Donald Goergen: "The *Summa Theologiae* does not develop any new directions (vis-à-vis the *Scriptum*); Thomas makes his implicit preference explicit. The motive—still uncertain, but now expressed as more probable because of Scripture—is sin as the reason for the Incarnation. There could have been an Incarnation, but, more probably, there would not have been as far as we can judge from Scripture." See Goergen, "Albert the Great and Thomas Aquinas," 537.

limited to this, so it would have been possible, even without sin, for God to become incarnate.[155]

In this succinct statement, Thomas reiterates the basic features of the early and middle phases of his thought: the need for revelation, revelation's support for the negative response, and the possibility of the affirmative. Indeed, Thomas is so consistent in his principles and arguments that his view of authoritative and speculative arguments can be summarized with perfect clarity. Only arguments from sacred authorities can deliver divine reasons for divine operations *ad extra*; they are beyond the order of natural power. Speculative arguments, on the other hand, can be supplied in defense of divine operations *ad extra* for worlds compossible with Thomas's God. But those arguments are merely possible, and authoritative sources should be preferred for "truths of faith." Even the speculative arguments from fittingness, which show the attributes revealed by God's acts in our *W*-world, are subordinated to the arguments from authority. The authoritative reasons establish the position; the speculative arguments investigate the rationality of the position. Thomas's thought on the reason for the incarnation is truly a summative achievement. As we will see in the next chapter, the key features of Thomas's approach to the motive for the incarnation are substantially the same as those developed by his Franciscan contemporary and Paris's most thorough thinker on the reason for the incarnation in the thirteenth century: Bonaventure of Bagnoregio.

<hr />

155. *ST* III, q. 1, a. 3, *corpus*: "Ea enim quae ex sola Dei voluntate proveniunt, supra omne debitum creaturae, nobis innotescere non possunt nisi quatenus in sacra Scriptura traduntur, per quam divina voluntas innotescit. Unde, cum in sacra Scriptura ubique incarnationis ratio ex peccato primi hominis assignetur, convenientus dicitur incarnationis opus ordinatum esse a Deo in remedium peccati, ita quod, peccato non existente, incarnatio non fuisset. Quamvis potentia Dei ad hoc non limitetur, potuisset enim, etiam peccato non existente, Deus incarnari."

FIVE

The Franciscans at Paris

Alexander of Hales (d. 1245)

The story of the Franciscans at the University of Paris begins with Alexander of Hales, who in 1236 joined the Order of the Friars Minor, thereby gaining his chair for the Franciscans at Paris.[1] Prior to his entry into the order, Alexander became the first Master of theology to give public lectures on Peter Lombard's *Sentences*. Moreover, he was likely the originator of the *divisio textus* and distinctions of Lombard's text.[2] The *Glossa in IV Libros Sententiarum*, redactions from his early lectures, includes Alexander's earliest reflections on the motive for the incarnation. Alongside the *Glossa*, we can also discern Alexander's teaching on the motive for the incarnation from his *Quaestiones disputatae "antequam esset frater"* (*Quaestiones antequam*).

The motive for the incarnation is also treated in the *Summa Halensis* (*SH*).[3] While this final text appears to be the work of Alex-

---

1. Weisheipl, *Friar Thomas D'Aquino*, 63–65; John Moorman, *A History of the Franciscan Order from Its Origins to the Year 1517* (Oxford: Clarendon Press, 1968), 131–33; Glorieux, *Répertoire des Maîtres*.

2. Ignatius Brady, "The Distinctions of Lombard's Book of Sentences and Alexander of Hales," *Franciscan Studies* 25 (1965): 90–116.

3. The *Summa Halensis* is variously referred to in the literature as the *Summa theologiae* of Alexander of Hales, the *Summa fratris Alexandri*, and the *Summa fratris minorum* or *Summa minorum*.

ander's students, it also reflects those students' attempts to record the teaching of their Master.[4] In what follows, I will begin with the first two texts (the *Glossa* and the *Quaestiones antequam*) in order to derive Alexander's teaching on the motive for the incarnation. I will then consider the topic as it is treated in the *Summa Halensis*. It is just as well, if not preferable, that the *Summa Halensis* reflects the thought of Alexander's students John of la Rochelle, Odo Rigaldi, William of Melitona, and others. Together with the subsequent text of Odo Rigaldi, the text gives a view of the state of the question on the motive for the incarnation among the Franciscan Masters between Alexander and Bonaventure.

Redaction A of the *Glossa*, book III, was composed circa 1225–1227.[5] It is difficult to discern Alexander's position on the motive for the incarnation from the text. In book III, d. 1, he considers "multiple causes for the incarnation of the Son." Much of his focus is on the phrase "of the Son."[6] Here, Alexander is addressing Peter Lombard's questions in the first distinction: why the Son and

4. The authorship of the *Summa Halensis* is difficult to discern. The debates up to the middle of the twentieth century are recited in Victorin Doucet, "The History of the Problem of the Authenticity of the Summa," *Franciscan Studies* 7, no. 1 (1947): 26–41; "The History of the Problem of the Authenticity of the Summa (Continued)," *Franciscan Studies* 7, no. 3 (1947): 274–312. Doucet concludes that book III was likely compiled prior to 1245, rendering possible Alexander's authorship or heavy involvement in the text's production. However, Walter Principe, citing an article by Carra de Vaux Saint-Cyr, holds to a much later date, suggesting that perhaps the *Glossa* of John of La Rochelle was a chief source of the relevant passages from book III of the *Summa Halensis*. It appears likely that, although Alexander's *Glossa* and *Quaestiones antequam* were sources for the treatment of the motive for the incarnation in the *Summa Halensis*, it was not authored by Alexander, but by his students. In keeping with this judgment, I will refer to the authors of these texts as "the brothers." Walter H. Principe, *Alexander of Hales' Theology of the Hypostatic Union*, vol. 2, *The Theology of the Hypostatic Union in the Early Thirteenth Century* (Toronto: Pontifical Institute of Mediaeval Studies, 1967), 15.

5. Alexander of Hales, *Glossa in quatuor libros Sententiarum Petri Lombardi*, edited by PP. Collegii S. Bonaventurae, vol. 3 (Quaracchi, Italy: Collegii S. Bonaventurae, 1954), 32*.

6. I will be following redaction A insofar as (1) the authorship of redaction L is uncertain and (2) L simply relocates the text of A later in distinction 1 of Book III. For a discussion of the text-critical issues in Alexander's *Glossa*, see Principe, *Alexander of Hales' Theology*, 16–20.

not the Father or Spirit became incarnate, whether the Father or Spirit could have become incarnate then or now, and so on.[7] It is notable, however, that all the arguments he considers have in view redemption from sin. For instance, Alexander supplies an argument from Romans 8:32; since all were created in the Word of God, they ought to be *recreated* through the same. Moreover, as Walter Principe observes, the *Glossa* does produce an argument that will recur in the discussion of the motive for the incarnation in the *Summa Halensis*. It arises, however, in Alexander's discussion of the Trinity at *Glossa* I, 31. This argument will be considered later, in the treatment of the *Summa Halensis*.

The disputed questions give a better view of Alexander's thought on the motive for the incarnation. The *Quaestiones antequam* are dated sometime between 1220 and 1236.[8] At q. 15, d. 2, m. 4, Alexander considers "whether the incarnation would have had a certain usefulness assuming there were no passion."[9] He first gives one argument for the negative by appeal to the *praechonium paschale*. Alexander then gives three counterarguments. First, he cites Pseudo-Augustine's *De anima et spiritu*; since the soul is created in both its sensitive and intellectual parts for glory, that through which it reaches glory should be both sensitive and intellectual.[10] Second, he argues that the greatest goodness should declare itself to creation in the greatest way, which requires incarnation in order that the greatest goodness would be manifest.[11] Third, the union of God with creatures brings about a perfect concatenation of the universe. Hence the incarnation would be appropriate even if there had been no passion.[12] Alexander favors these arguments for the affirmative

---

7. *Glossa* III, d. 1, n. 4.

8. Alexander of Hales, *Quaestiones disputatae "antequam esset frater,"* ed. PP. Collegii S. Bonaventurae, vol. 1 (Quaracchi, Italy: Collegii S. Bonaventurae, 1960), 36*.

9. *Quaestiones antequam* q. 15, d. 2, m. 4, n. 45: "Consequenter quaeritur, posito quod non esset passio, utrum incarnatio aliquam utilitatem haberet."

10. *Quaestiones antequam* q. 15, d. 2, m. 4, n. 46.

11. *Quaestiones antequam* q. 15, d. 2, m. 4, n. 47.

12. *Quaestiones antequam* q. 15, d. 2, m. 4, n. 48. Perhaps Alexander has in mind

response to the hypothetical question. Thus, he responds to the appeal to the *praechonium paschale*, while it is true, as the prayer states, that our birth would be to no gain unless we are redeemed, "regarding the fittingness of redemption, nevertheless the delight of humanity would be magnified were they to see their nature united to deity, even if there were no passion."[13] In sum, while we cannot see much of Alexander's position in these early texts, what is there appears very similar to what we saw in Grosseteste's *DCL*.

Summa Halensis

Alexander's thought on the motive for the incarnation is terse and inconclusive for the questions that concern us. The *Summa Halensis*, on the other hand, expands well beyond Alexander's teaching while retaining many of his central commitments. Following a series of inquiries on the necessity, possibility, and fittingness of the incarnation, the brothers ask, "Whether, if nature was not fallen through sin, there would be a reason (*ratio*) or fittingness (*convenientia*) to the incarnation?"[14] In the subsequent argument, Anselm's authority is eminent.

From time to time the brothers distinguish their thought from Anselm's. When they come to the question as to whether the Father or the Holy Spirit could possibly become incarnate (having determined that it is not suitable), the first argument for the negative position is drawn from Anselm:

Grosseteste's arguments for the incarnation for circular concatenation in *DCL* III.1.28.

13. *Quaestiones antequam* q. 15, d. 2, m. 4, n. 49: "Ad hoc quod obicitur: nihil nasci profuit etc., dico quod verum est: nihil nasci profuit quantum ad convenientem redemptionem; tamen magna delectatio esset homini, quod videret naturam suam unitam deitati etiam si non esset passio." N.b., Alexander also supplies a standard defense of Anselm's argument in *CDH* in d. 3, m. 1, when he inquires whether the incarnation was necessary for repairing the fall, to which he responds that it was fitting that God satisfy through the God-man.

14. *SH* IV, P3, In1, Tr1, Q2, T2, p. 41: "Consequens est quaerere de convenientia incarnationis, si non fuisset natura lapsa per peccatum, utrum scilicet esset ratio vel convenientia ad incarnationem."

In book I of *Cur Deus homo*, Anselm says: "Whatever is not fitting to God, it follows that it is impossible." But if another person than the Son became incarnate, it would follow that it is unfitting for God (because there would be a confusion of the dignity of persons); therefore it is impossible that another person than the Son become incarnate.[15]

This teaching is opposed by Peter Lombard in the *Sentences* III, d. 1. Lombard argues that the Father or Spirit could have become incarnate, though the Son was the most fittingly incarnate. The brothers therefore respond to Anselm's teaching with a distinction between two kinds of "divine possibility":

It must be said that what is "divinely possible" is two-fold, namely what is absolutely possible, and this mode is spoken of in *Sentences* III, that any divine person is able to become incarnate; and there is a possibility of suitability, and by this to become incarnate befits the Son alone.[16]

Already in the *Summa Halensis* we see that tensions are developing between Anselm's deployment of arguments *ex convenientia* and the arguments of other authoritative sources, in this case Peter Lombard.

It is difficult to determine the implications of this distinction for the brothers' subsequent reflections on the motive for the incarnation. Certainly, the category of suitability and fittingness is primary; the *responsio* is explicit: "Without prejudice it is conceded that even if there was not a fall of human nature, still the incarnation is fitting."[17] As we will see momentarily, their care for the modal status of their arguments show that the brothers are quite perceptive in

15. *SH* IV, P3, In1, Tr1, Q2, T1, D2, M1, C4, A2, p. 32: "I libro *Cur Deus homo*, dicit Anselmus: 'Quodlibet inconveniens Deo sequitur impossibile.' Sed, si alia persona quam Filius incarnaretur, sequeretur inconveniens Deo; ergo impossibile est aliam personam quam Filium incarnari. Media patet: Inconveniens enim est Deo quod sit confusio dignitatis personarum."

16. *SH* IV, P3, In1, Tr1, Q2, T1, D2, M1, C4, A2, p. 32: "Dicendum quod est 'posse divinum' dupliciter, scilicet posse absolute, et hoc modo dicitur, III *Sententiarum*, quod quaelibet persona potuit incarnari; et est posse de congruentia, et hoc modo soli Filio convenit incarnari."

17. *SH* IV, P3, In1, Tr1, Q2, T2, p. 42: "Sine praeiudicio concedendum est quod, etiamsi non fuisset humana natura lapsa, adhuc est convenientia ad incarnationem."

their understanding of the intricacies of the arguments of their day. Following Alexander, they deploy *convenientia* exclusively when considering the hypothetical question, avoiding necessity. This is evident in their phrasing of the question in the domain of possibility: "Can a fitting reason be found?" Moreover, as we will see, they appear to prioritize authoritative teaching over speculation, in a way that anticipates the mature application of *convenientia* in Aquinas.[18]

The brothers give four arguments in support of the conclusion that, even if there were not a fall of human nature, the incarnation would still be fitting.[19] First, the Good is diffusive of itself. Just as the Father diffuses his goodness in the generation of the Son without creation existing, if creation exists there should be the greatest possible diffusion of the Good in creation. The greatest possible diffusion in creation would be for the creature to be united to the Good itself.

Second, similarly to Grosseteste's argument at *DCL* III.1.22–24, the brothers argue that the incarnation, even in a world without sin, would be necessary for the full spiritual and intellectual beatitude of the human person. "If the entire human would be beatified in God, God must be corporeal and sensible."[20] Once again the brothers appeal to Pseudo-Augustine's *De spiritu et anima*.

Third, a suitability argument is given that is formally similar to the created goods arguments given by Grosseteste. The incarnation fills some logically possible category of existence that would otherwise be left vacant. It is a Christian variant of Arthur Lovejoy's principle of plenitude, which, as Simo Knuuttila and others have argued, underwent significant revision over the course of the thirteenth century.[21] Since there exists (1) three persons in unity

18. Certainly, the *Summa Halensis* shows nowhere near the consistency of application of the logic of *convenientia* that is found later in Thomas Aquinas. Nevertheless, there are notable developments. On the development of *convenientia* in the *Summa Halensis* see Barnes, "Necessary, Fitting, or Possible," 660–69.

19. *SH* IV, P3, In1, Tr1, Q2, T2, p. 41–42.

20. *SH* IV, P3, In1, Tr1, Q2, T2, p. 41: "Si ergo totus homo debet beatificari in Deo, oportet Deum esse corporalem et sensibilem."

21. Lovejoy defines the principle of plenitude as "not only the thesis that the

of substance, as in the Trinity, as well as (2) three persons in three substances, as in three human beings, there remains the possibility of (3) three substances in unity of person.[22] The incarnation actualizes this possible kind, bringing to completion the series of logical possibilities given two variables (substance and person) with two possible values (one and three). How? By the creation of a human nature composed of a body and soul (two natures) united to a divine person with a divine nature (one person and one nature). The argument is the same as the one given by Alexander with respect to the Trinity in *Glossa* I, 31.

Finally, the brothers give an argument from divine power. If the divine nature possesses a power for existence in multiple (three) persons, then divine persons also possess a power for existence in multiple natures. This can only be realized by union with a created nature, which is most fittingly a union between the Son with a human nature. And so, the incarnation is a fitting display of the perfection of divine power and personality.

We can note already the similarity between the *Summa Halensis* and Alexander's *Glossa* and *Quaestiones antequam*. The first two arguments of the *Summa Halensis* are the first two supplied in the treatment at *Quaestio* 15. In both cases, the first argument's appeal to the diffusion of the Good takes on a revelatory emphasis not found in Grosseteste's rendition; the highest good self-communicates to give the highest declaration to creatures (*per Quaestiones antequam*) or to reveal to us that the possibility of divine self-communication extends beyond what we could know (*per Summa Halensis*). The

---

universe is a *plenum formarum* in which the range of conceivable diversity of *kinds* of living things is exhaustively exemplified, but also any other deductions from the assumption that no genuine potentiality of being can remain unfulfilled, that the extent and abundance of the creation must be as great as the possibility of existence and commensurate with the productive capacity of a 'perfect' and inexhaustible Source, and that the world is better, the more things it contains." Lovejoy, *The Great Chain of Being*, 52.

22. Strictly speaking, there is a fourth possible combination: one person in one substance. This is satisfied by the existence of any individual human person. The brothers do not close this loop, however.

third argument of the *Summa Halensis* recalls the Trinitarian argument at *Glossa* I, d. 31. Moreover, the brothers' fourth argument is closely related to, and possibly derived from, that third, Trinitarian argument. Finally, the brothers' argument *ad oppositum* is the same as the argument in the *Glossa* III, d. 1, in its appeal to the *praechonium paschale*. It seems exceedingly likely, therefore, that the authors of *SH* III were directly engaged with Alexander's thought on the motive for the incarnation while developing their own position on the question.

Of the four arguments for the affirmative response to the hypothetical question in the *Summa Halensis*, the second argument from the authority of Pseudo-Augustine is reproduced in the body of the response. Here we see the brothers' preference for and concern with arguments from authority when it comes to the reason for the incarnation. For example, the brothers appeal to the authority of Bernard who, commenting upon Jonah 1:12, refers to Lucifer's foreknowledge of the incarnation as a condition of his envy and temptation of humans. According to Bernard, Lucifer tempted Eve "so that through sin human nature would be cut off from assumption and the ability to be unified to God."[23] Given Bernard's authoritative judgment that Lucifer foresaw the incarnation before he tempted human beings to fall, the brothers conclude that God must have intended the incarnation independently of the fall.[24]

In support of their position, the brothers, like Alexander, also supply the authority of Pseudo-Augustine, whose argument in *De spiritu et anima* they recite as follows:

For this reason God became man, that the whole man would be beatified in him, that man would advance both inwardly through intellect, and excel

23. *SH* IV, P3, In1, Tr1, Q2, T2, p. 42: "Unde invidia fuit causa casus diaboli et movens ipsum ad tentandum hominem, cuius felicitati invidebat, ut per peccatum demereretur humana natura assumptionem et unibilitatem ad Deum."

24. Grosseteste produced a similar argument from the prevision of Adam on the basis of Ephesians 5:32 at *DCL* III.1.20. Thomas Aquinas considers the same argument as the one articulated in the *Summa Halensis* and likewise draws it from Bernard's comment on Jonah 1:12 at *Scriptum* III, d. 1, q. 1, a. 3.

outwardly through sense, finding pasture in his Creator; interior pasture in the cognition of the deity; outward pasture in the flesh of the Savior.[25]

To this authoritative rehearsal of the earlier argument, the brothers addend the following comment: "And this reason (*ratio*) remains, and circumscribes the fall of human nature."[26] According to the *Summa Halensis*, we can be confident in the affirmative response to the hypothetical question on account of Bernard's authority and the ascription of a particular reason for the incarnation in a world without sin: to lead humanity to pasture. Authoritative, not speculative arguments, win the day. Having won the day by authority, speculative arguments can supply fitting reasons.

As a final note, the brothers reproduce an authority from Alexander that recurs in subsequent debates at Paris: the appeal to the *praechonium paschale*, the hymn sung for the Easter Vigil. Like Alexander, the *Summa Halensis* isolates a key moment in the Paschal prayer, which will be referenced in subsequent debates, in particular the "happy fault" (*O felix culpa*) arguments of Aquinas. The brothers give an intriguing, distinctive rendition of this argument from authority. The *Summa Halensis* claims that the hymn should be understood "supposing the guilt of the fall of nature," in which case an incarnation without redemption would be unprofitable. Nevertheless, incarnation without redemption would be fitting, if the fall of human nature were circumscribed. In that case, while redemption would not be necessary, beatitude would, and beatitude, according to the authority of Pseudo-Augustine, has as a necessary condition the sensitive soul's perception of God. And that perception is only made possible by the incarnation.

We can note, then, an important development in the brothers'

---

25. *SH* IV, P3, In1, Tr1, Q2, T2, p. 42: "Propterea Deus factus est homo, ut totum hominem in se beatificaret, ut sive homo ingrederetur intus per intellectum, sive egrederetur extra per sensum, in Creatore suo pascua inveniret, pascua intus in cognitione deitatis, pascua foris in carne Salvatoris."

26. *SH* IV, P3, In1, Tr1, Q2, T2, p. 42: "Haec autem ratio manet, etiam circumscripto lapsu humanae naturae."

application of Alexander's various arguments. First, the *Summa Halensis* shows an increased emphasis upon the authoritative arguments from Pseudo-Augustine and Bernard. Notable especially are the reasons supplied by the brothers for worlds that lack a fall. In the *Glossa*, the reason for the incarnation in worlds without a fall (*I*-worlds) is rather generic: the magnified delight of humanity. However, the *Summa Halensis* isolates the specific reason given in Pseudo-Augustine: that the human creature, in both its sensitive and intellective faculties, might "find pasture" in the Creator. This specific reason holds for worlds without a fall. The brothers' fixation on Pseudo-Augustine's authoritative argument likely explains the recurring appeals to the same argument in subsequent treatments of the motive for the incarnation by both Franciscans and Dominicans. Moreover, the brothers' interest in different classes of arguments, and their care to ground their argument in an authoritative source, rather than a speculative reason, anticipates the highly nuanced treatment of the motive for the incarnation we have already seen in Thomas Aquinas and will see in Bonaventure of Bagnoregio.

Odo Rigaldi (d. 1275/76)

Alexander was succeeded by his student John of la Rochelle in 1238, two years following Alexander's entry into the Friars Minor. John held the chair until he fell ill in 1244, finally succumbing in 1245, the same year of Alexander's death. John was then succeeded by Odo Rigaldi, another of Alexander's students. Like John, Odo was likely involved in the preparation of the *Summa Halensis*, although where and to what extent remains debated.[27] He held the Franciscan Chair until 1248, at which point he became Archbishop

27. The evidence suggests that John of la Rochelle's thought is heavily reflected in book III of the *Summa Halensis*. See Victorin Doucet, "*Prolegomena in librum III necnon in libros I et II Summa Fratris Alexandri*," Vol. 4, Pt. 2, *Alexandri de Hales Summa Theologica* (Quaracchi, Florentiae: Collegio S. Bonaventurae, 1948).

of Rouen.[28] Odo's comments on the motive for the incarnation reflect his engagement with Alexander, the *Summa Halensis*, as well as Guerric of Saint-Quentin.

In direct contrast with Alexander and the brothers, Odo prefers the negative response to the hypothetical question. The affirmative, he concludes, is against the piety of faith because, unless the Son were incarnate principally for our sin, we would not hold so great a gratitude as we might otherwise.[29] The argument is nearly identical to Guerric's spiritual attraction argument. Yet Odo, much like Grosseteste, leaves open the possibility of being convinced otherwise: "Unless I were to see more explicit reasons or authorities (*rationem vel auctoritatem*), I do not believe that the Son of God would have become man unless humanity had fallen."[30]

Odo considers and dismisses seven arguments for the affirmative response to the hypothetical question according to the same distinction: reasons (*rationes*) and authorities (*auctoritates*). Though he marks the distinction, like the brothers, he does not develop it. Odo considers four reasons and three authorities, all of which we have encountered in some form to this point. The first argument is a relatively routine argument from the principle that the Good is diffusive of itself. The second is a routine argument from creaturely capacity for union with God to the conclusion that God would fulfill that blessed capacity.

Odo interweaves his objections to both, but the critical point is made in response to the first. It is not necessary that the diffusion of Goodness be manifest in every possible good, but only that there be an eternal diffusion. This need is satisfied by the generation of

---

28. For a full account of Odo's life, with special attention given to his duties as Archbishop of Rouen, see Adam J. Davis, *The Holy Bureaucrat: Eudes Rigaud and Religious Reform in Thirteenth-Century Normandy* (Ithaca, N.Y.: Cornell University Press, 2006).

29. Odo's unedited treatment of the motive for the incarnation appears as an addendum to Bissen, "*De motivo incarnationis.*" It is otherwise unavailable in print.

30. Bissen, "*De motivo incarnationis,*" 335: "Dicendum, quod nisi videam rationem vel auctoritatem magis expressam, non credo quod Filius Dei factus esset homo nisi homo peccasset."

the Son from eternity. Moreover, the creation of the world itself is a sufficient manifestation of the diffusion of Goodness to that which is not God. After all, while God could make multiple worlds, God is not obligated to do so.[31] In this way, Odo distinguishes between the divine will (what God has done) and divine power (what God is capable of doing). This distinction between divine will and power pertains to any created good, at least insofar as the Good's diffusiveness is concerned. It therefore follows that the human capacity for union with a divine person is not necessary in any possible world, but is entirely within the domain of the divine will.

Odo considers two further speculative arguments for the affirmative to the hypothetical question. The third is similar to Grosseteste's created goods arguments from nature. Odo cites 1 Corinthians 11. Since "Man is the head of woman, and Christ the head of man," unless the Son becomes incarnate, man would lack his head, and the universe would be incomplete, "like a picture without a head."[32] The fourth argument we encountered in the *Summa Halensis*; in the incarnation we find three natures in one person, which completes the universe. The argument is slightly different here than in the *Summa Halensis*. In the latter, the argument is for the revelation of the extent of divine power. The brothers show a distinctive emphasis upon the revelatory effects of the incarnation. In Odo, the argument is for the completion of the universe, in keeping with Odo's concern with the critical theological issue of whether God is obligated to become incarnate in order to perfect some capacity of creation. Odo rebuts both arguments for the perfection of the universe with a single argument. Christ is not said to be *de universo*, but *supra totum universum*—not of the universe, but above the entire universe. The gift of Christ is *ex gratia*, as Guerric

---

31. Bissen, "*De motivo incarnationis*," 335: "Sufficienter autem manifestatur diffusio sive bonitas aeternaliter in generatione Filii et temporaliter in creatione mundi. Potuit etiam plures mundos facere, sed tamen non oportet; similiter nec in proposito."

32. Bissen, "*De motivo incarnationis*," 334.

says, not *ex natura*. And so the incarnation cannot be for the completion of the natural order.

Finally, Odo considers three authoritative arguments. He recites and rebuts the brothers' appeals both to Pseudo-Augustine's *De anima et spiritu* and to Bernard's interpretation of Jonah 1:12, which were the two favored authorities in defense of the affirmative response to the hypothetical question. Like Guerric, Odo includes a further argument from predestination by citing Romans 1:4.

Odo argues that the authorities pertaining to predestination fail because "God foresaw from eternity himself becoming human and (humanity's) sinning, and his repairing through incarnation."[33] The first authority (Pseudo-Augustine) does not obtain for possible worlds without sin because beatitude in these worlds, including corporeal beatitude, would come as a result of the overflow of glory from the soul into the body. This rebuttal leads Odo back to his central commitments from the *respondeo*. His comment shows how his position holds together: "Nevertheless, it is truly a great glory, though not essential, [that we are beatified] by the most brilliant and beautiful humanity of Christ our Lord."[34] The incarnation is entirely free from necessity. Nevertheless, the humanity of Christ is the most brilliant and beautiful created thing.

Odo concludes his reflection on the motive for the incarnation by returning to his central argument, his own rendition of Guerric's spiritual attraction argument: "But those who want to say that he would have become united to a creature, say that we owe him thanksgiving, because he assumed a passible and mortal nature, as a result of sin. Therefore we ought to give thanks, but not, however, as much."[35] It is therefore preferable, lacking any compelling ar-

---

33. Bissen, "*De motivo incarnationis*," 336: "Deus praeviderat ab aeterno se facturum hominem et illum peccaturum et se reparaturum per incarnationem."

34. Bissen, "*De motivo incarnationis*," 335: "Verum est tamen quod magnum est gaudium, sed non essentiale, in visione praeclarissimae et formosissimae humanitatis Christi Domini nostri."

35. Bissen, "*De motivo incarnationis*," 336: "Illi autem qui volunt dicere quod fuisset unitus creaturae, dicunt quod nihilominus debemus ei gratiarum actiones, quia

gument from authority or reason to the contrary, to say that Christ came to destroy sin and repair nature, and not otherwise.

Bonaventure of Bagnoregio (d. 1274)

In the 1250s, when Bonaventure composed his commentary on Lombard's *Sentences*, he saved his commentary on the third book for the very last.[36] Later, in 1259, on retreat in Mount LaVerna, the site of St. Francis's stigmatization, he composed the *Itinerarium mentis in Deum*.[37] In the *Itinerarium*, as the mind approaches the end of its journey, it arrives at the sixth step:

> Where it can behold in the first and highest Principle and in the Mediator of God and men, Jesus Christ, things the like of which cannot possibly be found among creatures, and which transcend all acuteness of the human intellect—when the mind has done all this, it must still, in beholding these things, transcend and pass over, not only this visible world, but even itself.[38]

He continues: "In this passing over, Christ is the way and the door; Christ is the ladder and the vehicle, being, as it were, the Mercy-Seat above the Ark of God and *the mystery which has been hidden from eternity*."[39]

Indubitably, Bonaventure's theology reflects what the Scotists call the "absolute primacy of Christ." But does Christ's place, at and beyond the apogee of all created existence, demand an affirmative response to the hypothetical question? Zachary Hayes thinks so:

---

tunc assumpsisset naturam passibilem et moralem, sicut fecit post peccatum; et ideo nihilominus tenetur ad gratiarum actiones, sed non tamen ad tot."

36. While it is quite clear that III came last, it is debatable whether the preceding sequence was I-II-IV or I-IV-II. See Ignatius Brady, "The Edition of the '*Opera Omnia*' of St. Bonaventure," *Archivum Franciscanum historicum* 70 (1977): 352–76.

37. Marianne Schlosser, "Bonaventure: Life and Works," in *A Companion to Bonaventure*, ed. Jay M. Hammond, J. A. Wayne Hellmann, and Jared Goff, 9–59, Brill's Companions to the Christian Tradition 48 (Leiden: Brill, 2014), 32–33.

38. Bonaventure, *Itinerarium mentis in Deum*, vol. 5, *Opera omnia*, ed. PP. Collegii S. Bonaventurae (Quaracchi, Italy: Collegii S. Bonaventurae, 1891), VII, 1. Translations taken from Bonaventure, *The Journey of the Mind to God*, ed. Stephen F. Brown, trans. Philotheus Boehner, OFM (Indianapolis: Hackett Pub. Company, 1993).

39. *Itinerarium* VII, 1.

It is virtually impossible for such a thoroughly Christocentric view to see the incarnation as an after-thought, for He in whose image all creation is shaped must somehow be involved in the world and its history from the start. It is not sufficient to say that He is involved precisely as the eternal Word, for the actual world is not only shaped in His image but remains incomplete until the *uncreated Word* becomes the *incarnate Word.*[40]

However, as Hayes recognizes, when Bonaventure considers the hypothetical question, although he mounts an array of arguments for the affirmative, he nevertheless prefers the negative. Why?

Bonaventure does not pose the question of the motive for the incarnation in the hypothetical form. His question concerns the order of motives in the de facto state of affairs. What is the *praecipua ratio incarnationis*—the primary reason for the incarnation? Bonaventure focuses on the primacy question rather than the hypothetical question. Notably, he is the first to pose the question in terms of primacy. This was likely due to Bonaventure's comprehensive sense for the arguments, considerations, and options raised by the hypothetical question. His response is notable for both its scope and depth. It remained influential as a result.

Though he raises a new question, Bonaventure interweaves his consideration of the primacy question with his treatment of the hypothetical question. He distinguishes two alternative responses to the primacy question: either (1) the primary reason for the incarnation is the redemption from sin, or (2) the primary reason for the incarnation is something else. If the former, a negative response to both the hypothetical question and the primacy question follows; if the latter, an affirmative response follows for both. It is therefore imprecise to say that "Bonaventure does not ask whether the Word would have become incarnate had Adam not sinned. This is a hypothetical question of little or no concern to him."[41]

---

40. Zachary Hayes, *The Hidden Center: Spirituality and Speculative Christology in St. Bonaventure* (New York: Paulist Press, 1981), 187.

41. Hayes, *The Hidden Center*, 187–88; Ilia Delio, "Revisiting the Franciscan Doctrine of Christ," *Theological Studies* 64, no. 1 (2003): 10. See also Pancheri and Carol's attempts to gloss these passages from III *Sent.* d. 1, a. 2, q. 2, by distinguishing be-

Bonaventure considers the primacy question, at some length, at III *Sent.* d. 1, a. 2, q. 2. The preceding article considers the possibility of hypostatic union. Article two moves from possibility to congruity. Like Thomas's *Scriptum, congruitas* is Bonaventure's preferred language, rather than necessity. In the first question of article two, he considers whether the incarnation is congruous on the part of God. That is, he asks whether and how the incarnation is congruent with the divine nature. The second question is the primacy question. This sequence, from possibility (a. 1) to congruity (a. 2, q. 1) to the *ratio incarnationis* (a. 2, q. 2), is the same as the sequence found in Thomas Aquinas's *Scriptum* III, d. 1, q. 1, aa. 1–3.

According to Bonaventure, in III *Sent.* d. 1, a. 2, q. 1, the incarnation is congruous on the part of God. Bonaventure's primary concern is what to make, modally, of arguments like Robert Grosseteste's, which move from divine attributes to the incarnation. Bonaventure argues that the incarnation is *congruous*, a significant revision of the necessary Grossetestean deductions. And so several of Grosseteste's arguments are recited. Infinite power, wisdom, and goodness manifests itself perfectly in an infinite effect, and since God's union with flesh is such an effect, it is congruous.[42] A perfect agent will bring its act to a complementary stasis, in this case by the union of the first (the Word) and last (humanity). Since the dignity of the divine nature is congruously shown by three persons existing in one nature without multiplying that nature, the dignity of the divine persons is congruously shown by three natures subsisting in one person without composition. For the perfect beatitude of humanity, both the exterior and interior senses must be beatified

---

tween (non-problematic) "hypothetical *expressions*" and (problematic) "hypothetical *facts*" in Pancheri, *The Universal Primacy of Christ*, 20.

42. Alexander Schaefer shows the importance of the three attributes *potentia, sapientia, et bonitas* in Bonaventure's larger cosmology and theology in "The Position and Function of Man in the Created World according to Saint Bonaventure (Part I)," *Franciscan Studies* 20, no. 3/4 (1960): 261–316; "The Position and Function of Man in the Created World according to Saint Bonaventure (Part II)," *Franciscan Studies* 21, no. 1/2 (1961): 233–382.

in the perception of God (à la Pseudo-Augustine). And finally, for God and humanity to be fittingly (*conveniens*) reconciled, a mediator who connects both divinity and humanity (i.e., a God-man) is congruous.

All the arguments supplied by Bonaventure in support of the incarnation's congruity derive from some divine attribute: power, wisdom, goodness, perfection, or dignity. Likewise, the arguments against the incarnation's congruity in the *sed contra* derive from divine attributes. For instance, the incarnation detracts from divine majesty, insofar as flesh derives from mud, which is contemptible. Similar arguments object that the incarnation is injurious, or vituperative, or detracts from divine wisdom.

The *respondeo* reiterates Bonaventure's central concern that the incarnation is congruous. "Congruous" here means that, while the incarnation reveals divine attributes, it is not necessitated by those attributes. Bonaventure gives four arguments in support of his determination that it was congruous that God should become incarnate, some of which reiterate the initial arguments for the affirmative. The arguments are oriented around four attributes: infinity, perfection, piety, and liberality. The incarnation is congruous with infinity in God's self, with perfection in working, with piety in liberating, and with liberality in repaying.[43]

Question one of article two, on the congruity of the incarnation on the part of God, anticipates the more extensive reflection on the motive for the incarnation in question two. In question one, Bonaventure supplies a number of reasons and divine attributes rendering the incarnation congruous. Some of those, such as divine liberality in remuneration or the fitting reconciler between God and humanity, pertain specifically to Christ's work of redemp-

---

43. III *Sent.* d. 1, a. 2, q. 1 (II, 20): "Et sic patet, quod opus incarnationis multum quidem per omnem modum Deum congruebat et quantum ad eius *infinitatem* et quantum ad eius *perfectionem* et quantum ad *pietatem* et quantum ad *liberalitatem*: ad *infinitatem* in se ipso, ad *perfectionem* in operando, ad *pietatem* in liberando et quantum ad *liberalitatem* in remunerando."

tion. Others, such as infinity and certain applications of perfection, seem to hold whether or not the need for redemption arises. Thus, the question of the primary reason for the incarnation, amongst those many reasons, arises naturally.

Bonaventure's treatment of the primacy question is the most thorough treatment of the motive for the incarnation at Paris in the thirteenth century. He draws together all the various threads of argument, considerations, puzzles, and subterranean anxieties in both the Dominican and Franciscan figures we have encountered to this point, and works them into a comprehensive synthesis. Whether his solution is satisfactory or not, the Seraphic Doctor's treatment at III *Sent.* d. 1, a. 2, q. 2, shows that he achieved an understanding of the issues at stake unparalleled in its precision, scope, and sensitivity.

The *respondeo* itself is lengthy, occupying four full columns in the critical edition. But his solution is concisely stated: "The primary reason for the incarnation seems to be the redemption of human nature, although many other congruent reasons are annexed to this reason."[44]

Bonaventure observes that, in his day, the Masters were divided between two options.[45] The first option (A) distinguishes two ways of speaking about the assumed flesh: (1) the flesh as regards substance, and (2) the flesh as regards the defect of passibility.[46] For the latter way of speaking, the primary reason for the incarnation is the redemption from sin. For the former, the primary reason is the perfection arising from the dignity of the incarnation. That perfec-

---

44. III *Sent.* d. 1, a. 2, q. 2 (III, 23): "Praecipua ratio incarnationis videtur fuisse redemptio humani generis, quamvis multae rationes aliae congruentiae huic rationi sint annexae."

45. Bonaventure is the first theologian to divide the positions in the way he does. This follows from the apparently Bonaventuran innovation with regard to the question, concerned as it is with the *primary reason* for the incarnation. While Aquinas's description of *alia opinarum* at the conclusion of *Scriptum* III d. 1, q. 1, a. 3, bears some similarities, Thomas is not nearly as precise or thorough as Bonaventure.

46. III *Sent.* d. 1, a. 2, q. 2 (III, 23): "De carne autem assumta est loqui dupliciter: aut quantum ad *substantiam*, aut quantum ad *defectum passibilitatis.*"

tion is both for humanity and the universe. On this final point, we find many resonances with the arguments from Grosseteste that I designated the created goods strategy.

Bonaventure expounds at some length on various perfections deriving from the incarnation for the assumed flesh considered substantially. That is, he considers several creaturely perfections that obtain in any possible world with incarnation. It is important to note that, in option A, these perfections are also achieved by the incarnation in those worlds, which, like our own, include an assumed flesh with the defect of passibility for the sake of redemption from sin. He divides those perfections into three categories: perfection of nature, perfection of grace, and perfection of glory. In the first case (perfection of nature), Bonaventure returns to his argument from question one that the incarnation unites the first (God) and last (humanity). In the second (perfection of grace), Bonaventure gives two goods of grace achieved by the incarnation. First, the incarnation perfects the entire church through union with Christ as its head. Second, the incarnation brings the perfection of merit, because "all merit depends upon and is improved by the merit of Christ." Finally, the perfection of glory is actualized insofar as the beatified "find pasture" both corporeally and spiritually, a clear reference to the recurring passage from Pseudo-Augustine's *De spiritu et anima*. Since these many perfections do not only pertain to humanity in a fallen state, they render the incarnation in possible worlds without a fall compossible (congruous) with Bonaventure's God.[47]

One more observation is made by Bonaventure with regard to option A. Earlier in the question, Bonaventure supplies five arguments in support of redemption from sin as the primary reason for the incarnation. Several of those arguments are from authoritative sources that state, quite clearly, that Christ came to redeem. It was generally accepted that the preponderance of authoritative

---

47. Note, here, that the function of *congruum* in Bonaventure is synonymous with Thomas's *convenientia* in the *tertia pars* of the *Summa Theologiae*.

evidence supports the negative response to the hypothetical question, against option A. Bonaventure summarizes the general strategy of those Catholic Masters who support option A when faced with these authorities; all of those authorities are said "with regard to the assumption of mortal and passible flesh." Scripture and the Saints, then, are simply speaking of the incarnation supposing the fall, and not supposing a persisting state of innocence. The same holds for the speculative (as opposed to authoritative) arguments that support option A.[48]

Bonaventure prefers the second opinion (B) taken by the Masters. Hence, he gives it a rather lengthy exposition. His exposition has a subtlety and theological vision on the motive for the incarnation unparalleled in any of the figures we have encountered to this point. Bonaventure and others taking option B hold that the primary reason for the incarnation is redemption from sin. All other congruent reasons are annexed to that primary reason. Thus, the position entails a negative response to the hypothetical question.[49]

Bonaventure's exposition of option B proceeds in several steps. First, he gives a concise reason for the incarnation:

And the reason is this: the incarnation of God is of such excessive dignity. And therefore, since there is there a certain excess, the mystery of incarnation would not have come about, unless it were preceded by an opposite excess, which (the mystery) corrected and restored. Hence, unless God had lost his sheep, he would not have descended from heaven to earth.[50]

---

48. III *Sent.* d. 1, a. 2, q. 2 (III, 24): "Rationes vero ad oppositum et auctoritates per hoc effugiunt, quia dicut, eas intelligi, secundum quod incarnatio dicitur carnis mortalis et passibilis assumtio. Loquitur enim Scriptura, et Sancti de incarnatione secundum eum modum, qui fuit post lapsum, non per eum modum, qui fuisset, homine persistente in statu innocentiae."

49. III *Sent.* d. 1, a. 2, q. 2 (III, 24): "Ista enim est praecipua respectu omnium, quia, nisi genus humanum fuisset lapsum, Verbum Dei non fuisset incarnatum."

50. III *Sent.* d. 1, a. 2, q. 2 (III, 24): "Et ratio huius est, quia incarnatio Dei est superexcedentis dignationis; et ideo, cum sit ibi quidam excessus, non fuisset introductum incarnationis mysterium, nisi praecessisset excessus oppositus per ipsum corrigendus et restaurandus. Unde nisi Deus *ovem suam perdidisset*, non de caelo ad terram descendisset."

This appeal to "excess" recalls the spiritual attraction argument of Guerric of Saint-Quentin and Odo Rigaldi, and is oriented around a similar vision of the divine beneficence that draws the sinner to God. As we will see, this commitment is consistent with Bonaventure's larger Christological vision.

Having stated his central argument, and before expounding it at some length, Bonaventure notes the feasibility of either option (A or B). His comments are worth citing:

> Which of these two ways of speaking is more true is known by the One who deigned to become incarnate for us. For which of these alternatives is preferable is difficult to see, since both options are catholic and sustained by catholics. Moreover, both options excite the spirit to devotion according to diverse considerations. But it seems that [option A] is more consonant with the judgment of reason, while [option B], it would appear, is more consonant with the piety of faith.[51]

He then proceeds to give four arguments in support of his final assertion that option B is more consonant with the piety of faith.

Before I turn to those arguments, however, we should note that Bonaventure, like those who came before him, expresses caution concerning his preference. We have observed this in several figures, most notably in Albertus Magnus, but also in Guerric, Thomas, and Odo. What was merely a hint of uncertainty in Grosseteste, which in no way shaped the form of his arguments, is integral to the responses to the hypothetical question by the time of Bonaventure. To call it a hesitation, as Bonnefoy has, does not quite convey how essential the assertion is to his position.[52] Like Albert and Thomas, Bonaventure's "hesitation" is demanded by his theological commitment to divine freedom.

---

51. III *Sent.* d. 1, a. 2, q. 2 (III, 24): "Quis autem horum modorum dicendi verior sit, novit ille qui pro nobis incarnari dignatus est. Quis etiam horum alteri praeponendus sit, difficile est videre, pro eo quod uterque modus catholicus est et a viris catholicis sustinetur. Uterque etiam modus excitat animam ad devotionem secundum diversas considerationes. Videtur autem primus modus magis consonare iudicio rationis; secundus tamen, ut apparet, plus consonat pietati fidei."

52. Jean Francois Bonnefoy, "La question hypothetique: utrum si Adam no peccasset ... au XIIIe siecle," *Revista esponola de teologia* 14 (1954): 351.

Bonaventure systematizes this commitment beyond anyone prior to him. Like Thomas, Bonaventure considers both options to be mere opinions. Like Albert, Bonaventure revisits and revises any and all arguments for and against his solution. Moreover, he takes up Guerric's "spiritual attraction" argument and moderates it, asserting that both options excite devotion in their own ways. And finally, Bonaventure engages in extensive hypothetical speculation to clarify not only his own preferred option B, but also to clarify option A in such a way that it retains its coherence and suasive power. As I will argue in the next chapter, Bonaventure's solution is a summative achievement of the debates we have been following across the thirteenth century. It is also an essential element of any theology of the motive for the incarnation.

Bonaventure gives four reasons for his assertion that option B is more consonant with the piety of faith. First, the authority of Scripture and the Saints states clearly that the Son came for the liberation and restoration of the human race. Moreover, no other reason is clearly given in these sources. In support of his position, Bonaventure cites Augustine multiple times, as well as Bernard and the *Gloss* on 1 Timothy.[53]

Second, God is more greatly honored if, per option B, God is not necessitated to act for the perfection or the completion of the universe. Option A argues that the incarnation in possible worlds without sin is fitting for the perfection of the universe (e.g., Grosseteste's created goods strategy). This implies, Bonaventure claims, that "in a certain way God is within the perfection of the universe."[54] However, with option B, God remains beyond every

---

53. While Bonaventure merely mentions "Bernardus," presumably the reference is to Bernard of Clairvaux's gloss on Jonah 1, which mentions Satan's foreknowledge of incarnation prior to his own fall, as in Thomas's *Scriptum* III, d. 1, q. 1, a. 3. The *Gloss* is a reference to the *Glossa Ordinaria* 114:626: "*Quia Christus Jesus.* Nulla causa veniendi fuit Christo, nisi quod peccatores salvos faceret."

54. III *Sent.* d. 1, a. 2, q. 2 (III, 25): "Nam praecedens dicit, quod Deum conveniebat incarnari ad perfectionem universitatis; et ideo quodam modo Deum intra perfectionem universi concludit."

perfection of the universe. "Christ is beyond (*supra*) every perfection of the universe, with regard to nature, grace, or glory."[55] Here, Bonaventure recalls Odo's teaching that Christ is *supra totam universam.*

Third, option B commends the *mystery* of the incarnation—the mystery that God would become incarnate to placate divine wrath and restore the entire creation for the fall of the noblest creature and offense against divine majesty. The argument recalls the incongruity of Guerric's spiritual attraction argument. In light of this great mystery, Bonaventure follows the third argument with a fourth; if God became incarnate to take away sin, rather than to complete an incomplete creation, then faithful affect is more inflamed.[56]

The four arguments for the concordance between option B and the piety of faith express the fundamental commitments of Bonaventure's position on the motive for the incarnation. To state them succinctly, the redemption from sin is the primary reason for the incarnation because:

(a) It is the only clear authoritative reason for the incarnation.

(b) It retains divine freedom over creation.

(c) It places Christ beyond all perfections of the universe.

(d) It commends the mystery of God's incongruous response to sin.

(e) It inflames the love of God in the heart of the faithful.

With these basic commitments in mind, we can now consider the various arguments for and against Bonaventure's preferred option B, as well as his rebuttals to the arguments for option A.

Bonaventure gives five reasons in support of his claim that re-

---

55. III *Sent.* d. 1, a. 2, q. 2 (III, 25): "Christum esse supra omnem perfectionem universitatis, sive quantum ad naturam, sive quantum ad gratiam, sive quantum ad gloriam."

56. III *Sent.* d. 1, a. 2, q. 2 (III, 25): "Etiam fidelem affectum magis inflammat. Plus enim excitat devotionem animae fidelis, quod Deus sit incarnatus ad delenda scelera sua quam propter consummanda opera inchoata."

demption from sin is the primary reason for the incarnation. The first three arguments, all from authority, substantiate Bonaventure's assertion, (a) above, that the primacy of redemption is clearly warranted by authority. He cites Paul's teaching in Galatians and Hebrews, as well as Augustine's *Gloss* on Jonah 1 and commentary on John 11. To these are later added the aforementioned citations from Augustine and Bernard. A fourth argument serves commitments (b) and (c) above; God assumed human nature neither because it was necessary nor on account of the dignity of human nature. The only need was a necessity of indigence arising from sin, our need for redemption. Otherwise God is not free over creation. Moreover, the dignity of humanity does not cause the incarnation, as angelic natures are more dignified than human natures. In fact, as Bonaventure puts it in the fifth argument, it is the indignity of fallen humanity, in need of liberation, that causes the incarnation. The fifth argument supports commitments (d) and (e) above, and follows Guerric by arguing that the primacy of redemption elicits greater gratitude than if the incarnation were required for the perfection of the universe.

These five reasons in support of the primacy of redemption from sin reinforce Bonaventure's central commitments. The nine arguments he supplies against his position, together with his rebuttals, further clarify his final solution. Bonaventure considers nine reasons for the incarnation prior to the redemption from sin: to satisfy some need of human nature, to manifest the divine nature, to actualize some created good independent of sin, and so on. He also considers one argument against his own position, and posits an original and highly influential argument from the predestination of Christ.

The majority of the nine alternative reasons Bonaventure recites are variations of Grosseteste's created goods strategies. The rebuttal to the second argument shows the basic features of Bonaventure's response to each of these Grossetestean arguments. The objector, citing a *Gloss* on Hebrews 2, argues:

If this dignity (of union with a divine person) is given to human nature, and human nature without the gift is frustrated, then if humanity had not sinned, so great a dignity would not have remained vacant, and humanity still would be united with divine nature. Thus, the liberation of human nature is not the primary reason (for the incarnation).[57]

If humanity possesses some capacity for union with a divine person, as it does in our de facto order, God would not frustrate human nature by denying that capacity its actualization.

Bonaventure's response is twofold. First, he refutes the principle that *any* created capacity must be actualized. A capacity is not frustrated simply because it isn't actualized (reduced to act), because there are many capacities which are not reduced to act and, nevertheless, creatures are not frustrated.[58] Second, he shifts from natural dignity and necessity to congruity or fittingness (*congruitas vel idoneitas*). Although the incarnation certainly confers a dignity upon human nature, the fittingness of the act derives "principally from the reparability of humanity."

And therefore, just as humanity would not have been repaired without having fallen, although (humanity) would have been reparable, so Divinity would not have been united, although it would have been unitable.[59]

But of course, reparability or unitability—capacity for reparation or unity—does not require actualization to avoid the frustration of the one bearing the capacity. Here Bonaventure is explicit; fittingness is distinct from necessity. He sometimes refers to these particular capacities as "fittingnesses" (*idoneitates*). Following Bonaventure's

57. III *Sent.* d. 1, a. 2, q. 2 (III, 22): "Si igitur haec dignitas data fuit naturae humanae, et humanae naturae nihil datum est frustra: ergo si non peccasset, talis dignitas non remaneret vacua: ergo adhuc uniretur cum divina natura: ergo liberatio generis humani non est ratio praecipua."

58. Of course, this is true if the capacity is not necessary to the natural integrity of the creature. Bonaventure's rebuttals to the created goods arguments demonstrate that he takes this into account.

59. III *Sent.* d. 1, a. 2, q. 2 (III, 26): "Illa idoneitas attenditur ex parte reparabilitatis hominis principaliter, quamvis ratione dignitatis et aliarum conditionum aliquo modo attenditur; et ideo, sicut homo non fuisset reparatus, si non cecidisset, quamvis esset reparabilis; sic Divinitati non esset unitus, quamvis esset unibilis."

suggestion, let us distinguish between natural capacities and fitting capacities. The former, it would seem, need to be actualized so that the creature will not be frustrated. The latter, however, are merely fittingly actualized. They are merely possible, in the sense that they need not be actualized. They are functionally similar to Thomas's obediential potencies.

The distinction between necessary and fitting capacities is critical for Bonaventure's rebuttals to the other created goods arguments. His general strategy is to show, first, that the relevant created good is only conditionally, accidentally, or occasionally (all terms he uses) actualized in the de facto order. This regularly involves him in counterfactual speculation as to the character of possible worlds without fall or incarnation (*X*-worlds). His goal is to demonstrate that relevant created goods would obtain in *X*-worlds in accidentally distinct modes. Second, Bonaventure often produces an argument that the incarnation contributes something commensurate with the accidental feature of the created good in possible worlds with sin and incarnation (*W*-worlds).

For example, Bonaventure appeals to Pseudo-Augustine's *De spiritu et anima* in support of beatitude as a reason for the incarnation prior to redemption from sin. Incarnation is necessary for the total beatitude of humanity. Bonaventure objects. Christ's body is not *essentially* necessary for the completion of beatitude, but only for a certain accidental delight. In support, he points out that not every human faculty (e.g., touch and taste) is granted its own corresponding object in beatitude. So, it cannot be necessary that every faculty requires an object for beatitude. Thus, he argues, in possible *X*-worlds the beatified would be beatified in their bodies. "For the glory of the exterior sense will be through the redounding of love arising from the superior part in the vision of God."[60] To think otherwise would be to derogate from the highest good.[61]

---

60. III *Sent.* d. 1, a. 2, q. 2 (III, 25): "Gloria enim sensuum exteriorum erit per redundantiam delectationis venientis a parte superiori ex visione Dei."

61. Here Bonaventure concurs with Guerric's judgment at *Quodl.* 7, a. 1, 14 (VG).

In III *Sent.* d. 1, a. 2, q. 1, Bonaventure argued for the congruity of the incarnation insofar as it manifests the infinite power, wisdom, and goodness of God. In question two, Bonaventure considers whether this reason would hold if humanity remained in a state of innocence. Once again, Bonaventure denies any need for God to "superadd" such a manifestation. These properties would be sufficiently manifest through the divine work of creation, distinction, and ornamentation.[62] In our world, God "superadded" the manifestation of divine wisdom, power, and goodness visibly through the incarnation as a consequence of the fall. Since humanity's internal light was obfuscated and turned toward sensible objects, God elected to manifest infinite wisdom, power, and goodness by taking on sensible flesh, just as Bonaventure had argued was congruous in the first question. And so, the incarnation is not necessary, but is rather apropos the condition of fallen humanity.

Several other created goods are given similar treatment. The incarnation is not necessary for merit. Divine grace is sufficient, and humans are able to receive divine grace simply by receiving the Holy Spirit and Son in their minds, as in angelic merit. While the incarnation is not necessary for merit, it is congruous with the condition of humanity after the fall, because after the fall humanity is in need of satisfaction. And Anselm has shown, in *CDH*, that satisfaction is most fittingly accomplished by the incarnation. Neither is the incarnation necessary for the headship of the church or for marriage between Christ and the church. Once again, Bonaventure makes an analogy with the angels, who have God as their head without natural conformity, and are united to God by charity rather than personal union.

Bonaventure also considers a variant of Grosseteste's argu-

---

62. Compare this point with Aquinas's argument at *Scriptum* III d. 1, q. 1, a. 3, where he argues, along similar lines, that infinite power, wisdom, and goodness are manifest in the creation of the most minute creature. Thomas modifies the argument slightly in *ST* III q. 1, a. 3, where he points to *creatio ex nihilo* as the manifestation of these properties.

ment for the completion of the circle of human generation. Unsurprisingly, he finds the argument unpersuasive. As he puts it, the generation of a human from woman alone is not for (*de*) the perfection of the universe, but beyond (*supra*) the perfection of the universe. Moreover, as he points out, if God does not become incarnate, nothing would prevent God from creating a human generated from a woman alone; this human simply would not be God. In objection six, Bonaventure considers a version of Grosseteste's argument, at *DCL* III.1. 5–6, that it is unfitting for an essence to derive from a privation.[63] Humanity would seem to receive advantage from a fault if the primary reason for the incarnation were redemption from sin. But this is not the case. The reason for the incarnation is not the malice of sin, but the great benignity and wisdom of God, manifest in the decision to restore human disobedience by satisfaction. In sum, Bonaventure recasts all the created goods arguments as arguments for congruity (akin to Thomas's arguments for fittingness), and refutes the Grossetestean claim that incarnation is a necessary condition of those goods. Such are the strategies Bonaventure advances against the Grossetestean deductions.

As we saw in the last chapter, Thomas's mature theology of the motive for the incarnation is carefully attuned to his larger theological emphases. He demonstrates profound insight into the issues confronting the theologian faced with the hypothetical question, and characteristically integrates them into his comprehensive theological vision. But the comprehensiveness is ordered primarily to Thomas's larger theological concerns over theology as *scientia* grounded in the articles of faith and proceeding according to *convenientia* in hypothetical speculation on the mysteries of faith. Bonaventure's early theology displays another kind comprehensiveness—on the full slate of issues entangled in his contemporaries' debates over the motive for the incarnation.

From what we have already seen, it is evident that Bonaventure,

63. See the treatment of this argument in chapter three above.

like Thomas, is aware of the distinction between the sources of his arguments as well as their relative importance. While weighing the positions (A and B), he notes that the former (A and the affirmative to the hypothetical question) is more warranted by speculative reasons, whereas the latter (B and the negative to the hypothetical question) is more warranted by revelation. Like the early Thomas of the *Scriptum* (and unlike the *Summa Theologiae*), Bonaventure considers authoritative arguments for both positions. For instance, he grants a place to the argument from *De spiritu et anima*, although only in an accidental sense, which is conditional upon the fall. In this way, the authoritative arguments for the alternative position are given a gloss similar to the revision of the speculative arguments he accepts "congruously": they are true for our world, given the condition of fall, and thus they show us something of the divine nature, usually divine beneficence.

There remains one very distinctive objection in question two. The fifth objects to Bonaventure's claim that the Son can become incarnate *occasionaliter* (conditionally) for the sake of expiation from sin. It seems to be unfitting that Jesus Christ, the most noble of creatures, should be conditionally created "since agents principally intend the nobler work."[64] It would seem, then, that the primary reason for the incarnation should not be redemption from sin, but rather the noble creature that is Christ's human nature itself, since agents intend their works in virtue of their relative nobility. Those familiar with the position of John Duns Scotus will notice the immediate resonances between the Seraphic and Subtle Doctors.

Intriguingly, Bonaventure does not accept the argument, although he admits it is rationally compelling. In fact, his response is rather thin, and does not reach to the heart of the objection as

---

64. III *Sent.* d. 1, a. 2, q. 2 (III, 23): "Si ergo inconveniens est, nobilissimam creaturam occasionaliter esse introductam, cum agens principaliter intendat opera nobiliora, videtur, quod inconveniens sit dicere, incarnationem factam esse propter hominis reparationem."

Duns Scotus will develop it. Bonaventure seems to understand the objection along the lines of the predestination objections we have encountered, for instance, in Grosseteste's argument on the fall of Satan. Thus, Bonaventure's response recalls Guerric and Odo's interpretation of Romans 1:4. Since God foresaw the fall of human nature from eternity, principle in God's intention is the conditional will to repair the damage of the fall by the incarnation. In short, foreknowledge of fall renders the conditional volition possible. But, of course, this does not address the argument for the primacy of Christ, in virtue of his exceeding nobility vis-à-vis all other noble works of God. For that argument, Bonaventure issues no rebuttal.

Recall the moment in the *Itinerarium* when the mind ascends to the final step, and discovers there Jesus Christ, "the like of which cannot possibly be found among creatures."[65] There Christ, the Mediator, brings the mind across, beyond its natural capacity for contemplation of God. Given this radical primacy, why does Bonaventure remain resolute in his preference for the redemption from sin as the primary reason for the incarnation? Consider the manner in which Christ, there at the mercy seat, carries the mind over into the final step of its journey into God:

He who turns his full countenance toward this Mercy-Seat and with faith, hope, and love, devotion, admiration, joy, appreciation, praise and rejoicing, beholds Christ hanging on the Cross, such a one celebrates the Pasch, that is, the Passover, with Him. Thus, using the rod of the Cross, he may pass over the Red Sea. . . he may rest with Christ in the tomb, as one dead to the outer world.[66]

At the height of the soul's ascent, Christ appears as the one whose nobility exceeds all other creatures, to take the soul across *by conformity to his Passion.*

Zachary Hayes has described Bonaventure's soteriology as one of "redemptive completion." Bonaventure conceives of the incar-

---

65. *Itinerarium* VII, 1.
66. *Itinerarium* VII, 7.

nation in the de facto order as simultaneously for both redemption and cosmic completion. Drawing upon the circular *egressio-reditio* pattern of Bonaventure's theology and his emphasis upon the exemplar causality of the Word, Hayes locates the created perfections achieved by incarnation (cosmic completion) on the redemptive shape of the Son's descent into flesh:

> In the obedience of the Second Man, the movement of *egressio* bends into a *reditio*, and the circle closes. But this cannot happen until the Word Himself has followed the aberrant creature through all the levels of being to its point of furthest distance from God.... In Christ, the broken image is restored in the incarnate Image; and creation, which in humanity was moving away from God, is touched by the cross at the furthest point of its flight away from God.... Through His incarnation and His passage through death, the Word has touched all levels of the hierarchy of being and restored the disrupted order. Reconciliation is not only moral but cosmic as well. Thus, the work of cosmic-completion takes the form of the redemptive work of Christ.[67]

Our observations from both the *Itinerarium* and the *Sentences* commentary fit with Hayes's description.

However, when Hayes comes to consider the motive for the incarnation, he is insistent that Bonaventure is in no way interested in the hypothetical order. Bonaventure does "try carefully to avoid anything external to God necessitating the divine in any way."[68] This concern, Hayes argues, leads Bonaventure to refute option A, as it seems to entail God becoming incarnate necessarily. On Hayes's reading, the Masters who hold option A "conclude that, in a certain way, the incarnation is necessary as the crown of creation," and this dimension of the argument Bonaventure finds unpalatable.[69] In order to overcome these negative implications of the

---

67. Hayes, *The Hidden Center*, 182. Hayes writes on this issue at some length in "Incarnation and Creation in the Theology of St. Bonaventure," in *Studies Honoring Ignatius Charles Brady Friar Minor*, ed. Romano Stephen Almagno, OFM, and Conrad L. Harkins, OFM, Theology Series 6 (St. Bonaventure, N.Y.: Franciscan Institute Publications, 1976).

68. Hayes, *The Hidden Center*, 188.

69. Hayes, *The Hidden Center*, 188.

created goods arguments in support of option A, Hayes points out that Bonaventure does not ask the hypothetical question. "This is a hypothetical question of little or no concern to him."[70] Rather, he asks the question of the primary reason for the incarnation in our de facto order, and there he permits the created goods, or cosmic completions, to persist as reasons for the incarnation alongside redemption from sin.

Fair enough, Bonaventure says explicitly that other reasons are annexed to redemption. But Hayes goes further. He resists the primacy question: "Bonaventure also sees the incarnation as the crown of creation; and as such it cannot proceed from God merely because of sin."[71] Hayes's replacement of Bonaventure's helpful term *praecipua* with "merely" only obfuscates the reading. If by "merely because of sin" is meant "for no other reason," of course Hayes is correct, as other reasons are annexed to it. But if by "merely because of sin" Hayes means "principally because of sin," it is difficult to understand how this position could be Bonaventure's. In fact, as I will make clear in the subsequent chapter, precision in hypothetical speculation allows the created goods arguments to avoid necessity while retaining their truth in our de facto state of affairs. Moreover, this strategy also allows us to interpret and appreciate Bonaventure's question regarding the primacy of redemption, which is difficult to express with precision absent the application of the possible worlds semantics I have been developing. So, Hayes is right to point to Bonaventure's vision of "redemptive completion," even if Hayes's analysis of the *praecipua ratio incarnationis* unnecessarily obscures the plain sense of the text.

---

70. Hayes, *The Hidden Center,* 187.

71. Hayes, *The Hidden Center,* 188–89. Hayes's analysis in *The Hidden Center* is accepted by Ilia Delio and developed into an argument that plays soteriological aims of the incarnation against cosmic ones, the latter superseding the former for the sake of modern theological considerations, such as ecology and interreligious dialogue, in ways anticipated by Hayes himself; Delio, "Revisiting the Franciscan Doctrine of Christ." See also Zachary Hayes, *Gift of Being: A Theology of Creation* (Collegeville, Minn.: Liturgical Press, 2001).

Matthew of Aquasparta (d. 1302) and
Richard of Middleton (d. c. 1308)

From the time of Bonaventure, Franciscan theologians at Paris generally accepted his basic solution. Matthew of Aquasparta and Richard of Middleton simply selected preferences from the options outlined by Bonaventure. Not until the proposal of John Duns Scotus did a new argument emerge, inaugurating a new moment in the debates over the motive for the incarnation at Paris.

Matthew of Aquasparta held the Franciscan Chair from 1275 to 1277.[72] His treatment of the motive for the incarnation, in *Quaestio* I of the Appendix to his *Quaestiones de Christo*, is deeply indebted to Bonaventure.[73] In brief, he takes Bonaventure's option A *sine praeiudicio*. Though his preference is not the same as Bonaventure's in his *respondeo* he follows Bonaventure's exposition of option A very closely, distinguishing between Christ's passible and impassible flesh. In Matthew's view, if Adam had not fallen, the Son would come in impassible flesh. However, as a result of the fall, the Son came in passible flesh. The subsequent argument of Matthew's *respondeo* follows Bonaventure's threefold classification of reasons for incarnation in impassible flesh: for the perfection of nature, grace, and glory. Perfection is the operative word, an emphasis that perhaps explains Matthew's preference for option A, against Bonaventure.

Regarding the perfection of nature, Matthew gives an argument from the unitability of human nature. If nature has a capacity for union with a divine person, and that capacity is not actualized, then nature would remain imperfect. This is the most basic form of the created goods arguments rehearsed by Grosseteste and Bonaventure. Matthew's second argument is for the circular concatenation of the universe—the union of the first, from which creation pro-

---

72. Glorieux, *Répertoire des Maîtres*.

73. Matthew Aquasparta, *Quaestiones disputatae selecta, Quaestiones de Christo* (Quaracchi, Italy: Collegii S. Bonaventurae, 1914).

ceeds, with the last, to whom creation returns. This was the only argument Bonaventure supplied from the perfection of nature. A third argument is given for the completion of the circle of generation in a human generated from a woman alone. Regarding the perfection of grace, Matthew recites Bonaventure's two arguments for the perfection of grace: for Christ's headship of the church, and for the meritorious nature of Christ's work. For the perfection of glory, Matthew gives the argument from Pseudo-Augustine's *De Spiritu et anima*, once again rehearsing Bonaventure. Finally, Matthew glosses the authorities cited for the opposite opinion according to the distinction between the passible and impassible flesh of Christ. In short, while Matthew prefers the opposite of Bonaventure's conclusion, it is not on the basis of any new understanding of the question, but simply a difference in how he weighs the evidence. The key features of his position are entirely Bonaventuran.

Richard of Middleton, Regent Master in the Franciscan Chair from 1284 to 1286, also prefers Bonaventure's option A.[74] At *Super* III *Sententiarum* d. 1, a. 2, q. 4, Richard asks whether the incarnation would have been if humanity had remained in a state of innocence.[75] Like Matthew, he favors the affirmative response. Unlike Matthew, Richard details the coherence of both Bonaventuran options. He begins with two speculative arguments—from the headship of the church and for the perfection of beatitude—in support of the affirmative. Subsequently, he gives two authoritative arguments in support of the negative, one from John of Damascus, the other from 1 Timothy 1:15. Richard then rehearses Bonaventure's distinction between the two options. He supplies further warrant from Anselm and Augustine in support of option B, which he notes "seems more concordant with holy authorities."[76] But he also

74. Richard Middleton, *Super quatuor libros Sententiarum Petri Lombardi questiones subtilissimae*, 4 vols. (Frankfurt am Main: Minerva, 1963).

75. *Super* III *Sententiarum* d. 1, a. 2, q. 4: "Utrum congruum fuisset Dei filium incarnari si natura humana permansisset in statu innocentia."

76. *Super* III *Sententiarum* d. 1, a. 2, q. 4: "Qui vult tenere opinionem secundam, quae magis videtur concors auctoritatibus sanctorum."

acknowledges that the alternative position (A) glosses those authorities according to the passibility of Christ's human nature.

Richard gives Bonaventuran rebuttals to the speculative arguments for option A, though he prefers it. That is, he speculates on possible worlds wherein God is head of the church and beatitude overflows from the intellectual into the sensitive soul. Like Bonaventure, then, he shows that both positions are defensible, even while stating his own preference. And so, if Matthew and Richard are any indication, Bonaventure's summative solution was quickly accepted by the Franciscans at Paris, who carefully read, considered, and then followed Bonaventure, even if they preferred other options on the hypothetical and primacy questions.

SIX ❧

Ratio Incarnationis

Now that we have encountered the various arguments and positions developed by the Dominican and Franciscan Masters, we can
characterize both the major developments in the debates over the
motive for the incarnation in thirteenth century Paris as well as the
relation of those debates to their predecessors in Anselm and Grosseteste. Once these various figures are drawn together, we can then
(1) give a concise dogmatic presentation of the summative solution
to the problem developed over the course of the thirteenth century in Paris, and (2) revisit the traditional characterization of the
motive for the incarnation as a debate between those who follow
Thomas and those who follow Scotus.

In order to achieve these aims, we need to isolate the primary
considerations observed in the preceding analysis of the debates
over the reason for the incarnation at Paris. These considerations
allow us to observe and characterize several important developments in the debates at the University of Paris over the course of
the thirteenth century. But before I isolate those considerations, let
us briefly recall the shape of the argument to this point.

In chapter one I formulated and clarified three questions.
These questions, I suggested, encompass the critical systematic
juncture of issues considered in the thirteenth century debates
over the motive for the incarnation. To wit:

- If humanity had not sinned, would God have become incarnate? (hypothetical question)
- What is the primary reason for the incarnation? (primacy question)
- How can we determine reasons for divine operations *ad extra?* (general question)

In chapter two, I derived Anselm's productive and problematic contribution of several "Anselmian theses" on the general question from the *CDH*. Chapter three detailed the ways in which Robert Grosseteste, in his *DCL*, developed those Anselmian theses into several arguments for the affirmative response to the hypothetical question. As we saw, Grosseteste pursued two strategies for determining divine reasons for divine operations *ad extra*. Grosseteste's strategies limn a set of challenges faced by theologians reflecting on the motive for the incarnation at the turn of the thirteenth century.

In light of Grosseteste's strategies, we can distinguish five important considerations that theologians of the thirteenth century worked with in formulating a position on the motive for the incarnation. As we saw, the function of divine attributes in Grosseteste's arguments restricted the domain of operations *ad extra* that are compossible with Grosseteste's God. One consideration (a), then, is the description of the divine attributes expressed or implied by theologians' responses to the hypothetical question and the primacy question. This consideration is integrally related to a second (b), the modal categories deployed. Consideration (b) includes both the particular senses of "necessity" and "possibility," as well as any other related categories developed in response to the question. The latter class would include concepts such as fittingness, suitability, probability, and congruity. In order to clarify the developments at Paris, I will utilize the concept "compossibility," as outlined in chapter one. I will also connect these modal categories with the first consideration by application of the phrase "compossible with *x*'s God."

The Parisian theologians' modal categories can be further refined by my possible worlds analysis, a third consideration (c). While my possible worlds semantics were not employed explicitly in the thirteenth century, the proliferation of counterfactual speculation in response to the hypothetical question render the debates amenable to such analysis. Moreover, my utilization of possible worlds semantics has already demonstrated their utility in clarifying arguments on the motive for the incarnation. With Grosseteste, possible worlds analysis allowed me to refine and query his arguments from divine attributes to divine operations *ad extra*. For instance, if Grosseteste's arguments are sound for the entire set of worlds compossible with Grosseteste's God (what I called a "confident" reading of Grosseteste), there will be an incarnation in every possible world compossible with Grosseteste's God. Therefore, the attribute of divine goodness, as Grosseteste applies it, severely restricts the domain of worlds compossible with Grosseteste's God. Theologians at Paris were disinclined toward such an interpretation of the divine attributes, though it took them time to reappropriate the Grossetestean arguments.

The fourth consideration (d) is a growing sensitivity exhibited by thirteenth century theologians to the sources of their arguments on the motive for the incarnation. It is therefore helpful to distinguish between two classes of arguments—authoritative and speculative—and their relative significance for each theologian. Authoritative arguments are those that rely upon the citation of some authoritative source, and usually raise issues of interpretation. Speculative arguments, on the other hand, do not rely upon authoritative sources for their argument (at least explicitly). Grosseteste's later applications of the created goods strategy, grouped under the heading of Christ's headship of creation, are good examples of speculative arguments. In those cases, a particular good is specified (e.g., the maximal union between creation and the Creator), and an argument is given to the effect that the incarnation is a necessary condition of that particular good. No direct appeals were made to authorities of the Christian tradition.[1]

---

1. There are, in some cases, appeals to philosophical authorities, but I will

Finally, it would be remiss to leave off a final consideration (e) of the actual response given by the theologians to their respective questions. While I have suggested that over reading the significance of a theologian's final response to the hypothetical question should be resisted, this is not to say their responses are unimportant. If, as I have argued, their responses gain importance once viewed in the larger context of argument, rebuttal, and development, that importance is significant. The question's importance is confirmed both by voiced anxieties about the hypothetical question and the transition to the primacy question, which never left behind the hypothetical, over the course of the thirteenth century.

Taken together, these five considerations will allow us both to synthesize the two preceding chapters, so that we can note key moments of development in the debates at Paris, and to clarify the positions of the Parisian theologians on the motive for the incarnation. The five considerations are:

(a) Divine Attributes
(b) Modal Categories
(c) Possible Worlds
(d) Authoritative and Speculative Arguments
(e) Responses

By tracking developments across these individual yet interrelated considerations, we can note the key moments within the Parisian debates and present, dogmatically, the final, summative solution to the motive for the incarnation developed at Paris in the thirteenth century.

---

include this class of arguments in the "speculative" category in light of the importance that appeals to authoritative Christian sources played in the debates.

Development at Paris

(a) Divine Attributes

Alexander's position bears marked similarities to Robert Grosseteste's *DCL*. He argues from divine goodness to the incarnation, citing the Dionysian dictum, "the Good is self-diffusive." However, Alexander tends to think of these arguments from divine attributes in terms of fittingness (*convenientia*) or usefulness (*utilitatem*). The brothers, in the *Summa Halensis,* reproduce Alexander's argument from the self-diffusion of divine goodness. The brothers also produce an intriguing argument from omnipotence: the incarnation actualizes the power of a divine person to be in three natures. But these reasons for the incarnation, derived from divine attributes, are not the ones the authors of the *Summa Halensis* find most compelling. Their preferred arguments derive from authority, most especially the argument from Pseudo-Augustine that incarnation makes it possible for both the sensitive and intellectual soul to "find pasture." They consider that reason applicable across all possible worlds without sin, but it remains unclear whether this is simply because God has willed it so (and thus it could be otherwise) or because God must actualize creation's capacity for union with God due to the perfection of the divine nature.

Alternatively, Guerric's strongest assertions are directed against the Grossetestean deductions that argue from divine attributes to the necessity of the incarnation for the perfection, beauty, or unity of the universe. For Guerric, deductive arguments from divine attributes to necessary divine operations *ad extra* vitiate divine transcendence and freedom, bringing God into servitude to creatures. Guerric's spiritual attraction argument follows from this insight. It is the incongruity of the incarnation's response to sin that he prefers to emphasize. Moreover, his final conditions for the incarnation are in a domain other than the perfections; they are in the domain of divine action (knowledge, capacity, and volition).

Odo Rigaldi departs similarly from Alexander and the brothers, not only in rejecting the affirmative response to the hypothetical question, but also in rejecting arguments from the self-diffusion of the Good. Odo grants that there must be some perfect diffusion, but thinks that this is satisfied by the essential diffusion of the eternal generation of the Son. God's nature as the summum bonum in no way obliges God to create a world, any more than it obliges God to create many worlds, and so Odo makes a distinction between divine will and power. This renders the actualization of created capacities a mere possibility, as God could do other than God has in fact done with any created effect, at least for those effects like the incarnation which are beyond the entire universe (*supra totum universum*).

Albert gives serious consideration to arguments markedly similar to Grosseteste's divine attributes arguments. But he consistently refuses to permit those arguments to arrive at necessity. His motivations are similar to Guerric's; Albert wishes to preserve divine freedom over any particular divine operation *ad extra*. Furthermore, Albert recognizes a difficulty overlooked by Guerric and partially addressed in Odo. Albert seeks to retain a qualified theological variant of the Aristotelian dictum "nature does nothing in vain," which he draws from Deuteronomy 32:4: "the works of God are perfect." The premise, in Grosseteste's application, produced deductions from created capacities to their necessary actualization. Albert's application is different. He distinguishes that which is *ex natura* from that which is *ex gratia*, and clearly states that the relevant consideration (the unitability of human nature with divinity) is *ex gratia*. Albert then argues that God is not bound to actualize the grace of union by the decision to create a creature with a nature unitable to God. Otherwise the union would not be grace. Like Guerric, Albert appeals to divine wisdom and divine volition. While divine perfection might be reflected in such decisions, the decision is not necessitated by that perfection.

Bonaventure, like Guerric, Odo, and Albert, refutes any argument that implies that the divine attributes obligate God to become incarnate. Like Odo and Albert, Bonaventure distinguishes between goods of nature and goods beyond (*supra*) nature. The latter cannot, by definition, be necessitated by God. In this way, Bonaventure follows Guerric et al. in emphasizing divine transcendence. Finally, and most importantly, Bonaventure's systematic application of *congruum* when giving Grossetestean arguments from the divine attributes make clear that those attributes, while they do not render divine operations necessary, do render them intelligible.

Thomas and Bonaventure hold the same position. For Thomas, the incarnation falls under the ordination of divine power. Therefore, a necessary condition for its actualization in any possible world will be a free volition issuing from the divine will. This principle holds for any other created effect falling under "the ordination of divine power." These would include created effects that are, to use Albert's terminology, *ex gratia*. On the other hand, created effects in "the natural order" are always fulfilled by God, due God's perfect goodness and liberality. While divine attributes supply necessary reasons for the fulfillment of these natural capacities, they only supply fitting reasons for those effects that are *ex gratia*. If God chooses to actualize those possible effects, then those effects will reveal attributes of the divine nature. Fitting reasons, then, reveal attributes of the divine nature, but are within the domain of the possible.

(b) Modal Categories

Already by the time of Alexander, the necessity attendant to the Grosstestean arguments was being supplanted by other modal categories. Alexander argues for the usefulness (*utilitas*) of the incarnation apart from the need for redemption. However, Alexander does not distinguish between necessity and possibility when he engages the Grossetestean arguments. The brothers express greater concern with the relation between fittingness, possibility, and necessity.

They distinguish between those things that are "absolutely possible" and those things that possess a "possibility of suitability," recasting the Grossetestean arguments in terms of the latter. In developing alternative modal categories from simply necessity or possibility, the brothers anticipate Aquinas and Bonaventure, although they are in no way as clear in their development or precise in their application.

For Guerric, the conditions for the incarnation are in the domain of divine action, especially divine capacity, and not in the domain of divine perfections. Thus, no necessary argument can be given on the motive for the incarnation. In his judgment, neither are the authoritative arguments determinative. He therefore produces probable reasons. He even explicitly acknowledges that his glosses of authorities and rational arguments are open to rebuttal, and so retains consistency with his ascription of probability to his position.

In comparison with the *Summa Halensis*, Odo's treatment is both an advancement and a regression. Perhaps in response to Guerric, Odo is far more assertive in rejecting any necessity that would restrict divine freedom and divine possibility. Thus, he distinguishes between goods of nature and goods of grace. He makes no appeal to fittingness, and so he straighforwardly rejects Grossetestean deductions, both deductions from divine attributes and deductions from created effects. Necessity is rejected, but fittingness and other forms of possibility remain undeveloped.

Albert's focus upon the unitability of human nature bespeaks his concern with possibility. He interweaves concerns over the metaphysical possibility of hypostatic union with his discussion of the motive for the incarnation. He is particularly eager to refute the possible union of angelic nature with divinity. But the possibility of union (unitability) with human nature is only that—a possibility. Hence, Albert refutes any Grossetestean demonstrations he encounters. His assertion that we could know the true answer to the hypothetical question only from revelation coincides with his conviction that the incarnation remains within the domain of the possible. No necessary demonstrations will succeed.

Bonaventure is the first figure to produce a complete modal proposal. It is remarkably similar to Thomas Aquinas's later proposal in the *Summa Theologiae*, although Bonaventure's earlier text uses *congruentia* where Aquinas would use *convenientia*. Bonaventure layers his reflection on the motive for the incarnation, inquiring first into its possibility, and second into its congruity. When he comes to the motive for the incarnation, he allows for two opinions (positions A and B), though he prefers the latter. This openness to a variety of responses characterizes Bonaventure's treatment of the motive for the incarnation and is critical to its own coherence. He engages in extensive counterfactual speculation to show that the incarnation is merely possible in worlds without sin; none of the reasons supplied obtain necessity. Therefore, it must be that multiple opinions can be held in response to the hypothetical question.

Thomas's great modal contribution is the consistent application of arguments *ex convenientia*. Earlier in Thomas's career he utilized *convenientia, probabilitas,* and *congruentia* variously to avoid the ascription of necessity to divine operations *ad extra*. By the time of the *ST* III, he settled on the category of *convenientia*. *Convenientia* arguments are reflections upon the acts of God in our *W*-world (with the fall and incarnation) that deliver insight into the divine nature. However, *convenientia* arguments do not determine God's course of action in our or any other possible worlds. They merely select one from a range of worlds compossible with Thomas's God, and articulate what would be revealed about that God by the various divine operations *ad extra* in those worlds in which God chooses to perform the operations. Therefore, *convenientia* remains within the domain of the possible, not the necessary.

(c) Possible Worlds

Alexander's various comments are too thin to render much of an analysis in terms of possible worlds. The brothers differentiate between two sorts of reasons: speculative and authoritative. The former reasons, many of which are variations of Grosseteste's reasons, are "fitting," which is to say, not necessary. Therefore, so far as those reasons are concerned, along with W-worlds (with a fall and an incarnation) like our own, both X-worlds (with neither a fall nor an incarnation) and I-worlds (with an incarnation but without a fall) are compossible with the brothers' God. Or, we might say, X-worlds are absolutely possible, but I-worlds are suitably, or fittingly possible. However, in light of the authorities cited, the brothers take it to be revealed that the incarnation would obtain even in possible worlds without a fall, insofar as a *ratio* is supplied (total beatitude, both intellectual and sensitive) for those worlds. In their words, this reason "circumscribes the fall of human nature."[2]

We can also refine Guerric's position by application of possible worlds semantics. Whereas only W-worlds and I-worlds are compossible with Grosseteste's God, X-worlds (with neither a fall nor an incarnation) are also compossible with Guerric's God.[3] Guerric's refutation of the created goods arguments favored by Grosseteste secures a larger domain of compossible worlds. Moreover, in keeping with his probabilistic reasoning, I-worlds remain compossible with Guerric's God. It is not that the union of Creator and creature is impossible in worlds without a fall, nor would such a union fail to contribute to the beauty of the universe. Were the Son incarnate in a sinless possible world, presumably the decorousness of that world

2. *SH* IV, P3, In1, Tr1, Q2, T2, p. 42.

3. The status of F-worlds (possible worlds with a fall and without an incarnation) also appear compossible, given Guerric's support of Augustine's argument in *Quodl.* 5, a. 1, 14 (V): "Verum est quod dicit Augustinus quod "alius fuit modus, sed nulus ita competens": nullo enim ita allicitur inimicus sicut per beneficia. Unde summa Dei benignitate summum debuit conferre beneficium, et haec est passio, quia *maiorem caritatem* etc." However, the magnitude of divine beneficence accomplished by an incarnation in a fallen world renders F-worlds improbable vis-à-vis W-worlds.

would be significantly enhanced by the hypostatic union, as in ours. Rather, Guerric's point is merely that a possible world without a fall or an incarnation would be satisfactorily decorous in the beauty of angelic spirits and human nature uniting creation as a microcosm. Likewise, the union of love (a union of wills) would suffice for the union of Creator and creature in X-worlds, which is not to say that this union could not be satisfied, and even augmented, by the union of a divine person with a creature.

It would seem that X-worlds, I-worlds, and W-worlds are all compossible with Odo's God. After all, Odo refutes all arguments from the divine attributes for the perfection of the universe and the perfection of beatitude. But there is the curious instance of his spiritual attraction argument. In Odo's treatment, the argument could be taken to entail that I-worlds are not compossible with Odo's God. That is, incarnation in possible worlds without a fall will not obtain since it would detract from the divine benignity that draws out the sinner's gratitude.

When Albert glosses 1 Timothy 1:15, he distinguishes between the phrases *in mundum* and *in hunc mundum*. That is, he distinguishes clearly between the cause of Christ's coming in this world (*in hunc mundum*) to redeem from sin through passion and death, and Christ's coming in another world. In the latter world, the reason for Christ's coming would be simply for the love of humanity and the unitability of human nature. Here Albert adverts clearly to a kind of possible worlds semantics. His assertion can be clarified with the vocabulary I have developed as follows: Our W-world is one of a number of worlds compossible with Albert's God. In some of those worlds, there is no fall, yet God becomes incarnate; they are I-worlds. In those worlds (or at least some of those worlds), Christ comes out of love for humanity and the unitability of human nature. Albert's arguments in the *Sentences* commentary can be rendered coherent with the *Quaestio* by noting that X-worlds are likewise compossible with Albert's God. This is because for any act that is *ex gratia*, such as the incarnation, it is sufficient that God wills it, so long as it does not violate the creature's nature. Presumably, then, in some possible worlds without a fall God wills to become incarnate (*I*-worlds), and in others God does not (*X*-worlds). This is consistent with Albert's assertion, at the close of the *Quaestio*, that it is possible to hold diverse opinions on the hypothetical question.

Bonaventure, simply put, holds all classes of worlds (*W*-worlds, *F*-worlds, *I*-worlds, and *X*-worlds) to be compossible with God. He supports both positions advocated by the Masters, even while preferring position B for its congruity with the piety of faith. Key here is his account of congruity, which anticipates Thomas's *convenientia*. Congruous reasons do not determine a particular created effect, but show the way in which that effect is consistent with the divine nature. The divine nature retains its properties across possible worlds; God has infinite power, whether that property is manifest in the creation of the world or in the assumption of human nature. Bonaventure also rejects the spiritual attraction argument if taken, as Odo seems to argue, as necessitating *I*-worlds (against *X*-worlds), since both positions on the hypothetical question are coherent *and attractive*. Nevertheless, since he leaves the argument from the predestination of Christ without full rebuttal, there is space for development of the rules for thinking through the set of worlds compossible with Bonaventure's God in light of his rule that "agents principally intend the nobler work." I will consider these possible revisions later, in light of Duns Scotus's arguments.

Finally, along with *W*-worlds like our own and *X*-worlds, it must be that *I*-worlds are also compossible with Thomas's God. As he says in the *corpus* of *ST* III, q. 1, a. 3, "the power of God is not limited to (becoming incarnate *if* the fall), so it would have been possible, even without sin, for God to become (incarnate)." *F*-worlds, with a fall and without an incarnation, are also compossible with Thomas's God, as elsewhere in the *Summa Theologiae* he rejects Anselm's necessary argument from satisfaction in the *CDH*.[4]

4. Aquinas's rejection of Anselm's argument has received considerable attention in secondary literature. In recent literature, see, for instance, Adam Johnson,

(d) Authoritative and Speculative Arguments

While Alexander does not demonstrate explicit reflection on the relative value of authoritative and speculative reasons, he does introduce the subsequently influential authority of the *praechonium paschale*. This text, which reappears especially among the Dominicans, may underlie the spiritual attraction arguments of Guerric and Odo. That is, the arguments of Guerric and Odo may be an exposition of the spirituality manifest in the *praechonium paschale*. Such a spirituality is, minimally, implicit in the liturgy. The *Summa Halensis*, on the other hand, reflects greater attention to the sources of arguments. The brothers seem to take the speculative reasons to arrive merely at fittingness, whereas the authoritative reasons, such as those given in *De spiritu et anima* or in St. Bernard, supply reasons sufficiently reliable to formulate a response to the hypothetical question. That is, the authorities supply reliable reasons for the incarnation in possible worlds without a fall—reasons independent of the fall.

Guerric asserts that no certainty can be given to any response to the question because Scripture is indeterminate. For this reason, he chooses the modal category of probability. The arguments from authority he cites, from Augustine and Paul, are all glossed in line with the argument from divine transcendence and the spiritual attraction argument that Guerric supplies in favor of the negative response. Authorities, Guerric supposes, are simply unclear, and can be interpreted in favor of a positive or negative response to the hypothetical question. He therefore leaves open multiple interpretations.

"A Fuller Account: The Role of 'Fittingness' in Thomas Aquinas' Development of the Doctrine of the Atonement," *International Journal of Systematic Theology* 12, no. 3 (2010): 302–18; Jerry Bracken, "Thomas Aquinas and Anselm's Satisfaction Theory," *Angelicum* 62, no. 4 (1985): 501–30; Matthew Cosgrove, "Thomas Aquinas on Anselm's Argument," *Review of Metaphysics* 27, no. 3 (1974): 513–30. Bracken's article is particularly insightful. In order to maintain focus, I am avoiding detailed analysis of what might be called the *ratio passionis*. This analysis of the *ratio incarnationis*, however, appears to be consistent with various theologians' wranglings with Anselm on the modal status and reason for the Passion, at least prima facie.

Albert is much less concerned with the sources of his arguments. Bonaventure, like Thomas, clearly distinguishes between the sources of his arguments as well as their relative importance. While weighing the positions (A and B), Bonaventure notes that the former (A and the affirmative to the hypothetical question) is more warranted by speculative reasons, whereas the latter (B and the negative to the hypothetical question) is more warranted by revelation. Like the early Thomas of the *Scriptum* (and unlike the later Thomas of the *Summa Theologiae*), Bonaventure considers authoritative arguments for both positions. For instance, he grants a place to the argument from *De spiritu et anima*, although only in an accidental sense, conditional upon the fall. In this way, the authoritative arguments for the alternative position are given a gloss similar to the revision of the speculative arguments he accepts "congruously": they are true for our world given the condition of a fall, and thus they show us something of the divine nature (usually beneficence).

Thomas is so consistent in his principles and arguments that his view of authoritative and speculative arguments can be concisely summarized: only arguments from sacred authorities can deliver divine reasons for divine operations *ad extra*, which are beyond the order of natural power. Speculative arguments, on the other hand, can be supplied in defense of divine operations *ad extra* for worlds compossible with Thomas's God. But those arguments are merely possible, and authoritative sources should be preferred for such things that are "truths of faith." Even the speculative arguments from fittingness, which show the attributes revealed by God's acts in our *W*-world, are subordinated to the arguments from authority. The authoritative reasons establish the position; the speculative arguments investigate the rationality of the position. In this way, Aquinas's method follows Anselm's method of faith seeking understanding.

(e) Responses

Alexander clearly prefers the affirmative response to the hypothetical question. Presumably, all the reasons for the incarnation supplied by Alexander are prior to redemption, and so he prefers the negative response to the primacy question. The brothers also advocate for an affirmative response to the hypothetical question. Not only does this imply a negative response to the primacy question, but the brothers also specify a reason prior to the redemption for sin: the pasture of the sensitive soul in the beatific vision. For the brothers, authorities are the primary means whereby we know divine reasons for divine operations *ad extra*. Thus, they distance themselves from the Grossetestean necessity and recast the speculative arguments as suitable or fitting. As a result, I have been reading the fitting arguments of the *Summa Halensis* as precursors to Thomas's *convenientia* arguments insofar as they demonstrate the coherence of particular divine actions with the divine nature.

For Guerric, the primary reason for the incarnation is the beneficent response to the fall, which, in virtue of its beneficence, draws the enemies of God back to God. Could this be another instance of Grosseteste's divine attributes strategy? Imagine an argument of the following form:

4.12 Incarnation for redemption from sin is more beneficent than incarnation for unity.

4.13 God is the most beneficent giver.

4.14 The most beneficent giver will choose to act in the most beneficent way.

4.15 Incarnation is for redemption from sin.

4.16 The primary *ratio* for the incarnation is for the sake of redeeming from sin.

Is this Guerric's argument? It seems not. All that we have seen of Guerric, his insistence on divine transcendence and his careful deployment of probability and rejection of necessity, mitigates against this reading. Moreover, Guerric's argument involves a response to a contingent event: the fall. The beneficence of God is expressed in the incongruity between the pride of Adam and the humility of Christ. In response to the fall, the Son becomes incarnate. God's volition, which is a free expression of God's beneficence, is a conditional volition, conditional upon the fall, and this conditional volition is the primary reason for the incarnation in our world.

Odo, in giving a negative response to the hypothetical question, gives an affirmative response to the primacy question. None of the arguments of Grosseteste, Alexander, and the brothers gain primacy vis-à-vis the redemption from sin, which is the most attractive option. All of Odo's central contributions serve to detract from the responses to the general question that precede him. However, there is an internal tension to Odo's position, similar to that of Guerric's. If the spiritual attraction argument functions along the lines of Grosseteste's deductive strategies, then we seem to have a violation of Odo's commitments to transcendence. That violation is reflected in a response to the general question that is substantially the same as Grosseteste's; we can determine divine reasons for divine operations by reasoning from divine attributes (in this case, divine beneficence).

While Albert makes an original speculation on possible worlds and notes that the incarnation could have diverse causes in diverse worlds, he does not consider the relationship between the two distinct causes considered in the two sets of possible worlds he specifies (*in mundum* and *in hunc mundum*): redemption and love. Given the way that Albert describes the cause of the incarnation *in hunc mundum*, it appears that his response to the primacy question would be that the redemption from sin by passion and death is the primary reason for the incarnation in our world. Other reasons might exist for other possible worlds, but Albert does not consider whether those reasons are present in our own world, nor how they would be related to the reason of redemption from sin.

Finally, Bonaventure takes up the primacy question explicitly. That question, together with Bonaventure's response, marks a summative moment in the series of debates over the motive for the incarnation extending back to Grosseteste. I will demonstrate, momentarily, this achievement and clarify the ways in which Bonaventure's response to the primacy question entails proposals in response to the general question as well as a response to the hypothetical question.

Thomas is clear that the negative response to the hypothetical question should be preferred. He also considers numerous reasons that are subordinate to redemption from sin, including those goods that are for the sake of the furtherance in good. In this light, we might anticipate a negative response to the primacy question for Aquinas, and in fact this is the very position developed by Thomists from Capreolus on.

But two important caveats must be made. First, Thomas's openness to other hypothetical situations, reflected in the consistent assertion of possible incarnations in worlds without sin, is required by the fundamental premises of Thomas's response to the hypothetical question, which he shares with Guerric and Albert. All goods that are not "capacities of natural power" have as a necessary condition of their actualization that God wills them. That condition holds across all worlds compossible with Thomas's God, and so God is genuinely free for incarnation in any compossible world. Second, Thomas is so hesitant with regard to counterfactual speculations that we do not detect any systematic reflection upon resemblance across possible worlds, which was found incipient in Grosseteste. Nevertheless, resemblance would explain his preference for the negative response to the hypothetical question. Thomas's argument holds for those possible worlds that resemble our own insofar as God has the same reasons for incarnation. But there would be no problems with God actualizing other possible worlds for a distinct set of divine reasons, because nothing requires God's having the reasons of the de facto order.

The Motive for the Incarnation in
Three Moments

In light of these five considerations, we can now distinguish three moments in the series of debates over the motive for the incarnation in thirteenth century. The first moment is represented by the thought of Robert Grosseteste and Alexander of Hales, and, to a lesser extent, by the *Summa Halensis*. The second moment runs from Guerric of Saint-Quentin to Albert the Great, and includes the position of Odo Rigaldi. The third moment is represented by Bonaventure of Bagnoregio and Thomas Aquinas.

Moment One

At Oxford, Robert Grosseteste produced a litany of arguments for the conclusion that the Son would become incarnate even if Adam had not sinned. His arguments reduce to two forms, or strategies as I have called them. In the former, the "divine attributes" strategy, Grosseteste argues from some divine attribute to the conclusion that God would become incarnate in possible worlds without sin. For instance, because God is the highest Good, and the Good is diffusive of itself, God would be diffuse in creation in the greatest possible way, which is by incarnation.

Grosseteste's "created goods" strategy builds on the first. Because God is perfect, etc., God will actualize any maximally good possibility in the order of nature or of grace. For instance, since the universe is possibly united to the Creator by hypostatic union (which we know to be the case from our W-world), and since that union would render the universe better than it would be otherwise (because it would be more unified), a perfect God would actualize that possibility independent of sin. In both strategies the attributes of the divine nature determine God's action to be "best" or "most perfect" in every possible world. Thus, the domain of worlds compossible with Grosseteste's God is restricted to W-worlds (with an incarnation and a fall) and *I*-worlds (with an incarnation but without a fall).

Alexander of Hales gives us very little, but what we have is highly amenable to Grosseteste's strategies. In fact, all three arguments Alexander supplies in support of his position are found with slight variations in Grosseteste. He also goes beyond Grosseteste in supplying an argument for the alternative position from the authority of the *praechonium paschale*. But Alexander does not find this argument on the hypothetical question compelling. And so, we can characterize the first moment in the thirteenth-century debates as one in which deductive arguments from divine attributes restrict the domain of worlds compossible with God to those which include incarnation. The Anselmian theses are upheld in Anselm's sense and his arguments from fittingness, including especially the gradation arguments, are rendered deductively.

The *Summa Halensis*, while upholding the affirmative conclusion on the hypothetical question shared by Alexander and Grosseteste, evinces a growing discomfort with the implications of the Grossetestean arguments. The brothers distanced themselves from Anselm on the distinction between divine will and power, giving an incipient form of the absolute-ordained power distinction. Like Lombard, they distinguish between God's power and will by arguing that God could, in fact, do otherwise than is done in our world. Thus, they distinguish between absolute and suitable possibility. While they lack the refined distinction of the third moment, we can detect the beginnings of a revision to the approach developed by Grosseteste and suggested by Alexander. The brothers therefore mark a transition between the first and second moments, and anticipate certain aspects of the summary solution of the third moment.

Moment Two

Guerric of Saint-Quentin holds two central commitments. The first is both Guerric's most fundamental commitment and the contribution that distinguishes the second moment from the first. Like the *Summa Halensis*, Guerric emphasizes divine freedom and transcendence. He straightforwardly rejects the Grossetestean arguments in order to retain God's freedom over creation. This is the central commitment of the second moment: God's freedom from necessary action in creation. Second, Guerric produces the highly influential spiritual attraction argument. However, that argument could be rendered as a divine attributes argument along the lines of Grosseteste. Moreover, Guerric gives us no way of accounting for the fact that Grosseteste's arguments, while failing as deductions from the divine attributes (otherwise divine freedom is vitiated), nevertheless supply reasons for the incarnation in our *W*-world.

Odo Rigaldi follows Guerric's rejection of the Grossetestean deductions and summarily rejects each Grossetestean argument he considers. Odo also supports Guerric's spiritual attraction argument for the negative response to the hypothetical question. If the second moment is characterized by emphasis upon divine freedom over creation, Odo reflects this emphasis and contributes a new dimension to the position. Among the created goods achieved by the incarnation in our world, Odo distinguishes between those that are "of the universe" (*de universo*) and those that are "beyond the entire universe" (*supra totum universum*). In this way, he refutes not only the divine attributes strategy, but also the created goods strategy, particularly the arguments from those goods that concern Christ as he is head of humanity. But once again, Odo does not give an account of those Grossetestean reasons in our *W*-world, and possibly undermines his emphasis upon transcendence in his affirmation of Guerric's spiritual attraction argument.

The most consistent expression of the second moment is given by Thomas's teacher, Albert the Great. He expresses utter commitment to divine freedom. Every argument for both the affirmative and negative is rebutted, and the only justification he gives for his preference (the affirmative response to the hypothetical question) is that it is more consistent with the piety of faith (possibly a reference to Guerric's spiritual attraction argument). Albert also develops Odo's distinction between that which is *de universo* and that which is *supra totum universum* by his parallel distinction between that which is from nature and that which is from grace. Moreover, he makes the first explicit reference to possible worlds in the debate over the motive for the incarnation when he distinguishes between reasons for incarnation "in a world" (*in mundum*) and "in this world" (*in hunc mundum*).

Moment Three

The third moment is summative, and Bonaventure is its finest expositor. Like the theologians of the second moment, he foregrounds divine freedom, insisting that God could do otherwise than the deductive reasons of Grosseteste and Alexander allow. However, unlike the second moment, he reappropriates the Grosseteste-an reasons by developing the category of congruity, a strategy that Thomas follows in his appeal to fittingness in the later *Summa Theologiae*. For both Bonaventure and Thomas, Grosseteste's arguments show the congruity that obtains between a specific divine operation *ad extra* and the divine nature. The operation is not necessitated by God's possession of the relevant attribute, but is nevertheless compossible with God's possession of that attribute. Unlike Anselm, Bonaventure and Thomas are clear that God's possession of an attribute, such as goodness, does not necessitate an action such as incarnation being elicited. It could be otherwise; there are other kinds of worlds compossible with that God. Congruous reasons do not violate this commitment to God's freedom. They retain the commitment that, across all possible worlds, God's decision to become incarnate has a free divine volition for that action as a necessary condition. And yet, congruous reasons still permit the faithful to reflect upon the actions of God in our *W*-world, and thereby to obtain knowledge of the divine nature on the basis of free divine actions.

Bonaventure's treatment of the motive for the incarnation also incorporates Guerric's spiritual attraction argument. But he does not permit the argument to attain Grossetestean implications. In fact, he states clearly that both options are spiritually attractive. Like Thomas, Bonaventure's position remains strictly preferential—language of belief, preference, and possibility are consistently applied. For Bonaventure, as with Albert, openness to both positions taken by the Masters is not cowardice, or lack of imagination, or deference. He demonstrates great ingenuity to sustain the genuine possibility of both responses. Bonaventure argues in more detail across hypothetical scenarios than any other theologian. Building upon Albert's distinction between *in mundum* and *in hunc mundum*, he considers various possible modes of beatitude, kinds of union between God and the church, and so on.

The third moment, then, is characterized by its openness to a broad range of possible worlds. This openness retains the possibility of multiple responses to the hypothetical question. That Thomas takes this course is most apparent in the *Scriptum*. As I have argued, the *Summa Theologiae* reflects substantially the same position. Thomas retains his preference for the authoritative arguments throughout his career (against speculative arguments). In the *Scriptum*, he notes that the authorities are susceptible to glossing against his own preferred response. In the *Summa Theologiae*, he simply asserts the possibility of either response to the hypothetical question. These assertions are consistent with his central commitment: God's motives are known only to God. In Thomas's judgment, it is of paramount importance to remain close to revelation. But, as he states explicitly in the *Scriptum*, even those revelations cannot be interpreted with certainty since they can also be glossed otherwise.

We can see, then, that to characterize Thomas's position as hamartiocentric is peculiar.[5] His arguments do not assert anything more than a preference. For all we know, it appears that redemption from sin is the reason for the incarnation such that, without

5. See, for instance, Gerald O'Collins, *Christology: A Biblical, Historical, and Systematic Study of Jesus*, 2nd ed. (Oxford: Oxford University Press, 2009), 208–11.

the fall, God would not have become incarnate. But it could be otherwise. Moreover, all the goods granted by the incarnation, which appear in the Grossetestean arguments, are granted in the de facto order by Thomas in the questions preceding the hypothetical question in the *Summa Theologiae.*

Thomas's preference for the negative response to the hypothetical question raises an important issue made explicit in the third moment of the debates: the distinction between authoritative and speculative arguments. Grosseteste had already noted this distinction and, finding no conclusive argument for whether or not God would have become incarnate had there been no fall, feels free to speculate on the question. By the time Bonaventure considers the primacy question, enough debate has passed for him to observe that the two positions on the hypothetical question and the primacy question are characterized by distinct evidentiary tendencies. Those supporting the negative to the hypothetical question (and affirmative to the primacy question) find more warrant from authority, while those supporting the alternative position find more warrant in speculative reasons. But, very importantly, Bonaventure notes that both positions have both authoritative and speculative support. Moreover, he lays out ways of rebutting both classes of arguments for both positions. For speculative arguments, he engages in hypothetical speculation to show they do not succeed. For authoritative arguments, he gives ways of glossing the authorities for both positions.

Unsurprisingly, in the third moment the question migrated from its hypothetical expression to the primacy question. This new question does not refute the possibility of hypothetical speculation, however. Instead, it aligns the developing insistence on divine freedom with the critical issue of the motive for the incarnation. By introducing the concept of *primacy,* Bonaventure focuses the question on the de facto order, but in a way that utilizes the resources of counterfactual speculation to analyze primacy among diverse reasons in that order.

Bonaventure's reformulated question allowed theologians to

speculate without necessitating divine operations *ad extra*. This development was coincident with a refinement of the modal categories of congruity and fittingness to resolve theological issues like the motive for the incarnation. As a result, the *question* of the motive for the incarnation was given precise articulation in the third moment: What is the primary reason for the incarnation? That is, in worlds that resemble our own as much as excepting sin makes possible (including, importantly, God possessing the same reasons for action), is there a reason for God to will an incarnation *prior* to humanity's need for redemption from sin?

Now we can succinctly describe the movement of the Parisian debates. Initially, theologians produced a series of reasons for the incarnation, which they thought would obtain even if the need for redemption did not. Subsequently, theologians objected to the form of those initial arguments: they were deductive reasons descending from divine attributes. They therefore rejected them in order to preserve divine freedom. Finally, theologians, while retaining the commitment to divine freedom, recast the initial reasons according to congruity or fittingness. At that time, Bonaventure was able to reformulate the question with greater precision.

The Summative Solution: A Dogmatic Presentation

Both Bonaventure and Thomas bring together the various arguments and concerns of the first two moments into a coherent synthesis. As I have argued, this summative position is expressed principally by Bonaventure, but also found in Thomas. The summative, third-moment solution can be expressed in six assertions:

(6.1) *No necessary reasons for the incarnation can be given.* The incarnation is a free divine operation. A necessary condition of its actualization is a free divine volition, where free means "it could be otherwise." Therefore, both *I*-worlds (with an incarnation and without a fall) and *X*-worlds (with neither an incarnation nor a fall) are compossible with God.

(6.2) *The hypothetical question is generically insoluble.* Arguments can therefore be supplied to show that none of the speculative arguments encountered obtain in all possible worlds (à la Bonaventure). Likewise, authoritative arguments can be glossed in favor of either interpretation.

(6.3) *Hypothetical speculation can (and should) be engaged so long as resemblance is upheld.* Given the supposition of a resemblance of divine reasons between the hypothetical world under consideration and our W-world (as far as excepting sin permits), counterfactual speculation is a precise way to clarify the order of reasons within our world.

(6.4) *The question of the motive for the incarnation can be asked more precisely in the form of the primacy question.* For the question of the motive for the incarnation to proceed while retaining a resemblance relationship between the counterfactual world under consideration and our own W-world (with the fall and incarnation), the concept of priority proves helpful. By focusing investigations on the conjunction of reasons surrounding the redemption from sin, and isolating the world(s) that resembles our own W-world as much as excepting sin permits, hypothetical speculations allow for reflection upon God's action in our world without restricting divine freedom.

(6.5) *Reasons from divine attributes are congruous or fitting.* These reasons, while actual reasons for God's incarnation in our world, express the *congruity* between a divine attribute and a freely willed divine action. The act retains a free divine volition as a necessary condition. This is true both for the Grossetestean arguments *as well as* for the spiritual attraction argument of Guerric and others. In whatever formulation, these reasons ought not hold for all possible worlds such that neither X-worlds nor I-worlds are compossible with the relevant description of God. Gradation arguments are particularly threatening on this point.[6]

---

6. N.b., this sort of revision would be the appropriate way to develop a "cautious" interpretation of Robert Grosseteste. Importantly, it avoids the overweening

(6.6) *These proposals render the question salutary for Christian reflection on the incarnation.* Reflection on the incarnation along these lines permits reason to interrogate the revelation of God in Jesus Christ, the object of faith. Thus, faith seeks understanding. Or, as Thomas put it in the *Summa contra Gentiles*, reasons are given that make the faith known for the training and consolation of the faithful.

Before I consider the reception of this summative solution, let us pause to consider its relation to the Anselmian theses, which were critical sources for the thirteenth-century debates over the motive for the incarnation. Most basically, the summative solution accepts Anselm's principles. Divine operations *ad extra* cannot be necessary; they must be free. But the summative solution also makes an important Lombardian revision to the concept of freedom anticipated in the *Summa Halensis* by distinguishing between divine power and divine will. As a result, while the attributes of the divine nature certainly restrict the domain of possible divine operations *ad extra*, a greater domain of compossible worlds emerges. Critical here is the rearticulation of congruity and fittingness by Bonaventure and Thomas. The position therefore refuses the application of the gradation arguments from fittingness as developed by Grosseteste. We can say, then, that fittingness arguments show the way in which some state of affairs is compossible with the divine nature. However, those arguments do not account for which particular state of affairs would be actualized by God. The divine will makes that determination, and so we can mark a distinction between divine will and divine power. This is reflected by the retention of a greater domain of compossible worlds (including X-worlds, contra Grosseteste).[7]

---

anti-hypothetical animus of the revised readings proposed by Unger and McEvoy, as recited in chapter three, while following Unger's helpful analysis of Grosseteste's certainty in Unger, "Grosseteste on the Reasons for the Incarnation," 35–36.

7. I am leaving off the important question of the compossibility of F-worlds. See the secondary literature on various figures in relation to Anselm in Rosato, "The Interpretation of Anselm's Teaching." Also, note the important argument from

John Duns Scotus (d. 1308)

In light of what we have encountered to this point, the treatment of the motive for the incarnation by John Duns Scotus is striking in its novelty. Bonaventure, while reframing the question and summatively resolving the first two moments of the debates, also introduced the original consideration of Christ's predestination, a topic tangentially treated in earlier appeals to Romans 1. When the argument from Christ's predestination was articulated by Bonaventure, he introduced a new premise to the debates: "Agents act principally for the nobler end." But his rebuttal did not address the premise. Instead, he rehearsed the standard rebuttal to Romans 1 that the prevision of sin was presupposed in God's predestination. This overlooked premise was taken up and developed by John Duns Scotus.

In what follows I will, first, outline the basic treatment of the question as advanced by John Duns Scotus by weaving together his treatment of the question in the *Ordinatio* III, d. 7, q. 3, in *Reportatio* III, d. 7, q. 4, and in the *supplementum* of *Ordinatio* III, d. 19, the three standard texts on the topic.[8] Once I have detailed Scotus's argument, I will consider its relation both to the questions we have been following and to the summative position on the motive for the incarnation, outlined above. In this way, I will clarify the

---

Duns Scotus at *Lectura* III, d. 20, q. 1, as well as the argument's evaluation in the literature, most recently in Andrew S. Yang, "Scotus' Voluntarist Approach to the Atonement Reconsidered," *Scottish Journal of Theology* 62, no. 4 (2009): 421–40; Steven S. Aspenson, "Anselmian Satisfaction, Duns Scotus, and the Debt of Sin," *Modern Schoolman* 73, no. 2 (1996): 141–58.

8. It should be noted that the *supplementum* of *Ordinatio* III, d. 19, was deemed inauthentic by no less reputable an authority than Charles Balić, in "*Duns Skotus lehre über Christi prädestination im lichte der neuersten forschungen*," in *Wissenschaft und weisheit* 3 (1936): 19–35. Balić's views, however, are not universally accepted on this score. See Odón Lottin, "*L'Ordination' de Jean Duns Scot sur le livre III des Sentences*," in *Recherches de théologie ancienne et médiévale* 20 (1953): 102–19. *Ord.* III, dd. 18–25, appear to be added from Lectura by an early anonymous redactor, and reproduced to complete Scotus's *Ordinatio* in subsequent editions, including the Wadding edition reimpressed by Vivès in 1894. For a fuller treatment, see *Ordinatio*, vol. 10, *Opera omnia*, ed. B. Hechich et al. (Vatican City: Typis Vaticanis, 2007), 42*–46*.

relationship between the new moment in the debates inaugurated by Scotus and the summative achievement of Bonaventure and Thomas.

Scotus's response has been rehearsed many times over.[9] In the *Ordinatio* III, his comments on the motive for the incarnation arise as the first *dubium* to the inquiry "whether Christ was predestined to be the Son of God," as Paul seems to assert in Romans 1. Following an analysis of the Pauline text, Scotus considers two *dubia*. First, he asks "whether (the predestination of Christ) necessarily follows upon the fall of human nature."[10] Second, he inquires "whether this nature's union with the Word or its ordination to glory was first."[11] His responses to these *dubia* give the fundamental premises for what would come to be known as the "Scotist" position on the motive for the incarnation.

Scotus considers the hypothetical question in the first *dubium*. His premise is straightforward: "The universally ordinate willer seems first to will that which is closest to the end."[12] As an example, Scotus states that God intends individuals to glory prior to grace (where prior means more proximate to the end). This principle will be all the more true when applied to Christ, since his soul is predestined to the *highest* glory.[13] Since Christ's soul attains the highest glory by union to a divine person, that soul is closest to the end (glory), and therefore first in the order of divine intentions. And so, God wills the glory of Christ's soul before the prevision of Adam's fall. The affirmative response to the hypothetical question and negative response to the primacy question follows.

---

9. Most recently in Pomplun, "The Immaculate World," 531–33. Pomplun's treatment is particularly attuned to speculation on the impassible flesh of Christ.

10. *Ord.* III, d. 7, q. 3, 286: "Utrum ista praedestinatio praeexigat necessario lapsum naturae humanae."

11. *Ord.* III, d. 7, q. 3, 289: "An prius praevidebatur huic naturae unio eius ad Verbum vel ordo ad gloriam."

12. *Ord.* III, d. 7, q. 3, 287: "Universaliter enim, ordinate volens prius videtur velle hoc quod est fini propinquius."

13. *Ord.* III, d. 7, q. 3, 287: "Multo magis est hoc verum de praedestinatione illius animae quae praedestinabatur ad summam gloriam."

Bonaventure, reflecting on the predestination of Christ, formulated a similar argument on the basis of Christ's nobility. Since "agents principally intend the nobler work," it would be unfitting for God to will the noblest creature conditionally.[14] Scotus's argument also hinges upon the value of Christ's soul: "But it does not seem on account of redemption alone that God predestined Christ's soul to such glory, since neither the redemption or glory of the souls to be redeemed are so good as the glory of Christ's soul."[15] Moreover, as Scotus points out, the alternative carries several problematic entailments. Not only would the predestination of Adam to glory, and presumably the predestination of all the blessed to glory, precede the predestination of Christ, but so would the prevision of the fall precede the predestination of Christ. This, to Scotus's mind, is most absurd.

Scotus clarifies the subtleties of his position with a subsequent question in the second *dubium*. Which is intended first, the glory of Christ's soul or the union of Christ's human nature with the Word? It is in response to this question that Scotus formulates a fundamental premise of the subsequent Scotist tradition:

> It is possible to say that, since that which is intended proceeds conversely in the action of the artist than the manner in which it is executed, and God unites Himself to a human nature in the order of execution naturally before He grants that nature the highest grace and glory, He intended it inversely. That is, God first willed that some nature, not the highest, have the highest glory . . . then secondly willed that nature to exist in the person of the Word.[16]

---

14. III *Sent.* d. 1, a. 2, q. 2 (III, 23).

15. *Ord.* III, d. 7, q. 3, 288: "Sed non propter illam solam videtur Deus predestinasse illam animam ad tantam gloriam, cum illa redemptio sive gloria animae redimendae non sit tantum bonum quantum est illa gloria animae Christi."

16. *Ord.* III, d. 7, q. 3, 289: "Potest dici quod cum in actione artificis sit contrarius processus in exsequendo ei, qui est in intendendo, et Deus prius natura ordine exsecutionis univit sibi naturam humanam quam contulit sibi gratiam summam vel gloriam, e converso posset poni in intendendo, ut sit Deus primo volens aliquam naturam non summam habere summam gloriam . . . et quasi secundo voluit illam naturam esse in persona Verbi."

Earlier, in response to the opening question of d. 7, q. 3, Scotus established the possibility of God's predestination of a nature rather than a person. Here, introducing the premise, "the order of execution is the inverse of the order of intention," Scotus argues that first in the order of intention is the volition for Christ's human nature to attain glory, followed by the volition for union with the second person of the Trinity.

This order of intentions is consistent with the order of intentions fleshed out more extensively in both the *Reportatio* III, d. 7, q. 4, and the *supplementum* to *Ordinatio* III, d. 19. In the *Reportatio* Scotus gives five *instantia*:[17]

First, God loved Himself. *Second*, He loved Himself for others, and this is a pious love. *Third*, he willed himself to be loved by another who is able to love him highest, speaking of love from someone extrinsic. *Fourth*, he foresaw union with that nature, which ought to love him highest, even if no one had fallen.... And therefore in a *fifth* instant he saw the mediator coming, suffering, and redeeming his people.[18]

So, God wills the greatest glory, or highest love of God, for the nature of Christ, prior to foreseeing the union of that nature with God.[19] The order of *instantiae* in the *Reportatio* is articulated slightly differently than the order in the *supplementum* to *Ordinatio* III, d. 19,

17. An excellent explication and defense of the *instantia* (or *signa*) *rationis* is given in the introduction to Bonnefoy, *Christ and the Cosmos*. Carol also gives an account and defense in *Why Jesus Christ?* 135–37.

18. *Reportatio* III d. 7, q. 4, 14–15: "Primo Deus diligit se; secundo diligit se aliis, et iste est amor castus; tertio vult se diligi ab alio qui potest eum summe diligere, loquendo de amore alicuius extrinseci; et quarto praevidit unionem illius naturae, quae debet eum summe diligere etsi nullus cecidisset.... Et ideo in quinto instantia vidit Deus mediatorem venientem passurum, redempturum populum suum."

19. There is some debate over whether Scotus upholds this sequence between the prior divine volition of Christ's soul to glory and subsequent volition for hypostatic union in light of the *supplementum* to *Ord.* III, d. 19. Those texts, as well as a brief discussion of Scotist evaluations of this matter, are discussed in Pomplun, "The Immaculate World," 8n23. Of course, whatever the order of these two *instantia*, they are both prior to the prevision of the fall and God's volition for Christ as redeemer, and so either option upholds the affirmative response to the hypothetical question and the negative response to the primacy question.

though both concur with the fundamental argument of *Ordinatio* III, d. 7.

I say that the incarnation of Christ was not occasioned by prevision (of sin), but was immediately foreseen by God from eternity as a good proximate to the end. . . Thus this was the order in divine prevision: that *first* God knew himself under the *ratio* of the highest good; *second* he knew all creatures; *third* he predestined some to glory and grace, and concerning those not predestined he had no positive act; *fourth* he foresaw all those fallen in Adam; *fifth* he foreordained and foresaw a remedy, how they would be redeemed through the passion of his Son, so that Christ in the flesh, just as all the elect, first had been foreseen and predestined to grace and glory, and then the passion of Christ was foreseen as a medicine against the fall, just as a physician wills first the health of a human, then wills the medicine for healing the human.[20]

In this case, the *instantiae* are articulated in terms of prevision and knowledge, whereas the *Reportatio* articulates them in terms of love. But in all three occasions where Scotus considers the motive for the incarnation, it is apparent that the prevision of sin and fall is subsequent to both the volition for the highest glory to Christ and the volition to personal union with Christ's human nature. And it is apparent that this order is justified by the fundamental orientation of the divine will to the divine glory and divine self-love. God's self-love is the first movement of the divine will, and every volition for an operation *ad extra* is ordered to this fundamental volition *ad intra*.

20. John Duns Scotus, *Ordinatio*, vol. 14, *Opera omnia*, ed. Luke Wadding (Paris: Vivès, 1894), III (suppl.), d. 19, 714: "Quantum ad primum, dico quod Incarnatio Christi non fuit occasionaliter praevisa, sed sicut finis immediate videbatur a Deo ab aeterno ... tunc iste (g) fuit ordo in praevisione divina; primo enim Deus intellexit se sub ratione summi boni; in secundo signo intellexit omnes alias creaturas; in tertio (h), praedestinavit ad gloriam et gratiam, et circa alios habuit actum negativum, non praedestinando; in quarto (i) praevidit illos casuros in Adam; in quinto (j), praeordinavit sive praevidit de remedio quomodo redimerentur per passionem Filii, ita quod Christus in carne (k), sicut et omnes electi, prius praevidebatur et praedestinabatur ad gratiam et gloriam, quam praevideretur passio Christi, ut medicina contra lapsum, sicut Medicus prius vult sanitatem hominis, quam ordinet de medicina ad sanandum." On the *supplementum* of *Ordinatio* III, see note 8 above.

A final note should be made concerning Scotus's treatment of the motive for the incarnation. Scotus famously speculates that, if Adam had not fallen, Christ would have become incarnate in impassible flesh. In the *Ordinatio*, he notes that "all authorities [for the opposite position] are able to be expounded thus: that Christ would not have come as redeemer, unless humanity had fallen, nor perhaps as passible."[21] Here Scotus follows Bonaventure very closely, like Matthew of Aquasparta and Richard Middleton before him. In the *Reportatio*, he reiterates and expands the point: "I say that glory is ordained to Christ's soul, and the flesh insofar as it is capable, just as it was conveyed to the soul in assumption. Therefore [glory] would have been conveyed immediately to the flesh, unless it was delayed for a greater good."[22] The redemption of fallen human nature is such a greater good; it is greater than the immediate glorification of Christ's flesh, but not of Christ's soul.

Consider now Scotus's position on the motive for the incarnation in relation to Bonaventure and Thomas, as well as the subsequent reception of Bonaventure's summative solution in the Franciscan tradition. In light of the latter context, Scotus is quite clearly developing Bonaventure's option A. The signature mark of the passible-impassible distinction is included, as well as the affirmative response to the hypothetical question and the negative response to the primacy question. However, it is notable that Scotus does not take the course of Matthew of Aquasparta or Richard Middleton in his argument. Whereas Matthew structured his arguments around the threefold perfections of Bonaventure's text, Scotus avoids entirely the arguments from the perfections of nature, grace, and glory. Instead, he develops exclusively one specific argument for the negative response to the primacy question, which was mentioned, but not rebutted, by Bonaventure.

21. *Ord.* III, d. 7, q. 3, 287: "Omnes auctoritates possunt exponi sic, scilicet quod Christus non venisset ut redemptor nisi homo cecidisset, nec forte ut passibilis."

22. *Reportatio* III, d. 7, q. 4, 15: "Dico quod gloria est ordinata animae Christi et carni, sicut potest carni competere, et sicut fuit collata animae in assumptione; ideo statim fuisset collata carni, nisi quod propter majus bonum illud dilatum."

Scotus's argument is, in fact, perfectly consistent with the summative solution laid out above. Indeed, Scotus presumes God's free volition to become incarnate, and merely argues for the proper order among the reasons for that volition (6.1). He focuses on the reasons in our de facto order, and employs hypothetical speculation only for the possible worlds resembling our own with respect to divine reasons (6.2–3). While Scotus departs from Bonaventure's primacy question, his investigation of the predestination of Christ continues a Bonaventuran approach to the question, while allowing further refinement according to the *instantia* (6.4). And while Scotus does not give an account of congruity or fittingness for the divine attributes arguments, given the context, it is sensible to assume that his silence on this point reflects an acceptance of the summative proposal of Bonaventure (6.5). Finally, Scotus's arguments confirm my assertion that the summative solution not only gives a satisfactory response to the issues of the first three moments, but also makes possible reason's fruitful interrogation of the revelation of God in Jesus Christ (6.6).

On Thomas and Scotus

In chapter one, I suggested that locating Thomas and Scotus in the larger context of thirteenth-century debates will allow us to reconsider the common presupposition that they were substantially divided on the motive for the incarnation. In light of my analysis, as far as Thomas and Scotus themselves are concerned, it is preferable to distinguish between their contributions, not as members of two camps, but as belonging to two distinct moments in the history of the debates over the motive for the incarnation. Thomas's arguments are nicely suited to the third moment, and while later Thomists developed his arguments into a refutation of Scotus, it was not inevitable that his arguments were developed in that direction. Indeed, in light of Scotus's coherence with Bonaventure and Bonaventure's similarity to Thomas, the actual arguments of

Thomas and Scotus on the motive for the incarnation are substantially coherent with one another. Minimally, we can say that we do not know what Thomas would make of Scotus's arguments, as by all indications he never encountered their like.

Of course, this is not to say there is not substantial disagreement between the positions of the Thomists and the Scotists taken up in later debates between the Franciscans, Dominicans, and (eventually) Jesuits. Later Thomists developed substantial rebuttals to Scotus's arguments, just as later Scotists made substantial developments to their founder's position. Intriguingly, some of the debates of the first and second moments reemerge in the debates over the *instantia rationis*. One can detect a hint of Guerric's spiritual attraction argument, for instance, when Reginald Garrigou-Lagrange, following Cardinal Cajetan, asserts:

> Therefore the whole teaching of St. Thomas, of St. Bonaventure, and others is summed up in these words: the motive of the Incarnation was formally the motive of mercy. As the Psalmist says: "Have mercy on me, O Lord, for I am weak." "Have mercy on me, for I am poor." "Have Mercy on me, O Lord, for I am afflicted."[23]

The appeal to mercy hearkens back to Guerric, Odo, and Bonaventure. And once again, in Garrigou's argument, it takes the form of an appeal to the divine attributes. For Garrigou, the debate over the reason for the incarnation is a debate between the mercy of God and the perfect ordination of the divine will. If this is the case, he reasons, the appeal to divine perfection underlying Scotus's "most ordinate willer" eventuates in the necessity of the incarnation. Interestingly, he argues, the Scotist *ordinatissime volens* is plagued by the Grossetestean necessities; Garrigou even raises the specter of Leibnitz and Malebranche against the Scotist arguments![24]

This brings me to my final judgment on the matter. Scotus's ar-

---

23. Garrigou-Lagrange, *Christ the Savior*, 94.
24. Garrigou-Lagrange, *Christ the Savior*, 99.

guments open a new moment in the history of the debates over the motive for the incarnation. If, as I have argued, Scotus's new arguments develop in line with the summative solution outlined above, three implications follow. First, arguments from the divine attributes and created or gratuitous effects, as outlined above, will not win the day. The disagreement between the Thomists and Scotists is not the same as the disagreement between Grosseteste, on the one hand, and Bonaventure, Thomas, and Scotus, on the other. Second, neither should we accept characterizations of a Christocentric Scotist position over against the hamartiocentrism of the Thomist school. While the position of Scotus renders an absolute primacy to Christ, Christ enjoys primacy in a significant sense in Thomas, as in Bonaventure. Third, while the Grossetestean arguments should be put to rest, the debates that have emerged between the Thomists and Scotists, focused upon the order of divine intentions without entailing God's necessary actualization of created potencies, should continue to flourish. In these debates, as in the reflections on the congruous reasons for the incarnation, faith seeks understanding, and the mystery of God's action in Jesus Christ is rendered more attractive. And thereby, the hearts and minds of the faithful are strengthened.

Bibliography

Primary Sources

Albert the Great. *Commentarii in* III *Sententiarum*. Vol. 28, *Opera omnia*. Edited by A. Borgnet. Paris: Vivès, 1894.

———. *Quaestio de conceptione Christi*. Vol. 25, Bk. 2, *Opera omnia*. Edited by Henryk Anzulewicz and Wilhelm Kübel. Münster: Aschendorff, 1993.

Alexander of Hales. *Glossa in quatuor libros Sententiarum Petri Lombardi*. Edited by PP. Collegii S. Bonaventurae. 4 vols. Quaracchi, Italy: Collegii S. Bonaventurae, 1951–57.

——— (?). *Doctoris irrefragabilis Alexandri de Hales Ordinis minorum Summa theologica*. Edited by PP. Collegii S. Bonaventurae. 4 vols. Quaracchi, Italy: Collegii S. Bonaventurae, 1924–48.

———. *Quaestiones disputatae "antequam esset frater."* Edited by PP. Collegii S. Bonaventurae. 3 vols. Quaracchi, Italy: Collegii S. Bonaventurae, 1960.

Anselm of Canterbury. *The Major Works*. Edited by G. R. Evans and Brian Davies. Oxford: Oxford University Press, 1998.

———. *Memorials of St. Anselm*. Edited by R. W. Southern and F. S. Schmitt. Auctores Britannici Medii Aevi 1. London: The British Academy, 1969.

———. *S. Anselmi opera omnia*. Edited by F. S. Schmitt. 2 vols. Edinburgh: Thomas Nelson and Sons, 1946.

Aristotle. *The Complete Works of Aristotle*. Edited by Jonathan Barnes. Translated by W. D. Ross. 2 vols. Princeton, N.J.: Princeton University Press, 1984.

Bonaventure. *Commentaria in quatuor libros Sententiarum Magistri Petri Lombardi*. Vols. 1–4, *Opera theologica selecta*. Edited by PP. Collegii S. Bonaventurae. Quaracchi, Italy: Collegii S. Bonaventurae, 1934–49.

———. *Itinerarium mentis in Deum*. Vol. 5, *Opera omnia*. Edited by PP. Collegii S. Bonaventurae. Quaracchi, Italy: Collegii S. Bonaventurae, 1891.

———. *The Journey of the Mind to God*. Edited by Stephen F. Brown. Translated by Philotheus Boehner, OFM. Indianapolis, Ind.: Hackett, 1993.

Capreolus, John. *Defensiones theologiae Divi Thomae Aquinatis*. Edited by C. Paban and T. Pègues. 7 vols. Tours: Alfred Cattier, 1900–7.

Glossa Ordinaria. Patrologia Latina 113–14. Edited by Jacques-Paul Migne. Paris: Garnier, 1852.

Grosseteste, Robert. *De cessatione legalium*. Edited by Richard C. Dales and Edward

B. King. *Auctores Britannici Medii Aevi* 7. London: The British Academy, 1986.

Guerric of Saint-Quentin. *Guerric of Saint-Quentin: Quaestiones de Quolibet.* Edited by J. Black and W. H. Principe. Studies and Texts 143. Toronto: Pontifical Institute of Mediaeval Studies, 2002.

———. *On the Truth of the Holy Scripture.* Translated by Ian C. Levy. Kalamazoo: Medieval Institute Publications, 2001.

Matthew Aquasparta. *Quaestiones disputatae selecta, quaestiones de Christo.* Quaracchi, Italy: Collegii S. Bonaventurae, 1914.

Notker Balbulus. *Patrologia Latina* 131, edited by Jacques-Paul Migne. Paris: Garnier, 1853.

Pascasius Radbertus. *De corpore et sanguine Domini: cum appendice Epistola ad Fredugardum.* Edited by Bedae Paulus. Corpus christianorum, continuatio mediaevalis 16. Turnholt: Brepols, 1969.

Peter Lombard. *The Sentences.* Translated by Giulio Silano. 4 vols. Toronto: Pontifical Institute of Mediaeval Studies, 2007–10.

———. *Sententiae in IV libris distinctae.* Edited by PP. Collegii S. Bonaventurae. Spicilegium Bonaventurianum 4–5. Grottaferrata, Italy: Collegii S. Bonaventurae, 1971–81.

Plato. *Plato: Complete Works.* Edited by John M. Cooper. Indianapolis, Ind.: Hackett, 1997.

Pseudo-Dionysius. *Pseudo-Dionysius: The Complete Works.* Translated by Colm Luibhéid and Paul Rorem. The Classics of Western Spirituality. New York: Paulist Press, 1987.

Richard of Middleton. *Super quatuor libros Sententiarum Petri Lombardi questiones subtilissimae.* 4 vols. Frankfurt am Main: Minerva, 1963.

———. *On the Cessation of the Laws.* Translated by Stephen M. Hildebrand. The Fathers of the Church, Mediaeval Continuation 13. Washington, D.C.: The Catholic University of America Press, 2012.

Rupert of Deutz. *De gloria et honore filii hominis super Mattheum.* Edited by H. Haacke. Corpus Christianorum continuatio mediaevalis 29. Turnhout: Brepols, 1979.

Scotus, John Duns. *Lectura* III. Vols. 20–21, *Opera omnia.* Edited by B. Hechich, B. Huculak, J. Percan, S. Ruiz de Loizaga, and C. Saco Alarcón. Vatican City: Typis Vaticanis, 2003–4.

———. *Reportatio Parisiensis.* Vol. 3, *Ioannis Duns Scoti, doctoris Mariani, theologiae marianae elementa.* Edited by Carl Balić. Sibenici: Kačić, 1933.

———. *Ordinatio.* Vols. 9–10, *Opera omnia.* Edited by B. Hechich, B. Huculak, J. Percan, and S. Ruiz de Loizaga. Vatican City: Typis Vaticanis, 2006–7.

———. *Ordinatio.* Vol. 14, *Opera omnia.* Edited by Luke Wadding. Paris: Vivès, 1894.

Thomas Aquinas. *De rationibus fidei ad Cantorem Antiochenum.* Vol. 40, *Opera omnia iussu Leonis XIII P.M. edita.* Rome: Typographia Polyglotta, 1968.

———. *Quaestiones disputatae de veritate.* Vol. 22, Bks. 1/1–3/2, *Opera omnia iussu Leonis XIII P.M. edita.* Rome: Typographia Polyglotta, 1970–76.

———. *Scriptum super libros Sententiarum.* Edited by P. Mandonnet and M. F. Moos. 4 vols. Paris: Lethielleux, 1929–47.

———. *Summa contra Gentiles.* Vols. 13–15, *Opera omnia iussu Leonis XIII P.M. edita.* Rome: Typographia Polyglotta, 1918–30.
———. *Summa theologiae.* Vols. 4–12, *Opera omnia iussu Leonis XIII P.M. edita.* Rome: Typographia Polyglotta, 1886–1906.
———. *Super Epistolas S. Pauli lectura, t. 2: Super primam Epistolam ad Timotheum lectura.* Edited by R. Cai. Marietti: Taurini-Romae, 1953.
Wyclif, John. *De veritate Sacrae Scripturae.* Edited by R. Buddensieg. 3 vols. London: Trübner for the Wyclif Society, 1905–7.

Secondary and Modern Sources

Adams, Marilyn McCord. "Elegant Necessity, Prayerful Disputation: Method in *Cur Deus Homo.*" In *Cur Deus homo: Atti del congresso Anselmiano internazionale: Roma, 21–23 Maggio 1998,* edited by Paul Gilbert, Helmut Kohlenberger, and Elmar Salmann, 367–96. Rome: Centro Studi S. Anselmo, 1999.
———. "The Primacy of Christ." *Sewanee Theological Review* 47 (2004): 164–80.
———. *Christ and Horrors: The Coherence of Christology.* Cambridge: Cambridge University Press, 2006.
Alston, William P. "Divine and Human Action." In *Divine Nature and Human Language: Essays in Philosophical Theology,* 81–102. Ithaca, N.Y.: Cornell University Press, 1988.
Anscombe, G. E. M. *Intention.* 2nd ed. Cambridge, Mass.: Harvard University Press, 1963.
Aspenson, Steven S. "Anselmian Satisfaction, Duns Scotus, and the Debt of Sin." *Modern Schoolman* 73, no. 2 (1996): 141–58.
Audet, OP, Th-Andre. "*Approches historiques de la Summa Theologiae.*" In *Etudes d'histoire litteraire et doctrinale,* 7–29. Universite de Montreal publications de l'institut d'etudes medievales 17. Montreal: J. Vrin, 1962.
Balić, Charles. "Duns Skotus lehre über Christi prädestination im lichte der neuersten forschungen." *Wissenschaft und Weisheit* 3 (1936): 19–35.
Barnes, Corey L. *Christ's Two Wills in Scholastic Thought: The Christology of Aquinas and Its Historical Contexts.* Toronto: Pontifical Institute of Mediaeval Studies, 2012.
———. "Necessary, Fitting, or Possible: The Shape of Scholastic Christology." *Nova et Vetera* 10, no. 3 (2012): 657–88.
Barth, Karl. *Church Dogmatics.* Edited by G. W. Bromiley and T. F. Torrance. Translated by G. W. Bromiley. New York: T&T Clark, 2004.
Bauerschmidt, Frederick Christian. "Incarnation, Redemption, and the Character of God." *Nova et Vetera* 3, no. 3 (2005): 459–72.
———. *Thomas Aquinas: Faith, Reason, and Following Christ.* Oxford: Oxford University Press, 2013.
Bissen, Johannes. "De motivo incarnationis." *Antonianum* 7 (1932): 314–36.
Boh, Ivan. "Divine Omnipotence in the Early *Sentences.*" In *Divine Omniscience and Omnipotence in Medieval Philosophy: Islamic, Jewish, and Christian Perspectives,* edited by Tamar Rudavsky, 185–211. Synthese Historical Library 25. Dordrecht: D. Reidel, 1985.

Bonnefoy, Jean Francois. "La question hypothetique: utrum si Adam no peccasset ... au XIIIe siecle." *Revista esponola de teologia* 14 (1954): 327–68.

———. *La primauté du Christ selon l'ecriture et la tradition.* Rome: Herder, 1959.

———. *Christ and the Cosmos.* Translated by Michael D. Meilach. Paterson, N.J.: St. Anthony Guild Press, 1965.

Bracken, Jerry. "Thomas Aquinas and Anselm's Satisfaction Theory." *Angelicum* 62, no. 4 (1985): 501–30.

Brady, Ignatius. "The Distinctions of Lombard's Book of Sentences and Alexander of Hales." *Franciscan Studies* 25 (1965): 90–116.

———. "The Edition of the '*Opera Omnia*' of St. Bonaventure." *Archivum Franciscanum historicum* 70 (1977): 352–76.

Brown, David. "'Necessary' and 'Fitting' Reasons in Christian Theology." In *The Rationality of Religious Belief: Essays in Honour of Basil Mitchell*, edited by William J. Abraham and Steven W. Holtzer, 211–30. Oxford: Clarendon Press, 1987.

Calvin, John. *Institutes of the Christian Religion.* Edited by John T. McNeill. Translated by Ford Lewis Battles. Vol. 1. Philadelphia, Pa.: Westminster Press, 1960.

Carol, Juniper B. *Why Jesus Christ? Thomistic, Scotistic, and Conciliatory Perspectives.* Manassas, Va.: Trinity Communications, 1986.

Cessario, Romanus. *The Godly Image: Christ and Salvation in Catholic Thought from St. Anselm to Aquinas.* Studies in Historical Theology 6. Petersham, Mass.: St. Bede's Publications, 1990.

Chrysostom, Fr. "La redemption est-elle le motif de l'incarnation?" *La France Franciscain* 14 (1931): 113–67.

Colish, Marcia L. *Peter Lombard.* 2 vols. Brill's Studies in Intellectual History 41. Leiden: Brill, 1994.

Cosgrove, Matthew. "Thomas Aquinas on Anselm's Argument." *Review of Metaphysics* 27, no. 3 (1974): 513–30.

Courtenay, William J. "Necessity and Freedom in Anselm's Conception of God." *Analecta Anselmiana* 4, no. 2 (1975): 39–64.

———. *Capacity and Volition: A History of the Distinction of Absolute and Ordained Power.* Bergamo: Pierluigi Lubrina Editore, 1990.

Crisp, Oliver. "John Calvin (1509–1564) on the Motivation for the Incarnation." In *Revisioning Christology: Theology in the Reformed Tradition*, 23–42. Burlington, Vt.: Ashgate, 2011.

Cross, Richard. *The Metaphysics of the Incarnation: Thomas Aquinas to Duns Scotus.* Oxford: Oxford University Press, 2002.

Davidson, Donald. "Actions, Reasons, and Causes." *Journal of Philosophy* 60 (1963): 685–700.

———. *Essays in Actions and Events.* Oxford: Oxford University Press, 1980.

Davies, Brian and Brian Leftow, eds. *The Cambridge Companion to Anselm.* Cambridge: Cambridge University Press, 2006.

Davis, Adam J. *The Holy Bureaucrat: Eudes Rigaud and Religious Reform in Thirteenth-Century Normandy.* Ithaca, N.Y.: Cornell University Press, 2006.

Delio, Ilia. "Revisiting the Franciscan Doctrine of Christ." *Theological Studies* 64, no. 1 (2003): 3–23.

Doucet, Victorin. "The History of the Problem of the Authenticity of the Summa." *Franciscan Studies* 7, no. 1 (1947): 26–41.

———. "The History of the Problem of the Authenticity of the Summa (Continued)." *Franciscan Studies* 7, no. 3 (1947): 274–312.

———. *Prolegomena in librum* III *necnon in libros* I *et* II *Summa Fratris Alexandri.* Vol. 4, Pt. 2, *Alexandri de Hales Summa Theologica.* Quaracchi, Italy: Collegio S. Bonaventurae, 1948.

Dreves, Guido Maria. *Ein jahrtausend lateinischer hymnendichtung: Eine blütenlese aus den analecta hymnica mit literarhistorischen erläuterungen.* Leipzig: O. R. Reisland, 1909.

Gaine, Simon. *Will There Be Free Will in Heaven?: Freedom, Impeccability, and Beatitude.* New York: Continuum, 2003.

Garrigou-Lagrange, Reginald. "*Motivum incarnationis fuit motivum misericordiae.*" *Angelicum* 7 (1931): 289–302.

———. *Christ the Savior: A Commentary on the Third Part of St. Thomas' Theological Summa.* Translated by Dom Bede Rose. London: B. Herder Book, 1950.

Gelber, Hester Goodenough. *It Could Have Been Otherwise: Contingency and Necessity in Dominican Theology at Oxford, 1300–1350.* Leiden: Brill, 2004.

Gils, P. M. "Textes inédits de St. Thomas. Les premières rédactions du Scriptum super Tertio Sententiarum." *Revue des sciences philosophiques et théologiques* 45 (1961): 201–28.

———. "*S. Thomas écrivain.*" Vol. 50, *Opera omnia iussu Leonis XIII,* 173–209. Rome: Cerf, 1992.

Ginther, James R. *Master of the Sacred Page: A Study of the Theology of Robert Grosseteste, ca. 1229/30–1235.* Burlington, Vt.: Ashgate, 2004.

Glorieux, Palémon. *Répertoire des Maîtres en théologie de Paris au XIIIe siècle.* Etudes de philosophie médiévale 17–18. Paris: J. Vrin, 1933.

Goergen, Donald. "Albert the Great and Thomas Aquinas on the Motive of the Incarnation." *The Thomist* 44, no. 4 (1980): 523–38.

Hayes, Zachary. "Incarnation and Creation in the Theology of St. Bonaventure." In *Studies Honoring Ignatius Charles Brady Friar Minor,* edited by Romano Stephen Almagno, OFM and Conrad L. Harkins, OFM, 309–29. Theology Series 6. St. Bonaventure, N.Y.: Franciscan Institute Publications, 1976.

———. *The Hidden Center: Spirituality and Speculative Christology in St. Bonaventure.* New York: Paulist Press, 1981.

———. *Gift of Being: A Theology of Creation.* Collegeville, Minn.: Liturgical Press, 2001.

Henriquet, F. M. "*Etudes de Rosny, OFM, Etudes Rigaud et la somme d'Alexandre d'Hales.*" Archivum Franciscanum historicum 33 (1940): 3–54.

Henry, Desmond Paul. *The Logic of Saint Anselm.* Oxford: Clarendon Press, 1967.

Hibbs, Thomas. *Dialectic and Narrative in Aquinas: An Interpretation of the* Summa Contra Gentiles. Notre Dame, Ind.: University of Notre Dame Press, 1995.

Honnefelder, Ludger. "John Duns Scotus on God's Intellect and Will." In *John Duns Scotus 1308–2008: The Opera Theologica of Scotus. Proceedings of "The Quadruple Congress" on John Duns Scotus, Part 2,* edited by Richard Cross, 73–88. Archa Verbi Subsidia 4. St. Bonaventure, N.Y.: Franciscan Institute Publications, 2012.

Horan, Daniel P. "How Original Was Scotus on the Incarnation? Reconsidering

the History of the Absolute Predestination of Christ in Light of Robert Grosseteste." *Heythrop Journal* 52 (2011): 374–91.

Jenson, Robert W. *Alpha and Omega: A Study in the Theology of Karl Barth.* New
York: Nelson, 1963.

Johnson, Adam. "A Fuller Account: The Role of 'Fittingness' in Thomas Aquinas'
Development of the Doctrine of the Atonement." *International Journal of
Systematic Theology* 12, no. 3 (2010): 302–18.

Knuuttila, Simo, ed. *Modalities in Medieval Philosophy.* London: Routledge, 1993.

———. *Reforging the Great Chain of Being: Studies of the History of Modal Theories.*
Synthese Historical Library 20. Dordrecht: D. Reidel, 2010.

Kretzmann, Norman. *The Metaphysics of Theism: Aquinas's Natural Theology in* Summa Contra Gentiles *I.* Oxford: Oxford University Press, 1997.

Lewis, David. "Causation." *Journal of Philosophy* 70, no. 17 (1973): 556–67.

———. "Counterfactual Dependence and Time's Arrow." *Nous* 13, no. 4 (1979):
455–76.

Long, R. James. "The Cosmic Christ: The Christology of Richard Fishacre, OP."
In *Christ among the Medieval Dominicans: Representations of Christ in the Texts and
Images of the Order of Preachers,* edited by Kent Emery and Joseph Wawrykow,
332–43. Notre Dame Conferences in Medieval Studies 7. Notre Dame, Ind.:
University of Notre Dame Press, 1998.

Lottin, Odón. "*L'Ordination' de Jean Duns Scot sur le livre III des Sentences.*" *Recherches de Théologie ancienne et médiévale* 20 (1953): 102–19.

Lovejoy, Arthur O. *The Great Chain of Being: A Study of the History of an Idea.* Cambridge, Mass.: Harvard University Press, 1964.

Marshner, William. "A Critique of Marian Counterfactual Formulae: A Report of
Results." *Marian Studies* 30 (1979): 108–39.

Matthews, Scott. *Reason, Community and Religious Tradition: Anselm's Argument and
the Friars.* Burlington, Vt.: Ashgate, 2001.

McEvoy, James. "The Absolute Predestination of Christ in the Theology of
Robert Grosseteste." In *Robert Grosseteste: Exegete and Philosopher,* 212–30.
Aldershot, Hampshire: Variorum, 1994.

———. *Robert Grosseteste.* Great Medieval Thinkers. Oxford: Oxford University
Press, 2000.

———. "Robert Grosseteste as Spiritual Guide." In *Robert Grosseteste and His
Intellectual Milieu: New Editions and Studies,* edited by John Flood, James R.
Ginther, and Joseph W. Goering, 87–101. Toronto: Pontifical Institute of
Mediaeval Studies, 2013.

Moltmann, Jurgen. *Trinity and the Kingdom.* Minneapolis, Minn.: Fortress Press,
1993.

Moonan, Lawrence. *Divine Power: The Medieval Power Distinction up to Its Adoption
by Albert, Bonaventure, and Aquinas.* Oxford: Clarendon Press, 1994.

Moorman, John. *A History of the Franciscan Order from Its Origins to the Year 1517.*
Oxford: Clarendon Press, 1968.

Müller, Gerhard Ludwig. "Incarnation." In *Handbook of Catholic Theology,* edited
by Wolfgang Beinert and Francis Schussler Fiorenza, 377–80. New York:
Crossroad, 1995.

Narcisse, Gilbert. *Les raisons de Dieu: argument de convenance et esthetique theologique selon Saint Thomas d'Aquin et Hans Urs von Balthasar*. Fribourg: Editions universitaires, 1997.

Nichols, Aidan. *Redeeming Beauty: Soundings in Sacral Aesthetics*. Ashgate Studies in Theology, Imagination, and the Arts. Burlington, Vt.: Ashgate, 2007.

Nielsen, Lauge Olaf. *Theology and Philosophy in the Twelfth Century: A Study of Gilbert of Porreta's Thinking and Theological Expositions of the Doctrine of the Incarnation during the Period 1130–1180*. Leiden: Brill, 1982.

O'Collins, Gerald. *Christology: A Biblical, Historical, and Systematic Study of Jesus*. 2nd ed. Oxford: Oxford University Press, 2009.

Pancheri, Francis Xavier. *The Universal Primacy of Christ*. Translated by Juniper B. Carol. Front Royal, Va.: Christendom, 1984.

Papineau, David. *Philosophical Devices: Proofs, Probabilities, Possibilities, and Sets*. Oxford: Oxford University Press, 2012.

Pomplun, R. Trent. "The Immaculate World: Predestination and Possibility in Contemporary Scotism." *Modern Theology* 30, no. 4 (2014): 525–51.

Principe, Walter H. *The Theology of the Hypostatic Union in the Early Thirteenth Century*. 4 vols. Toronto: Pontifical Institute of Mediaeval Studies, 1963–75.

———. "Guerric of Saint-Quentin, OP, on the Question: *Utrum Filius Dei esset incarnatus si homo non peccasset?*" In *Ordo sapientiae et amoris : Image et message de Saint Thomas d'Aquin à travers les récentes études historiques, herméneutiques et doctrinales : Hommage au Professeur Jean-Pierre Torrell OP à l'occasion de son 65e anniversaire*, edited by Carlos-Josaphat de Oliveira, 509–37. Fribourg: Studia Friburgensia, 1993.

Raedts, Peter. *Richard Rufus of Cornwall and the Tradition of Oxford Theology*. New York: Clarendon Press, 1987.

Randi, Eugenio. *Il sovrano e l'orologiaio: Due immagini di Dio el dibattito sulla "potentia absoluta" fra XIII e XIV secolo*. Florence: La nuova Italia editrice, 1987.

Robson, Michael. "Saint Anselm, Robert Grosseteste, and the Franciscan Tradition." In *Robert Grosseteste: New Perspectives on His Thought and Scholarship*, edited by James McEvoy, 233–56. Instrumenta Patristica 27. Turnhout, Belgium: Brepols, 1995.

———. "The Impact of the Cur Deus Homo on the Early Franciscan School." In *Anselm: Aosta, Bec and Canterbury: Papers in Commemoration of the Nine-Hundredth Anniversary of Anselm's Enthronement as Archbishop, 25 September 1093*, edited by D. E. Luscombe and G. R. Evans, 334–47. Sheffield: Sheffield Academic Press, 1996.

Root, Michael. "Necessity and Unfittingness in Anselm's Cur Deus Homo." *Scottish Journal of Theology* 40, no. 2 (1987): 211–30.

Rosato, Andrew. "The Interpretation of Anselm's Teaching on Christ's Satisfaction for Sin in the Franciscan Tradition from Alexander of Hales to Duns Scotus." *Franciscan Studies* 71 (2013): 411–44.

Rosemann, Philipp W. *Peter Lombard*. Great Medieval Thinkers. Oxford: Oxford University Press, 2004.

Schaefer, Alexander. "The Position and Function of Man in the Created World according to Saint Bonaventure (Part I)." *Franciscan Studies* 20, no. 3/4 (1960): 261–316.

————. "The Position and Function of Man in the Created World according to Saint Bonaventure (Part II)." *Franciscan Studies* 21, no. 1/2 (1961): 233–382.

Schlosser, Marianne. "Bonaventure: Life and Works." In *A Companion to Bonaventure*, edited by Jay M. Hammond, J. A. Wayne Hellmann, and Jared Goff, 9–59. Brill's Companions to the Christian Tradition 48. Leiden: Brill, 2014.

Serene, Eileen F. "Anselm's Philosophical Fragments: A Critical Examination." PhD Dissertation, Cornell University, 1974.

————. "Anselm's Modal Conceptions." In *Reforging the Great Chain of Being: Studies of the History of Modal Theories*, edited by Simo Knuuttila, 117–62. Synthese Historical Library 20. Dordrecht: D. Reidel, 2010.

Southern, R. W. *Robert Grosseteste: The Growth of an English Mind in Medieval Europe.* Oxford: Oxford University Press, 1986.

Torrell, Jean-Pierre. *L'Initiation à Saint Thomas d'Aquin: Sa personne et son oeuvre.* Fribourg: Editiones Universitaires de Fribourg, 1993.

————. *La théologie catholique.* Que sais-je? 1269. Paris: Presses Universitaires de France, 1994.

————. *Saint Thomas d'Aquin, Maître spirituel.* Fribourg: Editiones Universitaires de Fribourg, 1996.

————. "*Guerric de Saint-Quentin et ses quodlibet: Introduction historique et théologique.*" In *Guerric of Saint-Quentin: Quaestiones de quolibet,* edited by J. Black and W. H. Principe, 1–177. Studies and Texts 143. Toronto: Pontifical Institute of Mediaeval Studies, 2002.

————. *Spiritual Master.* Vol. 2, *Saint Thomas Aquinas.* Translated by Robert Royal. Washington, D.C.: The Catholic University of America Press, 2003.

————. *The Person and His Work.* Vol. 1, *Saint Thomas Aquinas.* Translated by Robert Royal. Washington, D.C.: The Catholic University of America Press, 2005.

————. *Encyclopédie Jésus le Christ chez saint Thomas d'Aquin: texte de la tertia pars (ST IIIa) traduit et commenté, accompagné de données historiques et doctrinales et de cinquante textes choisis.* Paris: Cerf, 2008.

Turrettini, François. *Institutes of Elenctic Theology.* Edited by James T. Dennison. Translated by George Musgrave Giger. Vol. 1. Phillipsburg, N.J.: Protestant and Reformed, 1994.

Unger, Dominic. "Franciscan Christology: Absolute and Universal Primacy of Christ." *Franciscan Studies* 2 (1942): 428–75.

————. "Robert Grosseteste, Bishop of Lincoln (1235–1253) on the Reasons for the Incarnation." *Franciscan Studies* 16, no. 1 (1956): 1–36.

————. "Select Questions on the Final Cause of the Incarnation." *Franciscan Approach to Theology: Report of the 38th Annual Meeting of the Franciscan Educational Conference* 38 (1957): 46–76.

Van Driel, Edwin Chr. *Incarnation Anyway: Arguments for Supralapsarian Christology.* American Academy of Religion Academy Series. Oxford: Oxford University Press, 2008.

Wawrykow, Joseph. "Wisdom in the Christology of Thomas Aquinas," In *Christ Among the Medieval Dominicans*, edited by Kent Emery, Jr., and Joseph Wawrykow, 175–96. Notre Dame, Ind.: University of Notre Dame Press, 1998.

————. "Hypostatic Union." In *The Theology of Thomas Aquinas*, edited by Rik Van

Nieuwenhove and Joseph Wawrykow, 222–51. Notre Dame, Ind.: University of Notre Dame Press, 2005.

Weisheipl, James A. *Friar Thomas D'Aquino: His Life, Thought, and Work.* 1st ed. Garden City, N.Y.: Doubleday, 1974.

———. "The Life and Works of St. Albert the Great." In *Albertus Magnus and the Sciences*, edited by James A. Weisheipl, 13–51. Studies and Texts 49. Toronto: Pontifical Institute of Mediaeval Studies, 1980.

Yang, Andrew S. "Scotus' Voluntarist Approach to the Atonement Reconsidered." *Scottish Journal of Theology* 62, no. 4 (2009): 421–40.

Index